Selling Fear

Selling Fear

Counterterrorism, the Media, and Public Opinion

BRIGITTE L. NACOS

YAELI BLOCH-ELKON

ROBERT Y. SHAPIRO

THE UNIVERSITY OF CHICAGO PRESS   CHICAGO AND LONDON

BRIGITTE L. NACOS is a journalist, adjunct professor of political science at Columbia University, and the author of numerous books, including several on terrorism and the media.

YAELI BLOCH-ELKON is lecturer/assistant professor of political science and communications at Bar Ilan University, Israel, and an associate research scholar at the university's Begin-Sadat Center for Strategic Studies (BESA), and at Columbia University's Institute for Social and Economic Research and Policy (ISERP).

ROBERT Y. SHAPIRO is professor of political science and ISERP faculty fellow at Columbia University and is coauthor, most recently, of *Politicians Don't Pander: Political Manipulation and the Loss of Democratic Responsiveness* (published by the University of Chicago Press).

The University of Chicago Press, Chicago 60637
The University of Chicago Press, Ltd., London
© 2011 by The University of Chicago
All rights reserved. Published 2011
Printed in the United States of America

20 19 18 17 16 15 14 13 12 11   1 2 3 4 5

ISBN-13: 978-0-226-56718-1 (cloth)
ISBN-13: 978-0-226-56719-8 (paper)
ISBN-10: 0-226-56718-4 (cloth)
ISBN-10: 0-226-56719-2 (paper)

Library of Congress Cataloging-in-Publication Data

Nacos, Brigitte Lebens.
    Selling fear : counterterrorism, the media, and public opinion / Brigitte L. Nacos, Yaeli Bloch-Elkon, and Robert Y. Shapiro.
        p. cm. — (Chicago studies in American politics)
    ISBN-13: 978-0-226-56718-1 (hardcover: alk. paper)
    ISBN-10: 0-226-56718-4 (hardcover: alk. paper)
    ISBN-13: 978-0-226-56719-8 (pbk.: alk. paper)
    ISBN-10: 0-226-56719-2 (pbk.: alk. paper)
    1. War on Terrorism, 2001–2009.   2. War on Terrorism, 2001–2009, in mass media.
3. National security—United States—History—21st century.   4. United States—Foreign relations—21st century.   I. Bloch-Elkon, Yaeli.   II. Shapiro, Robert Y., 1953–
III. Title.   IV. Series: Chicago studies in American politics.
    HV6432.N336 2011
    363.325′160973—dc22

                                                                    2010042779

♾ The paper used in this publication meets the minimum requirements of the American National Standard for Information Sciences—Permanence of Paper for Printed Library Materials, ANSI Z39.48-1992.

Contents

List of Illustrations vii

Preface and Acknowledgments xi

CHAPTER 1. The News as Commodity, Public Good, and
Political Manipulator 1

CHAPTER 2. Selling Fear: The Not So Hidden Persuaders 28

CHAPTER 3. Civil Liberties versus National Security 60

CHAPTER 4. Selling the Iraq War 93

CHAPTER 5. Preventing Attacks against the Homeland 125

CHAPTER 6. Preparing for the Next Attack 152

CHAPTER 7. Mass-Mediated Politics of Counterterrorism 182

POSTSCRIPT. President Obama: Underselling Fear? 201

Notes 211

References 221

Index 233

*Appendixes are available online at
http://www.press.uchicago.edu/books/nacos/.*

Illustrations

Tables

7.1   News messages by domestic sources on terrorism
      (percentage)   184
7.2   Number of TV news segments and messages   187

Figures

2.1   TV news coverage of official terror alert changes,
      by placement   39
2.2   TV news coverage of official terror alert changes, by airtime   40
2.3   TV news: Threat messages, by source   41
2.4   Concern about more major terrorist attacks   43
2.5   Concern about terrorist threat, by race   45
2.6   Concern about terrorist threat, by party ("Great deal")   47
2.7   Concern about terrorist attacks   48
2.8   Presidential approval and terrorism   49
2.9   Concern about more major terror attacks, October 2001–
      December 2004   52
2.10 Likelihood of attack in the next few months, October 2001–
      December 2004   53
2.11 Worry about becoming a victim of terrorism, October 2001–
      December 2004   54
2.12 Terrorism and approval of Bush, October 2001–
      December 2004   55
3.1   News: Sources in security/civil liberties news   73

3.2   News: Positions on security/civil liberties   74
3.3   News: Specific counterterrorism/homeland security
        |measures   75
3.4   Public opinion on trade-offs: Liberty vs. security   79
3.5   In order to curb terrorism in this country, do you think it will be
        necessary for the average person to give up some civil liberties?
        By party ID ("Yes, it is necessary")   81
3.6   In order to curb terrorism in this country, do you think it will be
        necessary for the average person to give up some civil liberties?
        By race ("Yes, it is necessary")   82
3.7   In order to curb terrorism in this country, do you think it will be
        necessary for the average person to give up some civil liberties?
        By education ("Yes, it is necessary")   84
3.8   The necessity to give up civil liberties in order to curb terrorism,
        October 2001–December 2004   86
3.9   Favor increased monitoring to prevent terrorism,
        October 2001–December 2004   87
4.1   Sources in pre–Iraq War news   103
4.2   Subjects of news media messages   106
4.3   Saddam Hussein/Osama bin Laden: ABC and
        administration   110
4.4   War on terrorism/terror: ABC and administration   111
4.5   Public opinion: Iraq and weapons of mass destruction   115
4.6   Public opinion: Iraq and Saddam Hussein's threat,
        October 2001–March 2003   116
4.7   Having U.S. forces take military action against Iraq to force
        Saddam Hussein from power? By race ("Favor")   117
4.8   Having U.S. forces take military action against Iraq to force
        Saddam Hussein from power? By party ID ("Favor")   118
4.9   Military action against Iraq to remove Saddam Hussein,
        October 2001–May 2003   121
5.1   Sources in terrorism prevention news   134
5.2   Areas of evaluation in prevention news   135
5.3   News message evaluations of prevention efforts   136
5.4   Public opinion: U.S. doing all it can to prevent future
        terrorist attacks   139
5.5   Confidence in government protection of one's residential area
        from terrorist attack, by race   142

5.6   Confidence in government protection of one's residential area
       from terrorist attack, by party ID   143
5.7   Confidence in the ability of the U.S. to prevent further terrorist
       attacks, October 2001–December 2004   145
5.8   Confidence in U.S. government to protect from future terrorist
       attacks, August 2005–March 2006   148
6.1   Sources in terrorism preparedness news   164
6.2   Evaluations of preparedness efforts in the news   164
6.3   Areas of preparedness/first responders in the news   165
6.4   News coverage of Hurricane Katrina and terrorism, September
       2005–February 2006   168
6.5   Public opinion: Terrorist attack and community emergency
       response plan   171
6.6   U.S. prepared for future terrorist attack, by race   172
6.7   U.S. prepared for future terrorist attack, by party ID   173
6.8   Community has adequate emergency plan, by party ID   174
6.9   Community has adequate emergency plan, by race   175
6.10   Terrorism and Katrina: Bush approval and stories citing
       "Hurricane Katrina," "failure," and "response," August 2005–
       August 2006   177
7.1   Threat of terror attacks and support for military action
       against Iraq   193
7.2   Civil liberties and worry about becoming a victim
       of terrorism   195

Preface and Acknowledgments

We're going to talk about *fear*. *Fear*, after all, is our real enemy. *Fear* is taking over our world. *Fear* is being used as a tool of manipulation in our society. It's our politicians who pedal policy. It's our Madison Avenue, who sells us things you don't need. Think about it: The *fear* of being attacked. The *fear* that there are communists lurking around every corner. The *fear* that some little Caribbean country that doesn't believe in our way of life poses a threat to us. The *fear* that black culture may take over the world. The *fear* of Elvis Presley's hips. Actually, maybe that one is a real fear. — Lecture by a fictional English professor in the early 1960s, played by actor Colin Firth in the film *A Single Man* (2009)

We came to write this book out of our common interest in the mass media, public opinion, and policymaking, and especially issues related to terrorism, counterterrorism, foreign policy, and national security. Our fundamental concern is the health of American democracy, which requires some influence of public opinion on government policies. One cannot talk about public opinion without talking about a nation's leaders and the free press that informs and guides the public. Democracy does not require that government always act in accord with the people's wishes, but it does, in our view, require that it provides the public with the best possible information so that it can form opinions that reflect its and the nation's best interest. Whether government leaders follow these wishes or not, they are obliged to explain the reasons for their decisions truthfully so that the citizenry can reward them or hold them accountable at the next elections. This breaks down, however, when leaders and the press do not fully inform and educate the public—by withholding information or by manipulating or deceiving the public in other ways.

This book examines a period of such a breakdown that occurred in the initial months and years after the terrorist attacks on the World Trade Center in New York, the Pentagon in Washington, and the fields of Pennsylvania. While the nation's response was one of patriotic unity, it was also one of *fear*. The events of 9/11 showed that the nation was vulnerable to the deadliest attacks from enemies who could strike again and might not be easily deterred. This posed a new kind of threat of the sort that in the past—ranging from the time of the Alien and Sedition Acts of our early republic, to the Palmer Raids after World War I and the Russian Revolution, to the anticommunist crusade of the McCarthy era and other times during the Cold War—led to government responses that encroached on fundamental rights and liberties and succeeded at manipulating public opinion.

What happened is reflected in the epigraph above. The book examines a period in which the American government used fear to control politics by manipulating the mass media and, through the media, public opinion. It describes how public relations strategies, the media's presentation of news, pollsters' decisions on what to ask about, and the public's perceptions and opinions all interacted with each other on terrorism-related issues for four years after the terrorist attacks of September 11, 2001. The administration of George W. Bush was able to effectively hype fear (and intimidate its critics), obscure civil liberties abuses, and downplay concrete issues of terrorism prevention and preparedness. This was substantially facilitated by a mostly captive media that conveyed the administration's positions and its justifications. The media were aroused to independent criticism concerning prevention and preparedness only after the disastrous response to Hurricane Katrina. For the most part, the media reported and amplified whatever messages the administration put out, and ignored topics and problems that the administration did not want to discuss. Overall, the press failed at its longstanding "watchdog" function suggested by the American Founders (especially Thomas Jefferson) and most widely asserted over the years by the profession of journalism in the United States. Other scholars noted this failure with respect to the invasion of Iraq, which we examine further by reporting additional evidence about media coverage and the effects of this coverage on the American public, confirming that such failures can affect democratic governance in profound ways.

Along the way we attempt to make some general theoretical and empirical contributions to political science and the study of public opinion and political communication. We also raise questions about the effects of partisan conflict and polarization that have continued stridently into Barack Obama's presidency. And at the end, we echo the challenges for the press in the United States as the news industry undergoes sweeping changes that may make increasingly more difficult the kind of close monitoring of government and public affairs—both the day-to-day "shoe-leather" reporting of events and new information and effective investigative journalism—that fell short during the time and in the ways we describe.

This book has been a long time in the making, and we are indebted to many people and institutions. We have been supported in many ways by Columbia University's School of Arts and Sciences, the Institute for Social and Economic Research and Policy (ISERP), the Department of Political Science, and the School of International and Public Affairs.

Nacos owes thanks to the Columbia and Barnard College students in her seminars on "terrorism and counterterrorism" and "communication and violence," whose inquisitiveness confirmed that there was a need to explore the relationships of counterterrorism policy, the mass media, and public opinion as systematically as in existing research on the centrality of communication in the calculus of terrorism. She is also grateful to Gregory Miller and Stephen Shellman, codirectors of the annual Summer Workshop on Teaching about Terrorism, for inviting her to give presentations at many sessions and sites, offering the opportunity to talk about the issues examined in this book and to get valuable feedback from established scholars and newcomers to the field. Bloch-Elkon thanks Bar Ilan University's Office of the President, the Dean's Office, and the Department of Political Studies for their Postdoctoral Fellowship. She is also grateful to Harvey M. Krueger for his support and encouragement in pursuing postdoctoral research at Columbia University. Shapiro is grateful to the Russell Sage Foundation where he was a 2006–7 visiting scholar working on partisan polarization and conflict in the United States.

For guidance and constructive criticism of the book itself, we are most grateful to anonymous reviewers who made the book far superior— much better structured and more readable—than its initial drafts. At the University of Chicago Press, John Tryneski and Rodney Powell were tremendously supportive and helpful, especially in moving us quickly to publication once we had the near final manuscript; Mark Reschke, Isaac Tobin, and Kristi McGuire assisted in other stages of the publication process and Laura Bevir with the index. We also thank the academic editors of the Chicago Studies in American Politics series, Benjamin Page, Susan Herbst, Jamie Druckman, and Larry Jacobs. Ben and Susan provided excellent comments and suggestions at crucial junctures.

Many individuals provided direct assistance as well as organizational and logistical support. We thank the following (who were students at the time) for able and important research assistance at various stages of our research and writing: Ping Song, Michael Anthony Duran, Daniel Carinci, Kaori Shoji, Katherine Krimmel, Jason Bello, Hana Greenberg, Steven Vainer, Gustavo Cano, Steve Thompson, James Kim, Alex Marchysan, Narayani Lasala Blanco, Charles McLaurin, Jamie Richardson, Mat Krogulecki, Richard Cho, Julia Rabinovich, and Daniel Enebeli.

We are also grateful to Kay Achar, Emily Prince, Michael Scott, Timothy Johnston, Nathalie Neptune, and Milly Behm at the Department of Political Science; Harpreet Mahajan at Columbia's School of International and Public Affairs; Peter Bearman (then director), Amira Ibrahim, and Christopher Weiss at ISERP; and Eric Wanner (president) and Suzanne Nichols at Russell Sage.

We could not have written this book without the public opinion data that we had available to us, as well as transcripts and summaries of news media coverage. These were originally collected by many survey sponsors and polling organizations, or were reported by news media outlets and archives that we credit in the text and in the appendixes available online. We owe special thanks to the Roper Center for Public Opinion Research and its associate director Lois Timms-Ferrara; Gary Langer, director of polling at ABC News; Jane Weintrop, head of Columbia's Electronic Data Service; David Berman (then at the National Center for Disaster Preparedness at Columbia's Mailman School of Public Health), Barbara Carvalho, and Lee Miringoff for reports and surveys conducted by the Marist College Institute for Public Opinion; Steven Kull, Clay Ramsay, and Evan Lewis at the Program for International Policy Attitudes, University of Maryland; and the Louis Harris Data Center at the University of North Carolina's Odum Institute.

Our heartfelt thanks go to our spouses and families, who with good cheer let us cloister ourselves for marathon stretches at our offices and home desks, huddled over our computers. We thank Bob's wife, Nancy Rubenstein, who gets additional credit for the title of the book; James Nacos, who suffered for several more years through Brigitte's never-ending preoccupation with terrorism and counterterrorism; Erez Elkon, for his patience, understanding, and support of Yaeli—and Liya, who patiently waited to enter the world until the day after we completed our data analysis; and Yaeli's parents, Uziyahu and Niza Bloch, for inculcating in her an ongoing quest for excellence. We owe them big time as always. They helped make the book all the better, along with the others mentioned above to whom we are in debt. But responsibility for all the shortcomings and deficiencies of the book and its analyses remains ours alone.

CHAPTER ONE

The News as Commodity, Public Good, and Political Manipulator

Everybody said it all day, a declaration of—of war, an act of war against the United States. Any number of politicians and commentators, us included, who were reminded that the last time there was an attack like this on the United States was Pearl Harbor which—which finally induced the United States to get fully involved in World War—in World War II. — Peter Jennings, ABC News anchor, September 11, 2001

Tuesday, September 11, 2001, began as a picture perfect day along the American East Coast. The sun was golden bright. The sky was blue and cloudless. On a clear day like this the view from the top of Manhattan's World Trade Center (WTC) over the metropolitan area was breathtakingly beautiful. At 8:48 a.m., when the workday began for thousands of men and women in the offices of the 110 stories of the Center's twin towers, a hijacked Boeing 767 crashed into the North Tower. Eighteen minutes later, a second Boeing 767 flew into the South Tower. Just before 10:00 a.m. the South Tower collapsed; 29 minutes later its twin crumbled. In between, at 9:40 a.m., a Boeing 757 flew into the Pentagon just outside of Washington, DC, and 30 minutes later another Boeing 757, probably on its way to Washington to destroy the U.S. Capitol, home of Congress, crashed to the ground in Somerset County, Pennsylvania. Within 82 minutes, the United States had suffered a series of synchronized attacks that added up to the most lethal strike in the history of terrorism.

Apart from eyewitnesses watching in shock and disbelief, hundreds of millions in America and abroad learned of the attacks from television, radio, or the Internet. They saw the horrific images of the World Trade Center, the symbol of America's financial and economic power, turning into a towering inferno before its towers collapsed. They saw a chunk of the Pentagon, the symbol of America's military might, in ruins. In the United States almost everyone followed the news of the attacks (National Geographic Society 2001; Nacos 2007) hour after hour, day after day. Evaluating the 9/11 TV coverage a few months later, one television critic concluded that "the first days after the terrorist attacks saw television at its near-best: solid coverage of the events, as well as a surfeit of political, social and historical background designed for an audience desperate to make sense out of the tragedies in New York, Washington and Pennsylvania" (Martin 2002). Indeed, in the hours and days after the strikes, anchors and correspondents, present and former government officials, historians, and other experts tried to explain what seemed beyond comprehension. There were efforts to provide historical context, assess the terror threat, and ponder sure or likely responses at home and abroad. In the process, the initial reporting touched on literally all major counterterrorism policies that the Bush administration and a compliant Congress would adopt in the following weeks, months, and years: the agreement that America was now at war; the need for reprisal against the Taliban, Afghanistan's rulers, because of their support for Osama bin Laden; the linking of Iraq to bin Laden and to the 9/11 attacks; the emphasis on security at the expense of civil liberties; and, last but not least, the outpouring of patriotism and calls for national unity and full support for the crisis-managing president and commander-in-chief.

It was striking that literally all of these frames were already present in the newscasts on September 11 itself. Even before President George W. Bush spoke of America's "war against terrorism" late that day, the attacks were cast as an act or acts of war—often compared to the Japanese attack on Pearl Harbor in 1941. With the horrific images of the burning and collapsing World Trade Center towers and with the destroyed part of the Pentagon shown constantly on full or split screens, "Pearl Harbor" and "war" were invoked repeatedly to explain the enormity of the day, with the anchors of the major networks leading the way as the following excerpts from the nonstop coverage on 9/11 underscore:

TOM BROKAW, anchor, NBC News: Twenty-four hundred people were killed when the Japanese attacked Pearl Harbor 60 years ago this year. This attack on America, this terrorist war on America, could be more consequential in terms of lives lost. And it could be, as well, consequential in other ways in terms of getting this country involved around the world. Pearl Harbor, of course, triggered World War II, one of the epic events in the history of mankind. This is not expected to do just that, but it will change this country in—in so many ways.

DAN RATHER, anchor, CBS News: Terror hits home. In the history of our country, we had "Remember the Alamo," then "Remember the Maine" during the Spanish-American War. We had "Remember Pearl Harbor," and now, "Remember the twin towers."

PETER JENNINGS, anchor, ABC News: Everybody said it all day, a declaration of—of war, an act of war against the United States. Any number of politicians and commentators, us included, who were reminded that the last time there was an attack like this on the United States was Pearl Harbor.

As Peter Jennings noted, people inside and outside the media agreed and repeated over and over that the attacks amounted to an act of war, a declaration of war, the equivalent of Pearl Harbor—or worse. And there was much talk about the need for a military response, the necessity to go to war. Reporting from the Pentagon, ABC News correspondent John McWethy said, "There is a pervasive sense of anger among the military officers I've talked to today. They have mentioned again and again, Pearl Harbor . . . They are ready to go to war. There is a sense of war here at the Pentagon." On the day of the attacks, anchors, correspondents, and reporters of the three networks mentioned the term "war" 57 times; "Pearl Harbor" 41 times, and "war zone" 11 times. In addition, experts, public officials, historians, and other sources used the term "war" a total of 29 times and "Pearl Harbor" 17 times.

Since Osama bin Laden was identified within a few hours after the attacks as the most likely mastermind by many seemingly authoritative sources, there was immediate talk of retribution against his Al Qaeda organization and its Taliban allies and hosts. An example was the following exchange between correspondent Andrea Mitchell and anchor Tom Brokaw during an early evening NBC News broadcasts on 9/11:

MITCHELL: Today, Afghanistan's Taliban leaders deny any involvement by Osama bin Laden. But as David Bloom alluded to earlier, intelligence officials and others are telling NBC tonight that they are 90% sure that bin Laden is involved. And, Tom, if that proves to be the case, there is no doubt in anyone's mind that the US will retaliate. Tom:

BROKAW: But the question is, how do they find Osama bin Laden, and who do they retaliate against?

MITCHELL: They cannot find Osama bin Laden. They have not been able to.

He is number one on the most wanted list of the FBI. They have warned the Taliban that they will respond against Afghanistan's leaders. So the attack would be against Afghanistan.

Just as swiftly, there was also finger-pointing in the direction of Saddam Hussein and Iraq. Former CIA director James Woolsey used his appearance on ABC News to discuss the possible involvement of state sponsors, mentioning both Iraq and Iran. But it was clear that he had mostly Iraq in mind when he mentioned the Iraqi government's alleged links to Osama bin Laden. To that end he said that "it's not impossible that terrorist groups could work together with the government, that—the Iraqi government has been quite closely involved with a number of Sunni terrorist groups and—on some matters had contact with bin Laden." As guest of PBS's *NewsHour with Jim Lehrer*, former Senator David Boren singled out Iraq as well, when he stated:

> I think obviously there are states that have reason to have strong feelings— Iraq, for example. We knew back during the Persian Gulf conflict—and that's when we had a lot of intelligence successes because a lot of efforts were broken up to mount terrorist attacks that Saddam Hussein among others was trying to recruit every terrorist organization in the world to serve his purpose. But I think now we're in a situation where we must respond so strongly and send such a very strong signal for the sake not only of our security but the stability and security of the world that nation states that condone terrorism, that harbor terrorists, let alone those that sponsor terrorism will pay a very heavy, heavy price.

Even the question of achieving greater security at the expense of civil liberties came up in the first hours after the strikes. Predicting that the attacks would inevitably bring about monumental changes, historian David McCullough said during a CNN special report, "I'm afraid that it will also mean a curtailing, trimming up some—maybe even eviscerating of the open society as we know it." This was also a topic when Linda Douglass of ABC News interviewed Senator Joe Biden:

> DOUGLASS: Senator Biden, a couple of the senators I've spoken to and members I have spoken to and members of Congress as well are saying that we are now at war. Senator Shelby, who is the ranking Republican on the Intelligence Committee, says we are now essentially at war, we have to be on

a war footing, we—and Senator Hagel has said that we've got to start securing our borders, locking down our airports, revisiting the way we protect our public institutions. What about that?

SEN. BIDEN: I hope that's not true. I would say it another way. I would say
we've come face to face with a new reality, a reality that we knew existed
and knew was possible, a reality that has happened in varying degrees to
other countries. But if, in fact, in order to respond to that reality we have
to alter our civil liberties, change the way we function, then we've truly
lost the war. The war is one that allows us—the way to conduct the war is
to demonstrate our institutions are functioning, that your civil liberties,
your civil rights, your ability to be free and walk and move around, in fact,
are not fundamentally altered.

A few hours after the attacks, Dan Rather characterized September 11,
2001, as "a day that will, as was the case with Pearl Harbor, live in in-
famy in American history." Such weighty assessments put their stamp
on the post-9/11 coverage. The news dramatized the terrorist strikes and
likely responses by touting the war metaphor and foreshadowing, if not
justifying, subsequent counterterrorism initiatives by the Bush administration, most notably, the Afghanistan War, the USA PATRIOT Act,
and the Iraq War. While the need for protecting the homeland and preventing further terrorist strikes was implicit in the discussion of possible curbs on civil liberties, specific terrorism prevention and preparedness policies were not topics in the immediate coverage except for some
tough remarks about possible failures in the intelligence community.
This came up in a conversation between ABC News anchor Peter Jennings and security expert Vince Cannistraro:

JENNINGS: And this is, among other things, a desperate failure of intelligence
in both the human and technical area. Am I right?
MR. CANNISTRARO: There's no question about it, Peter. It's a—it's a major intelligence failure. The inability to anticipate this kind of—of a terrorism
event on U.S. soil. I—I think that they were focused on bin Laden in Afghanistan. They were focused on US facilities abroad, and I don't think
they believed that bin Laden or a consortium of groups collaborating together had the capability or the willingness to do this kind of thing.

This particular exchange seemed to predict a robust scrutiny of the
counterterrorism practices before the attacks and perhaps critical exam-

inations of soon to be proposed and adopted post-9/11 counterterrorism policies. But there were stronger signs of a watchdog press unwilling to bark and instead to provide the stage for a strong rally around the flag. Almost immediately after the attacks, the news reflected what appeared to be the nation's collective, patriotic reflex. There were numerous promises and appeals for national unity and unequivocal support for the president. Like other networks, the *NewsHour with Jim Lehrer* on PBS aired Senate Majority Leader Tom Daschle's full statement with the following promise of bipartisanship:

> And we will speak with one voice to condemn these attacks, to comfort the victims and their families, to commit our full support to the effort to bring those responsible to justice. We, Republicans and Democrats, House and Senate, stand strongly united behind the President and will work together to ensure that the full resources of the government are brought to bear in these efforts.

On CNN, former assistant FBI director James Kallstrom said, "we, as a country, as a nation, need to stand together." Referring to the ability of presidents to rally the nation around their leadership, historian Doris Kern Goodwin said during an NBC News broadcast, "what historians have noted is that whenever one of these crises occurs, a leader is able to make the people feel they belong to the country as one. Even the logo that you've been using all day, every time I see that, 'Attack on America,' I feel a sense of being an American."

And then there were outright signs that media personnel shared these emotions and joined the rally around the president. Nothing attested more to this than the emotions of Dan Rather who had the reputation of a tough-nosed newsman: Six days after the attacks, as guest on the *Late Show with David Letterman*, an emotional Rather shed tears as he discussed 9/11 and said, "George Bush is the president, he makes the decisions, and, you know, just as one American, he wants me to line up, just tell me where."[1]

Decision Makers, the Media, and Patriotism

Scholars tend to distinguish between news coverage of foreign or international politics and policies on the one hand and domestic politics and policies on the other. But as international interdependence proliferated on the heels of globalization, the domestic-international divide has increasingly become blurred when it comes to developments and issues related to trade, financial markets, health, environment, and other areas (Deese 1994; Schneider 1994; Huntington 1997). This convergence of the international and domestic realms is particularly salient with respect to transnational terrorism. What happened on September 11, 2001, was a case in point. The attacks occurred on U.S. soil, but they were masterminded and carried out by foreigners. Thus, the crisis triggered by the event was both domestic and international in nature and resulted in the most powerful patriotic "rally-around-the-flag" response since Pearl Harbor and the nation's entry into World War II. President Bush's public approval shot up more than 35 percentage points, from 51% before the attack to 90% less than two weeks later, reaching record high levels since presidential approval ratings were first measured in the 1930s.[2]

While the initial rally was extraordinary in magnitude, a spontaneous outpouring of support was hardly surprising. After all, conventional wisdom has it that Americans line up behind their presidents in times of serious international crises. But contrary to this common assumption, not all such crises lead to greater presidential approval. John Mueller (1985 [1973], 209) established the following criteria for events that are likely to trigger rallies:

> In general, a rally point must be associated with an event which (1) is international and (2) involves the United States and particularly the president directly; and it must be (3) specific, dramatic, and sharply focused. It must be international because only developments confronting the nation as a whole are likely to generate a rally-round-the-flag effect.

In the past, not even all events that fulfilled Mueller's requirements resulted in such rallies (Brody and Shapiro 1989; Edwards 1990; Hugick and Gallup 1991). Similar incidents, such as the USS *Pueblo* seizure by North Korea in 1968 and the seizure of the SS *Mayaguez* by the Khmer Rouge in 1975, led to very different public reactions: Whereas President Lyndon Johnson's approval dropped after the *Mayaguez* seizure, President Gerald Ford's increased following the takeover of the *Pueblo*. Why such vastly different public responses? Based on their research, Richard Brody and Catherine Shapiro (1989; Brody 1991) offered a plausible explanation that links public reactions to the mass-mediated responses of

opinion leaders: Rallies occur, when the news reflects that opinion leaders (administration officials, members of Congress, and others) either
support the president or abstain from criticism. With respect to the ori-
gin of mass opinion in general, John Zaller (1992, 8) concluded, "when
elites uphold a clear picture of what should be done, the public tends to
see events from that point of view."

In the immediate aftermath of the 9/11 strikes, the news reflected a
broad consensus on the need to suspend bipartisanship for the benefit
of a united front as reflected in the following exchange between NBC's
Tom Brokaw and former secretary of state James Baker in the afternoon
of September 11, 2001:

> BROKAW: Mr. Baker, let's talk a little bit about where we go from here in—in
> this country internally, how the president talks to America, and how the
> political leadership, Republican and Democrat, begin to deal with each
> other after this attack.
> MR. BAKER: Well I think any time you have a crisis such as this, it brings all
> Americans together and it tends to bring all Americans together in sup-
> port of their president regardless of their party or their political affilia-
> tion. It happens in war-time, and it happens at I'm quite confident, in cir-
> cumstances like this.

At this early stage, the die seemed cast for unilateral presidential decision making unfettered by oppositional voices inside and outside of
government. The question was what reporting mode would emerge over
the following months and years.

News as Commodity, Public Good, and Political Spin

During the first decade of the 21st century an increasing number of
newspapers and news magazines across the United States closed down
or went bankrupt. The remaining print media as well as radio and television networks' news divisions struggled to avoid great losses in the face
of the severe meltdown of financial markets and the economy as a whole.
The loss of advertising revenues and the emergence of the Internet as
major source of mostly free information contributed to the mainstream
media's predicament and offered a stark reminder that the "news is a

commodity" and "a product shaped by forces of supply and demand" (Hamilton 2004, 7).

If the news is understood as commodity, one would expect that the content of the product—what is reported and how—depends on business judgments. Here, the contemporary crisis of the press refers to news providers' problems and failures in the economic marketplace. In the competition for audience share, even organizations once committed to quality public affairs news have moved increasingly away from reporting what professional journalists, editors, and producers deem *important* for the enlightenment of fellow citizens to what profit-oriented corporate managers consider *interesting* for the entertainment of news consumers. As a result, "hard" news has been crowded out by "soft" news (Bennett 2001, 12–15) and has become increasingly a blend of information and entertainment—"infotainment" in the guise of news reporting.

But news media organizations differ from other enterprises because, as Walter Lippmann (1997 [1922], 203–4) recognized nearly 90 years ago, the "community applies one ethical measure to the press and another to trade or manufacture." This double standard is the result of "the first American revolution in information and communications" and a series of trailblazing steps at the birth of the nation, when "the United States established free speech as a constitutional principle, and the Constitution itself was written and published so that ordinary citizens could read it. Instead of taxing newspapers, the government subsidized them. It created a comprehensive postal network [with low postal rates for the shipment of newspapers]" (Starr 2004, 107). In short, the free press was supported and subsidized by the public arm so that citizens had the opportunity to be well informed and able to make educated decisions in matters of public affairs. The media's responsibility to cover a certain amount of public affairs became an obligation for broadcasters who were legally charged with providing public interest programming in return for the right to use the airwaves. If the news is understood as a public good, one would expect news professionals to adhere to journalistic ethics, providing public affairs information and monitoring government on behalf of the citizenry—in addition to offering "soft news" and entertainment.

In reality, the news is neither purely a commodity nor solely a public good. Instead, "while it is true that media markets focus on profits, within media companies there exists some slack between the interests of owners, managers, and reporters. Journalists have some leeway to provide stories that are not profit-maximizing but do provide broad social returns" (Hamilton 2004, 261). As Robert Entman put it, "news organizations and personnel are driven by economic pressure and incentives; professional customs, norms and principles; and normative values" (Entman 2000, 14).

Crucial therefore is to what extent journalists, editors, producers, and other media professionals utilize the slack between business interests and journalistic norms to publicize important public affairs news that is independent of the interest and manipulation of powerful forces in society, most of all those in government. As for the nature of journalism ethics, there is no doubt: The "Statement of Principles" of the American Society of Newspaper Editors, the organization that pioneered codified journalism ethics, spells out the meaning of press freedom in a strong democracy ("Freedom of the press belongs to the people.") and the responsibility of media professionals that comes along with that right and the obligation to serve the public interest, not special interests:

> The primary purpose of gathering and distributing news and opinion is to serve the general welfare by informing the people and enabling them to make judgments on the issues of the time. Newspapermen and women who abuse the power of their professional role for selfish motives or unworthy purposes are faithless to that public trust. The American press was made free not just to inform or just to serve as a forum for debate but also to bring an independent scrutiny to bear on the forces of power in the society, including the conduct of official power at all levels of government.[3]

How do the competing necessities of the news as public good on the one hand and news as commodity on the other relate to the coverage of spectacular terrorist acts and counterterrorist responses? Infotainment thrives on the images and themes that terrorist incidents offer: drama, tragedy, shock, fear, panic, grief—ideal ingredients for turning real-life terror into breathtaking thriller and heartbreaking soap opera that captivate audiences. Similarly, news narratives and images that amplify the threat of terrorist violence and the war metaphor are likely to hold the attention of audiences in targeted societies. Thus, when guided by the imperatives of the press as commodity, media organizations' self-interest would be well served by magnifying and prolonging the fear and anger associated with the specter of war as expressed by "Attack on America" and "America's New War" on television screen banners and headlines in print soon after the 9/11 attacks. Conversely, when guided by the responsibilities of the news as a public good, the media would be less tempted to pump up emotions and would prefer to offer competing perspectives on terrorism and policy responses, after initially "supplying an immediate, and perhaps knee-jerk, solidarity schema" in the wake of a major crisis (Hoskin and O'Loughlin 2007, 104). But there are other factors that affect news production as well.

Strategic Government Communications and Press (In)dependence

In tracing the political origins of modern communications and the press, Paul Starr (2004, 1) recognized that "the communications media have so direct a bearing on the exercise of power that their development is impossible to understand without taking politics fully into account." If anything changed in the course of history, the media's importance mushroomed to a point where decision makers in particular have come to internalize strategic communications strategies and tactics in order to enlist public support for their agendas (Rose 2000; Kernell 2007; Stroembaeck 2008). Perhaps no other president understood the relationships between power and communications better than Richard Nixon. His White House battled the print press and the increasingly influential television networks as "twin evils" to which he "was in no mood to surrender" (Nolan 2005, 74). According to Theodore White (1973, 327, 336), what was at issue between Nixon and the press "was simple: it was power."[4] More specifically, "it was the struggle over the agenda that bothered [presidential speech writer Patrick] Buchanan—and over and over again the struggle between President and press came down to this struggle, Who controlled what went before the American people?" While the president-press conflict was extraordinarily hostile during the Nixon years, since then literally all presidents and many other governmental decision makers have complained about the media's agenda-setting power at the expense of their own agendas.

But contrary to the notion of vast political power in the hands of an autonomous press, the mainstream media have not always, nor most of the time, exercised their constitutionally guaranteed freedom when reporting on public affairs. Instead, they have given high level government leaders ample room to manipulate the news. As Lance Bennett, Regina Lawrence, and Steven Livingston (2007, 49) concluded, the media take their cues to a significant extent from influential government officials and stay "within the sphere of official consensus and conflict displayed in the public statements of the key government officials who manage the policy areas and decision-making processes that make the news." What Bennett (1990) termed news "indexing" speaks to the media's tendency to make news decisions based on their assessments of the power dynamics inside government. The focus here is particularly on the White House and, depending on the specific policy area, on other important administration beats (i.e., Departments of State and Defense) and Congress albeit to a lesser extent. To be sure, depending on the policy at issue, other officials may enter the tier of those deemed to be key players in the political power game.

By relying mostly or solely on the most influential government insiders, the media allow them and their institutions to frame the news, set the range of the mass-mediated debate, and influence the politics of policymaking and the policies themselves. Because it is most ubiquitous in foreign policy and war reporting, news "indexing" explains why major international crises (of the kind described above) trigger—or fail to trigger—rallies around the flag. The decisive factor is the level of consensus or disagreement among influential officials within the administration and Congress as reflected in the news.

Unlike the "indexing" explanation, the *durable propaganda* or *hegemony model* considers the mainstream media as an instrument of America's power elite who include the top echelon of the economic, military, and political domains. As C. Wright Mills (2000 [1956], 215) explained, the media are "among the most important of those increased means of power now at the disposal of elites of wealth and power; moreover, some of the higher agents of these media are themselves among the elites or very important among their servants." Later, Herman and Chomsky (2002, xi) reemphasized that "among their other functions, the media serve, and propagandize on behalf of the powerful societal interests that control and finance them." While the propaganda model assumes a far larger circle of powerful elite influences on the news than the "indexing" framework, when it comes to the nitty-gritty of reporting practices, the two are not incompatible. According to Herman (1993, 45), "the mainstream media tend to follow a state agenda in reporting on foreign policy," and their "adversarial posture reflects tactical differences among the elite." And whereas "indexing" incorporates the influence of "spin operations" in the most influential government beats, the propaganda school, too, recognizes the media's vulnerability to "news management" on the part of government.

After a wave of anti-American terrorist attacks abroad in the 1980s, proponents of the propaganda model noted that terrorism experts with no apparent links to government agencies were frequent news sources. In reality, these high profile experts did not offer a diversity of views and alternatives to government positions, because they were part of the "terrorism industry"—the "revolving door relationships with governments and government intelligence agencies" or "private security companies"; thus they "rarely depart[ed] from the assumption of the Western model of terrorism" (Herman and O'Sullivan 1989, 190, 194).

Whether expert members of the "terrorism industry" supporting government positions or retired generals touting the Iraq War as a leg of the "war on terrorism" echoing their confidential and undisclosed briefings by Pentagon leaders, these seemingly nongovernmental sources participated in the post-9/11 news management or "spin" that are part and parcel of both explanatory models.

Compared to the nuances involved in the politics of counterterrorist policymaking that the press could cover, the news media's narrowly focused narratives on terrorist incidents and their perpetrators are less complex.

Publicity as the Oxygen of Terrorism

Even before the attacks of 9/11 in New York and Washington, there was a growing perception that transnational terrorism had changed and that the "new" terrorism associated with religious fanaticism was more likely than its older counterpart to inflict catastrophic harm on its targets. Following the 1995 sarin gas attack in the Tokyo subway by the doomsday cult Aum Shinrikyo, then U.S. Senator Sam Nunn warned that this event signaled the beginning of "a new era" in terrorism. The notion of a new and far more dangerous terrorism gained momentum after 9/11 (Simon and Benjamin 2001; Laqueur 2003). While agreeing that this contemporary threat was real and serious, others argued that it was not terrorism itself but rather the environment in which terrorists operated that had changed—most of all, due to advances in communication and information technology (Crenshaw 2006; Spencer 2006; Nacos 2007b).

Regardless of whether the 9/11 attacks or the earlier 1990s incidents indicated the advent of a new form of terrorism, one thing had not changed: In the early 21st century, as in the past, *publicity* remained the oxygen for this kind of political violence. As two scholars noted, the "immediate victim is merely instrumental, the skin of a drum beaten to achieve a calculated impact on a wider audience" and that "an act of terrorism is in reality an act of communication" (Schmid and de Graaf 1982, 14). Whether they attack, threaten violence, or communicate their demands, terrorists need access to mass media and to what we call the *political communication triangle*, that is, the interconnectedness of the media, public officials, and the general public (Nacos 2002; Cohen 2008, chap. 2). Once they have the attention of each of these three corners, terrorists market their brand of violence, intimidate their foes, and court those in whose names they claim to act. Both international and domestic communication links come into play, including the Internet. Recognized terrorist organizations have no difficulty in disseminating their messages to domestic and international publics and decision makers. Thus for years Al Qaeda's taped messages were delivered to the global Al Jazeera TV network or posted on jihadi Web sites; either way, the international and domestic news media reported the content of these communications prominently and repeatedly.

Terrorists want societies and their governments to overreact and inflict great cost on themselves. In a 2004 videotaped message, for example, Osama bin Laden boasted that it was easy to provoke the United States, "lure it into perdition," and inflict "human, financial, and political losses on America." More importantly, he threatened that "we are continuing to make America bleed to the point of bankruptcy, by God's will" (Lawrence 2005, 240–41).

Ultimately, those who commit terrorism and those who respond to terrorist violence compete for media attention. Just as terrorists market their brand of violence and the threat of further attacks, political leaders in targeted societies market their overblown threat assessments to enlist support for their counterterrorism policies. To put it differently, publicity is the oxygen of both terrorism and counterterrorism.

Communication That Unites and Divides

Communication scholars distinguish between communication as transmission and communication as ritual. Whereas transmission means disseminating information "farther and faster, eclipsing time and tran-
scending space" (Carey 1992, 17) in order to persuade message receivers,
ritual communication refers to the "sacred ceremony that draws persons
together in fellowship and communality" (Carey 1992, 18). However,
there are also "rituals of excommunication" that divide and separate
communities rather than draw them together (Carey 1998). While typically applied to a society domestically, these concepts are equally useful
in the global setting—especially in view of recent technological advances
that provide more and increasingly effective vehicles for transmission as
well as for ritual communication and excommunication.

Both the purveyors of terrorist violence and of counterterrorist responses are well versed in using all facets of communication in order to
persuade. Moreover, they are equally savvy in utilizing ritual communication both to draw communities together and to divide and demonize.
The concept of communication as ritual in the case of terrorism fits what
Daniel Dayan and Elihu Katz (1992) defined as "media events." Televised
live, preplanned, and preannounced, these unifying events (e.g., John F.
Kennedy's funeral, the royal wedding of Charles and Diana, or the
Olympic Games) are "co-produced by broadcasters and organizers"—
the latter meaning governments or other bodies (Katz and Liebes 2007,
164). Regarding terrorist spectacles during the 1980s, Gabriel Weimann
(1987, 21) suggested that "there are attributes shared by certain terrorist events and the conceptualization of media events." Later, Elihu Katz
and Tamar Liebes concluded that disruptive, threatening events, such as
disasters, terrorism, and wars have actually upstaged ceremonial "media
events," and that terrorist events "are obvious co-productions of perpetrators and broadcasters" (Katz and Liebes 2007, 164). While agreeing
that the attacks of 9/11 were "shocking global media events," Douglas
Kellner (2005, 25) argued that these catastrophic strikes were exploited
by Osama bin Laden and President George W. Bush to pursue their
respective agendas. In the United States the president tried to unite a
shell-shocked nation behind him, and in the Arab and Muslim world bin
Laden attempted to unite the community of anti-American extremists.
But besides such ritual communications of fellowship and shared senti-

ments, both sides also conveyed ample messages of division and excommunication within and among communities. For bin Laden and his circle, apostates within the Muslim community were considered just as dangerous as the Crusaders and Zionists; for President Bush and his supporters, fellow Americans critical of his security policies were abettors of terrorists or no different from them. To put it differently, President Bush and his top advisers on the one side and Osama bin Laden and his fellow Al Qaeda leaders on the other engaged in demagoguery in the sense of "polarizing propaganda that motivates members of an ingroup to hate and scapegoat some outgroup(s)" (Roberts-Miller 2006, 462).

It was not only President Bush who "articulated the escalating patriotism, vilification of the terrorists, and demand for stern military retaliation," as Kellner (2006, 165) put it. The news media in turn followed a melodramatic storyline that pitted the victimized nation against an ultimate enemy. Some news organizations went further than others in this respect. Based on a qualitative content analysis of Fox News on the afternoon of September 11, 2001, Elisabeth Anker (2005, 35) concluded that the "melodrama defined America as a heroic redeemer with a mandate to act because of an injury committed by a hostile villain." While the virtuous nation and its heroes received a great deal of prominent news coverage, so did the villain-in-chief Osama bin Laden and the members of his suicide teams who killed themselves in order to murder thousands of innocent Americans. Indeed, in the months immediately following the 9/11 attacks, bin Laden was mentioned more often in television news than President Bush (Nacos 2002). This degree of attention to bin Laden's messages of hate and threat fit the story line about "the evil-doer," as President Bush called the Al Qaeda chief; it provided a perfect contrast to the commander-in-chief who dispatched military forces to Afghanistan to hunt down bin Laden and, later on, sent more troops to remove from power another threatening source of "evil," Iraq's Saddam Hussein.

The Opportunities and Limits of Virtual Reality

More than 80 years ago, before the advent of radio and television, Walter Lippmann (1997 [1922]) observed that what people know about the world around them is mostly the result of secondhand knowledge acquired by reading newspapers. In modern-day mass societies, people are just as dependent on the news; they have "nowhere else to turn for information about public affairs and for cues on how to frame and interpret that information" (Neuman, Just, and Crigler 1992, 2). Even when individuals witness events, such as a devastating terrorist attack or massive antiwar demonstrations, or when people are affected by social and economic developments such as high unemployment or increasing energy costs, they still depend on the news to explain the reasons, consequences, and political significance of what they and others experience personally. As Benjamin Page and Robert Shapiro (1992, 340) put it, the public "often responds not to events or social trends but to *reported events*."

Given this dependence on the mass media, it is hardly surprising that communication scholars found strong correlations between the media's issue agenda and the public's. After examining the effects of television news on TV audiences, Shanto Iyengar and Donald Kinder (1987, 112) concluded that

> Americans' views of their society and nation are powerfully shaped by the stories that appear on the evening news. We found that people who were shown network broadcasts edited to draw attention to a particular problem assigned greater importance to that problem—greater importance than they themselves did before the experiment began, and greater importance than did people assigned to control conditions that emphasized different problems.

Research has also established that "by calling attention to some matters while ignoring others, television news influences the standards by which governments, presidents, politics, policies, and candidates for public office are judged" (Iyengar and Kinder 1987, 63). Specifically, the news can cue or "prime" audiences to evaluate a president based upon heavily and prominently covered events, problems, or developments. Given that American presidents are widely regarded as the nation's protectors-in-chief and leaders during major crises, it is likely that priming provides citizens with the parameters within which they judge the performance of a president in the face of terrorist acts and threats. In the past, the approval ratings of presidents increased—often significantly—during and after terrorist incidents and in the wake of military responses to terrorism (Brody and Shapiro 1989; Nacos 1996, 2002, 2006). Moreover, since some research has shown that mass-mediated messages from presidents with approval ratings greater than 50% tend to be especially persuasive on public opinion (Page and Shapiro 1984, 1992, chap. 8), it is entirely possible that there were linkages between and among the events of 9/11, President Bush's national addresses and appeals, the news coverage of them, the president's public approval rating, and public attitudes toward Washington's counterterrorist policies.

However, mass-mediated reality does not always affect, move, or sustain public attitudes along the lines of political spin and media hype. Addressing the links between media and public opinion during crises and with respect to presidential rallies, Richard Brody (1994, 211) observed that "the public does not exclusively rely on media." Moreover, just as individuals can and do embrace persuasive messages, they can also resist them, if they collide with their own concerns and partisan predispositions (Zaller 1992, 266). Based on his analysis of news about the Monika Lewinsky scandal and President Bill Clinton's approval gains in the immediate aftermath of this breaking news, John Zaller (1998, 188) suggested that "more attention needs to be given to the general question of when Media Politics (in the sense of trying to mobilize public support through mass communication) matters and when it doesn't, and to do so in a manner that doesn't presuppose the answer." While he did not understate the importance and effectiveness of "the new style of Media Politics," he also cautioned that "the effects of Media Politics on political outcomes must be demonstrated on a case-by-case basis, because sometimes the effects are real and lasting and other times they are not" (187).

This book examines the opportunities and limits of the reality depicted and shaped by media politics. Its chapters contribute to understanding further the government-media-public opinion nexus and its impact on news reporting, by focusing on a set of interconnected domestic and foreign policy issues following the 9/11 attacks. This was a period in which the United States struggled as the world's superpower, possibly teetering, and its domestic politics experienced increasing partisan and ideological conflict that extended to foreign policy as well (see Shapiro and Bloch-Elkon 2008a; Snyder, Shapiro, and Bloch-Elkon 2009). In this global and domestic setting, we explore what influenced news reporting on terrorism and counterterrorism, and to what extent this reporting affected, or failed to affect, public opinion. Writing about the characteristics of "the media-opinion-foreign policy system" in the post–Cold War era, Robert Entman (2004, 120) suggested that "methodical analysis of media content and other data is necessary to generate a more precise and comprehensive understanding of that system." Our research adds to this understanding beyond the purely foreign policy context.

Research and Method

As mentioned above, there has been limited systematic study of the relationships between and among political elites, the news media, and public opinion concerning counterterrorist policies. A lot has been written, of course, on leadership and terrorism politics and policymaking (e.g., Martin and Walcott 1988; Woodward 2002; Clarke 2004), and as noted earlier there has been significant research on terrorism and the news media (see Schmid and de Graaf 1982; Alali and Eke 1991; Paletz and Schmid 1992; Weiman and Winn 1994; Nacos 1996, 2002). Various authors have also tracked and analyzed public opinion toward various aspects of terrorism, including prevention efforts (e.g., Weiman and Winn 1994; Bloch-Elkon 2007; Nacos 2007a, chap. 6) and the tension between these efforts and the defense and protection of civil liberties (Davis and Silver 2004; Davis 2007; Berinsky 2009, chap. 7). But there has been little study of how elite level politics, the media, and public opinion are interconnected conceptually and empirically. We attempt to fill this gap by examining five policy areas, related to terrorism and especially counterterrorism after 9/11. These issues have both domestic and foreign policy dimensions, and thus they provide good cases for examining and comparing the relevant theoretical perspectives described earlier. The analysis of each focuses on news media coverage of government leaders and other political actors; public attitudes concerning policy responses to 9/11 and the threat of further violent acts of this kind; and the possible dynamics of media coverage and public opinion. The first issue or case we study, unlike the others that examine specific counterterrorist policies, is the *threat of terrorism*. That is, we examine (1) the threat assessments and terrorism alerts issued by the Bush administration, along with the public warnings from Al Qaeda leaders; (2) television news coverage of these alerts and threats; (3) the American public's perceptions of the seriousness of the terrorist threat; and (4) the possible relationship between the news coverage and public attitudes. In subsequent chapters we continue our analysis of media coverage, public opinion, and their possible relationships for the following issues: the post-9/11 *curbs on civil liberties in the name of fighting terrorism*; the *buildup to the invasion of Iraq* as part of the "war on terror"; terrorism *prevention* efforts on American shore; and *preparedness* for terrorist attacks at home as well.

We outline here the general features of the methodology that we used in our analysis of these five issues. We describe the issue- or case-specific data and methods in the separate chapters that follow.

Because television news is still the most important source of political information for the majority of the public (Pew Project for Excellence in Journalism 2009), we focus on it in our analysis of the content of news coverage. While the overall audience of cable TV news has steadily grown in the last decade, the nightly network news broadcasts of ABC News, CBS News, and NBC News still outpace—by far—prime time news and talk programs on cable television (Pew Project for Excellence in Journalism 2009). This was even more so the case for the earlier period of our study. Since the central parts of our analyses are devoted to the immediate post-9/11 period through the end of 2004, we did not examine prominent Internet blogs and social networks because most of them emerged in later years. In discussing the technological transformation of the media and its consequences for the traditional news sector, Ken Auletta (2010, 38) provided the following time frame:

> Just six years ago, when George W. Bush was finishing his first term [early 2005], there was no Facebook, no Twitter, no YouTube; dozens of regional newspapers and TV stations were highly profitable and seemed at least to themselves, inviolable. Between 2006 and 2008, daily online news use jumped by a third, which meant that one-quarter of Americans were getting news online.

Since our systematic analysis of the media ends December 31, 2004, we used TV news programs of the three networks for our quantitative content analysis of news coverage. However, we added samples of PBS's *NewsHour with Jim Lehrer* and cable news and talk programs to our qualitative analysis of network news and considered the possible impact of blogs and social networks on the range of mass-mediated debates in more recent times. The latter is relevant for an assessment of terrorism and counterterrorism news and public opinion in the early phase of the Obama presidency that we offer in a postscript briefly comparing the Bush and Obama years.

For our quantitative content analyses of terrorist threats and alerts, security versus civil liberties, terrorism prevention, and emergency preparedness, we utilized relevant post-9/11 news for a period of 39 months from October 1, 2001, through December 31, 2004. In the case of the buildup to the Iraq War, we examined news coverage up to the invasion in March 2003, about an 18-month period.

For our content analyses of terrorism threats/alerts and the Iraq War case, the number of pertinent news segments was far too large to work with full news transcripts. For these cases we and the students who assisted us coded the content of news abstracts available from the Vanderbilt University Television News Archive. Our reading of these summaries indicated that they contained the basic information that we needed in our content coding process. We also used the summaries to retrieve network news on the issue of terrorism prevention, although the number of relevant news segments was quite small. Again, the synopsis of terrorism prevention news provided us with the information we required. This did not apply for the coverage of terrorism preparedness and the civil liberties issues arising in response to the events of 9/11. In these cases, we retrieved full transcripts from the Lexis/Nexis electronic archives for our content coding and analysis. For all five issues we used a sample of full transcripts of relevant news segments for our qualitative analyses.

We coded the television news coverage for each issue in a systematic way. First, we recorded basic information, such as the network that broadcast a particular news segment and the date of the broadcast, and in the case of terror threats and alerts the placement and length of relevant segments in the broadcasts. Our unit of coding and analysis was the *message*, that is, the statements made by or attributed to news sources directly (see Page, Shapiro, and Dempsey 1987; Nacos 1990; Page and Shapiro 1992, chap. 8). Our coders identified the *sources* of each of the messages, such as the president, the secretary of homeland security, members of Congress, experts, members of the general public, foreign sources, and media sources (anchors, correspondents, reporters, etc.).

Next, we categorized the type(s) of message(s) contained in each news segment. For example, in our study of terrorism prevention, the positions expressed by sources were coded as positive, negative, or neutral/ambiguous with respect to terrorism prevention efforts on the part of federal, state, and local governments as well as the private sector. In addition, our coders identified areas or sites vulnerable to terrorist attacks—such as airports, seaports, buildings, bridges, infrastructure, etc.—and also the possible means of attack—such as weapons of mass destructions, missiles, etc.—that were mentioned by sources in these broadcasts. Since these coding processes were fairly straightforward, our reliability tests showed high intercoder agreement, ranging overall between 86% and 94% following a series of test codings.

One question that came up at the outset concerned the attribution of messages conveyed by anchors, reporters, and other on-air media personnel. To begin with, the descriptions, summaries, and assessments of the media sources tend to provide a large part of the news (Nacos 1990) and fill significant—often the greatest—chunks of television airtime. For example, based on their analysis of television network news Stephen Farnsworth and Robert Lichter (2007, 91–92) found that "during the 2004 [presidential] campaign, two-thirds (67%) of all speaking time was allotted to journalists, with the remainder split between candidates (12%) and other on-air sources (21%) such as voters, pundits, and policy experts." Their research revealed that media personnel had an even greater share of the total campaign coverage during the presidential campaigns of 2000 (74%), 1996 (73%), and 1991 (71%). An additional reason for a large proportion of media-based sources was the hiring of retired military officers and former intelligence officials as network analysts who assessed and commented on the post-9/11 threat of terrorism and the war on terrorism abroad. When expressly introduced as network analysts—as they were in many but not all instances—we coded them as media-based sources.

Whether in print, radio, or television, in most instances journalists do not take discernable positions but rather describe, summarize, and introduce the news and newsmakers. This news context was coded in our analysis as not favoring or opposing particular positions but rather providing neutral or ambiguous descriptions. If a reporter mentioned, described, or summarized policy positions expressed by other sources— for example, a U.S. Senator speaking out in favor of invading Iraq—we attributed the policy message described to the best fitting source category, in this case "members of Congress." In this example, the reporter's narrative that added to the Senator's statement was coded as "media source" and as "no position/neutral." If an anchor or correspondent said outright that there was no longer any doubt that Iraq had weapons of mass destruction, the message "Iraq has WMD" was coded along with "media source."

Our analysis of public opinion focused on the macro or *aggregate* level, not the micro or individual level (see Page and Shapiro 1992; Erikson, MacKuen, and Stimson, 2002; Baumgartner, De Boef, and Boyd-stun 2008). For our analysis of attitudes and opinions after 9/11 concerning terrorism and counterterrorism responses, we assembled the results of public opinion surveys from September 11, 2001, through December 31, 2005, and in some cases through December 2006. Our sources for these public opinion data were the "iPOLL" archive of the Roper Center for Public Opinion Research at the University of Connecticut (the source we relied on most heavily in our chapters), the "Polling the Nations" archive, the Marist College Institute for Public Opinion, and other polling organizations. We collected responses to identical questions, preferably asked by the same survey organizations and repeated over time in order to track short- and long-term trends. It is worth noting that searching with the keyword "terrorism" produced 400 survey items (from the iPOLL archive), asked during the more than 21 years, from January 1, 1980, when the Iran hostage crisis made headlines, to September 10, 2001, the day before the 9/11 attacks. In contrast, for the little more than four years from September 11, 2001, to December 31, 2005, the same keyword search produced a total of 3,235 survey questions.[5] Even allowing for the fact that the number of opinion polls conducted in the United States increased since the 1980s, the differences are striking. This upsurge in terrorism- and counterterrorism-related polling did not include large increases in data on all terrorism-related issues. While we found an abundance of survey data for some matters (e.g., the terrorist threat, the buildup to the Iraq invasion), there was a paucity of such data for others (especially terrorism prevention and preparedness). The opinion data that we focus on can be found in the online appendixes (available at http://www.press.uchicago.edu/books/nacos/). The general appendix includes the presidential "approval" questions that we examined, and the remaining appendixes pertain to specific chapters. In analyzing opinion trends, when we had data for more than one time point in a particular month, we used the monthly *average*.

In addition to analyzing how the American public collectively viewed counterterrorism responses after 9/11, we also looked at some subgroup breakdowns of survey data to probe differences and similarities based on partisanship, race, gender, and in a few cases education and age. In addition to comparing subgroups at one time point, we were interested in the extent to which the 9/11 patriotic rally and reactions to new information in the months and years that followed were stronger among some groups than others. As Robert Erikson and Kent Tedin (2001, 2005) concluded, "group characteristics can clearly make a difference in how people see the political world." At the same time it was also possible that the influences at work on *aggregate* public opinion over time, concerning some or all of the issues we examined, were so strong that they affected all subgroups about equally, leading largely to in-tandem or "parallel" patterns of change or stability (see "parallel publics" in Page and Shapiro 1992, chap. 7).

In light of studies that have demonstrated the agenda-setting, framing, and priming effects of news content, as well as relationships between the news and the public's policy preferences, we explored the associations we could observe in comparing trends in public opinion with trends in our measures of news content. For the issues and time periods we examined, however, we did not have sufficient time series data for comprehensive multivariate statistical analysis to allow us to draw the strongest possible inferences as we would have liked about cause and effect relationships (e.g., see Erikson, MacKuen, and Stimson, 2002; Baumgartner, De Boef, and Boydstun 2008). We often have only intermittent public opinion data (that is, missing time points), which we indicate with *broken or dotted lines* in our graphs ("figures") comparing trends in public opinion and news media coverage. However, *cumulatively*, our close examination of the issues in each chapter, the results of our media content analyses, and the frequency and degree to which we could connect short- and long-term changes in public opinion with events, changing conditions, and news coverage, provide substantial evidence for the interplay of politics, the press, and processes of influence and manipulation that are the focus of the book (for a similar marshalling of evidence, see Page and Shapiro 1992, chaps. 3–6).

Organization of the Book

Terrorists, policymakers, and scholars have long assumed that the mere threat of terrorist attacks affects societies. For this reason, most definitions of terrorism refer to the *threat* of violent political acts against civilians and noncombatants. But thus far research has not demonstrated how actual threats by terrorists and terrorism alerts and threat assessments by government officials are reported by the media and affect the publics in nations that have experienced such attacks. Chapter 2 presents evidence that the warnings and terrorist alerts issued by the Bush administration and the widely publicized threats made by Al Qaeda appeared to influence the American public's perceptions of the terrorist threat in the years after 9/11.

In his numerous post-9/11 statements and warnings Osama bin Laden communicated his conviction that the United States and other Western democracies undermined civil liberties, political openness, and other freedoms in the name of providing greater protection at home against terrorist strikes. In other words, he was aware of the dilemma that liberal democracies face in their response to terrorism: overemphasis on security and curbs on civil liberties can weaken the most fundamental values of these societies and play into the hands of their terrorist foes. Based on their observations, not systematic research, critics blamed the news media for their "inadequate" coverage of the Bush administration's post-9/11 restrictions on civil liberties.[6] Our examination of this issue in chapter 3 substantiates this criticism, as reflected in patterns and trends in the content of television news coverage and our analysis of public opinion after 9/11 regarding the tension between maintaining domestic security and protecting civil liberties.

Much has been written and said about the media's failure to provide the American public with a full and critical account of the available evidence justifying the invasion of Iraq. Albeit belatedly, the *New York Times* and the *Washington Post* admitted publicly that their reporting was heavily tilted in favor of the Bush administration and its arguments supporting war at the expense of attention to credible sources and arguments, that contradicted the administration's and its backers' "evidence" and claims justifying the war. In contrast to research that examined news coverage and public opinion during the actual invasion and subsequent occupation of Iraq, especially the Pentagon's policy of embedding reporters within various military units, our analysis in chapter 4 focuses on the period leading up to the invasion of Iraq. During those 18 months, a robust and more balanced mass-mediated debate about the Bush administration's justifications for war might have boosted the antiwar sentiments and forced the White House to reconsider its plan to attack. Instead, the administration's ability to set and change the media agenda during the months preceding the invasion manifested itself in direct news references to the greatest "evil-doers" in the "war against terrorism" during this period: at first mainly Osama bin Laden, and later predominantly Saddam Hussein.

In addition to battling the terrorists on their turf, one might also expect that *prevention* at home—protecting the nation from further domestic terrorist attacks—would have been a major concern for policymakers and a major topic in debates about counterterrorism reported in the media after the attacks on the World Trade Center and the Pentagon. Chapter 5 reveals, however, that prevention efforts received surprisingly little attention in the news media and apparently from Washington decision makers as well; it was also of only sporadic interest to opinion pollsters. These findings raise the question of whether such inattention to protecting the homeland from further catastrophic attacks might affect the nation's vigilance as the years passed since 9/11.

Further, given that it is unlikely that prevention of terrorism can be perfected to the point that terrorists cannot succeed, countries that are at risk must be well prepared to respond to terrorist attacks. As we describe in chapter 6, there was a stunning lack of attention to the state of such *preparedness* in the public debate reported in the media after 9/11—just as there was little interest before 9/11 in the politics of policymaking in this area. This changed abruptly, however, as the result of the bungled government response to Hurricane Katrina in New Orleans that laid bare the soft underbelly of America's disaster preparedness. It took this show-stopping natural disaster for critics inside and outside the news media to take up the state of terrorism preparedness on the local, state, and federal level, since terrorists—unlike hurricanes—hit without warning. Subsequently, the public's confidence in the country's—and their own communities'—preparedness for terrorist strikes and other catastrophic events declined. The case of Katrina illustrated the kinds of conditions and contexts in which the press and the public can respond independently from government efforts to control issues and debates.

The concluding chapter summarizes our findings, focusing on the similarities and differences in the issues we examined, and whether and to what extent the results lend support for the theories we set out to assess. In exploring whether the end of the Cold War would result in a more independent news media, Robert Entman (2004, 5) noted that the "collapse of the Cold War consensus has meant that differences among elites are no longer the exception but the rule. Patriotic deference to the president does not come automatically or last indefinitely, and hegemonic control is a tenuous feature of some but not all foreign policy news" (see also Entman 2003). If there was a trend toward greater independence in the mainstream media in the 1990s, the decade after the Cold War ended, our study provides important test cases to gauge whether media practices had indeed changed and had been testaments to a more independent fourth estate, or whether they continued to fit the "indexing" or "propaganda" modes—or a combination of the two.

In our conclusion, we reflect further on public opinion trends and divergences among subgroups and the dynamics between terrorism and counterterrorism news and public attitudes toward presidents and their policies in response to terrorist attacks and threats.

Last, we speculate about the prospects of "marketing" terrorist threats and counterterrorism in a changing media and communications landscape, in which conventional news organizations compete with a growing number of other influential information and opinion providers, especially the vastly expanding "blogosphere" and virtual social networking. Influential bloggers—or whatever they might be called in the future—may become, if they do not constitute already, watchdogs that bark louder than their counterparts in the traditional media and provide an extra check on government that is needed in normal times and in periods of crises. But one also wonders whether the partisan and ideological polarization in American politics and its magnification in cyberspace deprive presidents and other decision makers from finding support for effective and sensible counterterrorism measures. In this context, we include our postscript with an early assessment of the Obama presidency and how it compares to the Bush administration with respect to the issues we studied.

CHAPTER TWO

Selling Fear

The Not So Hidden Persuaders

This great Nation will endure as it has endured, will revive and will prosper. So, first of all, let me assert my firm belief that the only thing we have to fear is fear itself—nameless, unreasoning, unjustified terror which paralyzes needed efforts to convert retreat into advance. — Franklin D. Roosevelt, Inaugural Address, March 4, 1933

On Wednesday, September 19, 2001, eight days after the attacks of 9/11, Ron Fournier of the Associated Press asked President Bush during an ad hoc exchange between president and press, "Will you be able to tell all Americans whether they are going to be safe while you prepare to retaliate, or could terrorists strike again while we prepare for war?" The president replied, "Life around the White House or around the Congress is not normal, is not the way it used to be because we're very aware that people have conducted an act of war on our country." If anything, this was an understatement in the face of the grim crisis atmosphere in Washington, DC, New York City, and elsewhere across the country.

The next day, the White House heightened the perception of a nation under siege by announcing that Vice President Richard Cheney would not attend the president's speech before a joint session of Congress that evening but would remain in an undisclosed "secure location." Hours later, when the president's motorcade arrived at Capitol Hill, the area looked like a fortress rather than the seat of the legislature in a stable democracy. Heavily armed soldiers, SWAT teams, police officers, and police dogs patrolled along and between several layers of cement barriers and wire fences. Emergency responders sat in parked ambulances and fire trucks. Fighter jets and helicopters guarded the airspace above. As one seasoned reporter observed, "the Capitol looked as if it had sud-

denly moved to Beirut or Mogadishu" (Milbank 2001, 22). The degree
of security here and elsewhere was unprecedented and magnified the already tense atmosphere of fear and anxiety. Again and again interrupted
by thundering applause, the president's speech in the House chamber
was a rallying cry for a united nation going to fight the war against terrorism that he had declared hours after the attacks. Repeatedly, he addressed the sentiments that the 9/11 strikes triggered. "I know many citizens have fears tonight," he said, "and I ask you to be calm and resolute,
even in the face of a continuing threat." Pointing to the enormity of what
had "just passed," the president said that it was "natural to wonder if
America's future is one of fear," but he firmly promised that "this country will define our times, not be defined by them."

This was a far cry from President Franklin D. Roosevelt's categor-
ical declaration that "the only thing we have to fear is fear itself." In
contrast, President Bush expressed empathy for fellow Americans' fears
linking each of his several fear references to the looming threat of terrorism and the need to fight a determined war against terrorists and
their supporters. The speech was enthusiastically received and favorably
compared to FDR's declaration of war in response to Pearl Harbor. CBS
News anchor Dan Rather declared, "No president since Franklin Del-
ano Roosevelt, after the Japanese attacked Pearl Harbor, has delivered
anything approaching a speech such as this. And there may be those who
observe that no president in the history of our country has ever delivered
a speech such as this." ABC News correspondent Sam Donaldson told
anchor Peter Jennings, "Peter, this was a fierce speech. It sounded fierce,
the president looked fierce. I mean, if you look back at the old film of
Franklin Roosevelt asking that Congress for a declaration of war, you
do not see the same type of fierce presentation." Tom Brokaw of NBC
News seemed to allude to the emotional effects of 9/11 that kept many
Americans awake at night. "With all apologies to Robert Frost," he said,
"this speech tonight means that we have miles to go before we sleep easily again."

Even if anchors, correspondents, and other instant commentators had
not been preoccupied with figuring out what the president's speech revealed about the next steps in the war against terrorism abroad, they
couldn't have anticipated the future role of a new cabinet-level office
whose creation the president announced on this occasion. Charged with
coordinating dozens of departments and agencies involved in terrorism
prevention and response, the new White House Office of Homeland Se-

curity was to be headed by Pennsylvania governor Tom Ridge. President Bush introduced him as "a military veteran, an effective Governor, a true patriot, a trusted friend." If the White House expected that this "true patriot" would follow the party line, Ridge was the right man for the job most of the time—but not all the time. First as director of homeland security and later as secretary of the newly created Department of Homeland Security (DHS), he became an important player in what he himself characterized as "the politics of terrorism" (Ridge 2009) or, more precisely, in the politics of counterterrorism.[1] In this role, he and his staff disagreed repeatedly with other administration officials' eagerness to issue public alerts indicating that attacks were likely or imminent. Before Memorial Day 2003, for example, Ridge and Attorney General John Ashcroft held press conferences on the same day. In response to questions about threats and security, Ridge told reporters that there was no reason to heighten the alert level. A few hours later, Ashcroft warned of an imminent, major attack on the United States by a team led by Adam Gadahn, a U.S. citizen who had joined Al Qaeda. According to Ridge,

> Ashcroft's warning . . . seemed to us at DHS to be overstated, to put it charitably. Pat Hughes, our intelligence chief, and others were convinced of this.
>
> During the next regular morning meeting in the Oval Office, I was told by the president bluntly that counterterrorism is one of the administration's highest priorities, and that a united front had to be presented (Ridge 2009, 228).

Besides Ashcroft, Secretary of Defense Donald Rumsfeld was a strong advocate of raising the threat level at any opportunity. Inside the Pentagon, Rumsfeld made no bones about his motives. In the many so-called snowflakes memos to his staff the secretary "wrote of the need to 'keep elevating the threat [of terrorism] . . . and develop 'bumper sticker statements' to rally public support for an increasingly unpopular war" (Wright 2007 1).

Even when there was agreement on the need to issue threat alerts, Ridge was not always comfortable with those decisions as he revealed in his memoir:

> We had our own comedy act in the Bush administration. On three or four occasions before we adopted a formal process to review intelligence and issue alerts, [Attorney General John] Ashcroft and [FBI Director Robert] Mueller, and I hosted press conferences, each time with warnings to the public about

new intelligence, each time with the empty feeling that we weren't presenting any specific information that people could act on, each time leaving the podium thinking, "What the hell did I just say" (Ridge 2009, 81).

When it comes to analyzing intelligence, reasonable people can differ about the meaning of often sketchy information and the credibility of sources. But in discussing threat assessments on the part of those who fight terrorism, Albert Bandura took note of the likelihood that such judgments can be influenced by the desire to justify counterterrorism policies. As Bandura (2004, 129) put it:

> Lethal countermeasures are readily justified in response to grave threats that inflict extensive human pain or that endanger the very survival of the society. However, the criterion of "grave threat," although fine in principle, is shifty in specific circumstances. Like most human judgments, gauging the gravity of threats involves some subjectivity. . . . Assessment of gravity prescribes the choice of options, but choice of violent options often shapes evaluation of gravity itself.

In the post-9/11 period, the administration's eagerness to rally support for America's new war was not completely separate from the official threat warnings and alerts it issued; they were also tools in the politics of counterterrorist policymaking. This was also true for the color-coded alert system that Tom Ridge introduced in early 2002 and explained as a means to end the confusion about the meaning of various types of alarm soundings. It is telling that Ridge, Ashcroft, and other high-ranking officials could not agree on the proper threat color for the day the new system was announced. Ashcroft insisted on the "high risk level" orange, Ridge opted for "significant risk" yellow, still others in the administration preferred blue for "general risk." It was left to President Bush to decide—in favor of Ridge's choice. In other words, officials with access to the same intelligence came to very different threat assessments.

As for Ridge's declared objective to improve the nation's understanding of various threat levels, even comprehensive news coverage did not explain clearly the meaning of the five-color alert scheme as the following CNN report shows:

[Anchor Wolf] BLITZER: But first, a new terror threat warning system is in place in the United States, and the country is now on level "yellow." That means an elevated risk of attack. Homeland Security Director Tom Ridge unveiled the color-coded system earlier today, and we get more details now from CNN's Jeanne Meserve. (BEGIN VIDEOTAPE)

JEANNE MESERVE, CNN CORRESPONDENT (voice-over): During the Cold War, radios had specially marked civil defense frequencies, where the public could get information about imminent danger. Now a new warning system for a new enemy: terrorists.

TOM RIDGE, HOMELAND SECURITY DIRECTOR: We can fight them not just with conventional arms, but with information and expertise and common sense.

MESERVE: The Attorney General will evaluate the credibility, specificity and gravity of terrorist threats, and set a color-coded threat level that will be relayed to federal agencies, state and local officials, the private sector and, in most instances, to the public. Green for times of low risk, blue when there's a general risk. When the level rises to yellow there is an elevated risk. Orange indicates a high risk and red means there is a severe threat. Each level triggers specific responses. For instance, at level red, transportation systems could be stopped, just as they were on September 11. And the threat levels can be targeted, geographically or otherwise.

RIDGE: The system will not eliminate risk. No system can. We face an enemy as ruthless and as cunning and as unpredictable as any we've ever faced. Our intelligence may not pick up every threat.

MESERVE: One goal of the system is to create a common language to eliminate confusion that has cropped up since 9/11.[2]

By introducing what was meant to be "a common language to eliminate confusion," Ridge and the administration became the butt of jokes. Late night comedian Jay Leno said that "this color coding thing is so confusing. Yesterday the alert went from blue to pink; now half the country thinks we are pregnant"[3] His colleague Conan O'Brien joked, "Tom Ridge announced a new color-coded alarm system. Green means everything's okay. Red means we're in extreme danger. And champagne-fuchsia means we're being attacked by Martha Stewart."[4] In hindsight, Ridge (2009, chap. 5) himself described the green-blue-yellow-orange-red selection as "the colors of fear (and laughter)"—also the title of one chapter in his memoir.

Jokes aside, the media-reported threat warnings in general, whether issued by influential officials in Washington or by terrorist leaders, were no laughing matter for the public nor for state and local leaders and emergency responders in the months and years after the 9/11 attacks. And in spite of the blurry distinctions between several color categories, news organizations were not inclined to downplay Washington's frequent threat communications nor, for that matter, threats issued by Osama bin Laden and other Al Qaeda leaders. On the contrary, for the media this was the right stuff to refresh continually the terrible images and narrative of 9/11 and the fears of further attacks that kept news audiences engaged (Nacos 2007a; Hoskin and O'Loughlin 2007).

The White House and TV Networks' Self-Censorship

A month after 9/11 and following a request that National Security Adviser Condoleezza Rice made during a conference call with leading news executives of ABC, CBS, CNN, FOX, and NBC, the networks agreed to edit future videotapes released by Osama bin Laden and to omit inflammatory passages and hate speech. Rice expressed concern that the videotapes contained secret messages for Al Qaeda operatives inside the country and inflamed Muslims abroad. There was apparently no resistance by the networks. According to one report, the agreement "was described by one network executive as a 'patriotic' decision" (Carter and Barringer 2001).

During a White House briefing a few days later, Rice responded to a reporter's questions about the possibility of hidden messages:

> QUESTION: You asked the networks last week to use careful consideration before broadcasting the messages that were coming from Al Qaeda and bin Laden. At the time, you said that you had people who were analyzing these for possibly secret coded messages. What have the analysts found?
>
> RICE: The analysts continue to look at these messages, and they are continuing to see what we could learn from them. The point to the networks—and let me just say that I think the networks have been very responsible in the way that they have dealt with this. My message to them was that it's not to me [sic] to judge news value of something like this, but it is to say that there's a national security concern about an unedited 15 or 20 minute spew of anti-American hatred that ends in a call to go out and kill Americans. And I think that that was fully understood. We are still concerned about whether there might be some signaling in here, but I don't have anything more for you on that yet.

QUESTION: Any specific phrases or anything that you were concerned about
that you think may, in fact, be (OFF-MIKE)

RICE: We're doing the analysis, I can't promise you that we'll be able to talk
about what we think may be here, but I can tell you that I don't have anything for you right now on that.

It did not matter that no secret codes had been found to justify curbs
on bin Laden's communications and that the Arab news network Al
Jazeera and other foreign satellite networks showed the complete videotapes in the Arab and Muslim world. If there was opposition to the vol-
untary curbs, it was not reported and therefore not heard by the public.
Dan Rather seemed to speak for many in the media, when he said, "By
nature and experience, I'm always wary when the government seeks in
any way to have a hand in editorial decisions. But this is an extraordinary time. In the context of this time, the conversation as I understand it
seems reasonable on both sides" (Carter and Barringer 2001). Even when
edited and only shown in excerpts, all the messages from bin Laden, his
deputy Ayman al-Zawahiri, and other Al Qaeda figures continued to receive a great deal of news attention. Yet, there were no further requests
to restrict the coverage of these sorts of communications. Perhaps Rice
and other White House officials came to understand that the interests of
President Bush and Osama bin Laden converged, in that both sides fur-
thered their agendas by keeping the U.S. public's fears and perceptions
of threat at high levels. As noted earlier, Secretary of Defense Rumsfeld
was convinced that the threat alerts increased public support for military actions abroad.

Bin Laden, too, expressed confidence that public fear in America
would influence U.S. policies resulting in hellish human, economic, and
political costs (Lawrence 2005, 240–41). Commenting on Americans'
reactions to the attacks of 9/11, bin Laden said with obvious satisfac-
tion, "America has been filled with terror from north to south and from
east to west, praise and blessings to God" (Lawrence 2005, 104). In the
years thereafter, he and other Al Qaeda leaders issued many threats
and warned of further devastating attacks against Americans at home
and abroad. Well versed in the psychology of fear, terrorists know that
violent incidents and the mere threat of more attacks in the aftermath
of major ones can accomplish one of their primary goals: namely, to
heighten fear and anxiety among their target populations and thereby
force governments to react—and often overreact. By overcovering ter-

rorism, the media become "terrorists' weapon of choice" (Hoskin and O'Loughlin 2007, x) and open a front for their psychological warfare. As Martha Crenshaw (1986, 400) recognized, the "political effectiveness of terrorism is importantly determined by the psychological effects on audiences." Terrorism has been compared to theater because terrorists perform their violent acts for those who watch, for their audience; they have little interest in the immediate victims who are merely props in their performances. While the theater metaphor is instructive, modern-day terrorists aim for and reach global audiences that transcend the crowds in the largest theaters. Yet, the central components of terrorists' communication strategy have not changed but continue to be best summarized as "publicity, propaganda, and psychological warfare—the three P's of terrorism" (Schlagheck 1988, 3). Nineteenth-century anarchists and radical social reformers recognized that they could send powerful messages to audiences through violent acts; they therefore defined terrorism as "propaganda by deed" or "propaganda of the deed." They wanted their terrorist attacks to drive fear into targeted societies and to make them amenable to the revolutionary changes they sought. Contemporary terrorists have the same mass-mediated objectives.

In sum, then, hyping threat and fear is central to terrorist and counterterrorist rhetoric—it is part of a mass persuasion effort directed at audiences in whose interest terrorist organizations and the governments in targeted countries claim to act. According to Anthony Pratkanis and Elliot Aronson (1991, 165), such persuasion is especially effective "when (1) it scares the hell out of people, (2) it offers a specific recommendation for overcoming the fear-arousing threat, (3) the recommended action is perceived as effective for reducing the threat, and (4) the message recipient believes that he or she can perform the recommended action." This is what Al Qaeda's and the Bush administration's appeals to fear tried to do. Both sides emphasized the terrorist threat and dwelled on reasons for being fearful; both sides detailed how the enemy could and would be defeated; and both sides invoked high values (in the case of Al Qaeda, religious devotion; in the case of the Bush administration, patriotism) in their unifying ritual communications. Conversely, demagoguery and rituals of excommunication were utilized by bin Laden and Al Qaeda to threaten Americans, Westerners, and infidels among Muslims, and they were used by President Bush and other administration officials to demonize the terrorist enemy and thereby widen the gap between the good in-group and the evil out-group.

To be sure, not all fear appeals succeed, but in the face of catastrophic events that rise to the level of "media events" or "media spectaculars," the mass public pays attention and reacts to threats issued by friends and foes alike.

Researching Threat Messages, Media Coverage, and Public Opinion

Anecdotal accounts and what we have described so far contribute to our understanding of the complex relationship involving political leaders, terrorism threats, the media, and public reactions. However, what is needed is systematic research to affirm or contradict such accounts and to examine these relationships further. Therefore, we undertook a fuller study of news content and public opinion concerning the post-9/11 terrorist threat.

For our news content analysis we searched the Vanderbilt University Television News Archive for network news segments that mentioned threat(s), alert(s), or warning(s) in the context of terrorism. We retrieved a total of 373 relevant story abstracts, of which ABC News aired 32%, CBS News 34% and NBC News 34% of the stories—a testament to network news' uniformity. We retrieved a smaller number of full transcripts from the Lexis/Nexis archives for a qualitative analysis of relevant news segments.[5]

In this particular case, we were interested in the placement and length of terrorist threat messages and possible differences in news coverage of the administration's raising and lowering the alert levels. Since our focus was also on news messages and their sources, our coders identified the sources of these threat messages, such as the president, the secretary of homeland security, the director of the FBI, members of Congress, experts, foreign sources, and last, media sources (anchors, correspondents, reporters) whose descriptions and comments tended to make up the largest proportion of news sources (Nacos 1990, 1996; on the increase of news personnel as sources, see Hallin 1992; Jamieson 1992; Patterson 1994; Steele and Barnhurst 1996 Cappella and Jamieson 1997; Jacobs and Shapiro 2000). Our coders categorized further the *type* of messages attributed to sources in each news segment. Specifically, we differentiated messages about increases versus decreases in the administration's color-coded alert levels, messages about general threat assessments, and warnings by Osama bin Laden and other Al Qaeda figures.

In addition, we searched open sources on the Internet for dates, reports, and transcripts of audio- and videotaped messages released by bin Laden and other Al Qaeda leaders, and for statements by U.S. administration officials alerting the public to specific terrorist threats or describing threats against the American homeland in more general terms. We coded these segments independent of television news coverage and identified them according to sources and message types, in order to examine possible consequences of these original threat communications and whether they were also publicized by the mainstream media. The British *Guardian*'s timeline of bin Laden tapes was helpful here, as were the online archives of the White House, the Department of Homeland Security, and the U.S. Federal News Service.

As for public opinion, we assembled national opinion poll results that revealed the public's more general concerns about future terrorism and catastrophic terrorist attacks in particular, and perceptions related to individuals' own communities and to themselves and their families. Out of 35 survey questions that were repeated through the years, we focused on responses to seven items that addressed concern about terrorist attacks over different time horizons, terrorism affecting individuals personally, terrorism as most the important issue facing the country, and approval of President Bush's handling of terrorism and his presidency in general.

In addition to using these data to describe and track public opinion, we explored the possible relationships involving public perceptions about terrorism, threat pronouncements by Al Qaeda leaders, terrorism alerts and assessments by U.S. administration officials, and news coverage of such threats.

Television News: Covering and Magnifying Terrorist Threats

"The United States is back on orange alert," Dan Rather said at the top of the *CBS Evening News* on May 20, 2003. According to Rather, "President Bush today approved raising the national terror alert from yellow, meaning an elevated risk of a terror attack, to orange, meaning there is now considered to be a high risk." In the following three and a half minutes Washington correspondent Bob Orr explained that officials in

Washington "say they have no concrete information pointing to any imminent terror attack anywhere in the U.S. But it's fair to say here in Washington, the level of worry is as high as it's been since September 11th." After comments by Asa Hutchinson (the undersecretary of homeland security) and Randall Larson of the Anser Institute for Homeland Security, Rather asked CBS News Pentagon correspondent David Martin, "David, how imminent is a possible terror attack to be?" Martin's alarming answer was "Very imminent, Dan, if you believe the intelligence, which consists primarily of intercepted conversations among known al-Qaeda operatives talking among themselves about something big that is going to happen in the next two or three days." Ten days later, Jane Clayson, sitting in for Dan Rather as anchor of the *CBS Evening News* announced, "In this country, the terror alert level, raised to orange after the attacks in Saudi Arabia this month, was lowered today to yellow, elevated risk. The Department of Homeland Security says intelligence indicates the threat of an imminent attack has decreased." Forty-three words in two sentences in a nonlead segment were devoted to inform the audience that there was less reason to worry about a terrorist attack compared to the 642 words that were spoken to alarm Americans 10 days earlier that there was an "imminent" threat of terrorism in the United States.

ABC's *World News Tonight* and NBC's *Nightly News* covered these two official announcements in similar ways. On *World News Tonight*, the heightened terror alert of May 20, 2003, was dramatized by correspondent Pierre Thomas:

> An FBI bulletin obtained by ABC News points to two recent e-mails, intercepted by US intelligence. One message warns of a possible devastating attack in the next 48 hours and urged all Muslims to leave all cities, especially Boston, New York and the commercial coastline. A separate intercepted message targets Washington, and again points to possible attacks against New York and the nation's beaches. The FBI made an immediate decision to share the e-mails with police across the country.

In what followed, current and former federal and local officials then commented on the raised threat alert. In all, 734 words were spoken. When the official alert was lowered 10 days later, Peter Jennings announced it in two sentences and 25 words, "The Department of Homeland Security has lowered its terrorist threat level today from orange to yellow. Ten days ago, you will recall, they raised it." Over at NBC News, anchor Tom Brokaw introduced the comprehensive lead story by telling his audience that the decision to jack up once again the nation's security alert had been made in the White House. Reporting from Washington, correspondent Pete Williams revealed that intelligence leading to the higher terror alert was received during the interrogation of suspected Al Qaeda members arrested in Saudi Arabia after recent bombings in Riyadh; the segment then turned for comments to Hutchinson of the Department of Homeland Security and New York's police commissioner Raymond Kelly. Finally, reporting from the State Department, Andrea Mitchell spoke about possible terrorist targets inside and outside the United States. When the threat level was lowered 10 days later, the *Nightly News* did not include a report on the change.

Taken together, the three networks aired 18 reports on the Bush administration's decisions to raise the national terror alert level and 15 segments on the lowering of the color-coded alarm. In addition, the networks reported three times on raised terror alerts for New York and twice for other cities, while two newscasts mentioned the lowering of regional alerts. True to the media's tendency to highlight shocking, sensational, and disconcerting news, all 23 announcements of increases in the national or local terrorism alert levels—100% of them—were reported at the top of newscasts (figure 2.1). Conversely, ABC, CBS, and NBC reported decreases in these threat levels much less prominently, airing only 13% of such announcement as short lead stories and 87% further down in their broadcasts. When the Bush administration raised the nationwide terrorism alert, the networks devoted an average of 5 minutes and 20 seconds to such reports; when the terror alerts were lowered, the average news segment lasted only 1 minute and 34 seconds (figure 2.2). The difference was even more pronounced for regional or local alerts: the average airtime for raised threat levels was 2 minutes and 56 seconds

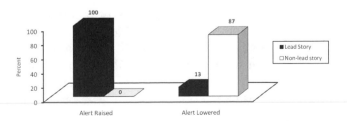

FIGURE 2.1. TV news coverage of official terror alert changes, by placement

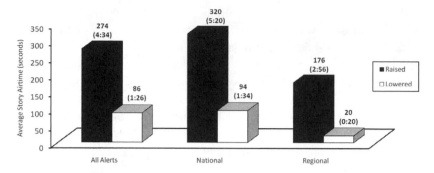

FIGURE 2.2. TV news coverage of official terror alert changes, by airtime

versus only 20 seconds for news segments on lowering the official alert level. When the three networks aired reports about threat advisories that did not involve changes in the color-coding, the average length of these stories was still fully 2 minutes and 20 seconds.

No doubt, then, that the news magnified the administration's terrorism alerts by reporting these announcements mostly in lead stories and long segments, while downplaying the lowering of alert levels or not covering them at all.

How did the networks cover the frequent audio- and videotaped messages from bin Laden and his close associates? For the 305 instances in which the release of new Osama bin Laden/Al Qaeda messages were originally reported or repeated, cited, analyzed, or commented on, about half of these messages (51%) appeared in lead stories. When the bin Laden/Al Qaeda messages were reported in lead stories, they were typically discussed or analyzed by experts, administration officials, other domestic actors, and, on a few occasions, foreign sources. The average length of these segments was close to four minutes (3 minutes and 51 seconds). Only 25% of these explicit and implicit threat messages were translated statements by bin Laden and other Al Qaeda leaders, or summaries of them by anchors and correspondents; 6% were comments attributable to foreign sources, and more than two-thirds (69%) came from domestic sources reacting to hostile remarks from Al Qaeda's leaders. In the TV newscasts we examined, 28% of President Bush's statements concerning terrorism threats and alerts were reactions to communications by bin Laden or other Al Qaeda leaders, as were 22% of those by experts and 100% by CIA officials. This high degree of attention to Al Qaeda's communications is powerful evidence for the tendency of targeted societies to repeat—and even amplify—the propaganda of their terrorist foes and thereby, unwittingly, assist terrorists in their efforts at intimidation.

Typically, anchors, correspondents, and reporters describe public affairs news and characterize the importance of events or developments and what political actors have stated. As a result, more information is conveyed by these media-based sources than by the newsmakers who are covered and by others who react to and comment on what has unfolded (again, see Hallin 1992; Jamieson 1992; Patterson 1994; Steele and Barnhurst 1996; Cappella and Jamieson 1997; Shapiro and Jacobs 2000). As figure 2.3 shows, this was also the case in the years after 9/11 with respect to covering terrorism: media personnel were 30% of the sources reporting on terrorist threats regardless of whether these warnings came from the Bush administration or from Al Qaeda leaders. Administration officials accounted for a total of 20% of all domestic and foreign sources, with President George W. Bush receiving 3%. Among other administration officials, the secretary of homeland security (4%) was most prominent in TV newscasts. Following these administration officials, terrorism and counterterrorism experts were the next most often cited nonmedia group, accounting for 14% of all sources. This was hardly surprising because the television networks had signed up these experts in droves as news consultants after 9/11. While not identified as experts, former government officials and members of the military were also cast in the roles of experts. Much less visible in the on-air terrorism debate, members of Congress made up 4% of the total news sources.

All three networks paid attention to ordinary Americans and offered them opportunities to express their feelings about the usefulness of terrorism warnings (8% of all sources). And while federal departments and agencies issued all the alerts, local and state officials reacted

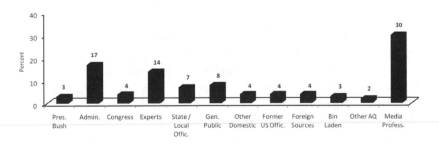

FIGURE 2.3. TV news: Threat messages, by source

to announcements from Washington, especially when warnings were issued for particular areas (i.e., New York City, Los Angeles). As a result, mayors, governors, police commissioners, and others in the emergency response communities were 7% of the news sources.

All in all, television news coverage of the threat of terrorism was dominated by American sources (91%)—only 9% were foreigners. But most of these were bin Laden and other Al Qaeda leaders, 5% of all sources, and they were more frequently newsmakers on this topic than were members of the U.S. Congress. More important, television network news presented bin Laden as a news source as often as President Bush, each at 3% of the total.

The Threat in the Public's Mind

How the public perceives the risk of terrorist attacks matters, particularly in the aftermath of major attacks, because individuals' risk assessments affect their support for counterterrorist policies (Lerner et al. 2003; Huddy et al. 2005; Kushner 2005). Elaborating on psychological causes and using experiments and survey analysis in the United States and Mexico, Jennifer Merolla and Elizabeth Zechmeister, in *Democracy at Risk: How Terrorist Threats Affect the Public* (2009), showed how perceptions of threat trigger authoritarian attitudes, lead to intolerance toward disliked groups, increase social distrust, curtail support of civil liberties, increase the likelihood of support for leaders dealing with the threat at hand, and affect opinions toward foreign policies. We consider some of these further below and in later chapters.

Beginning with the Iran hostage crisis at the end of the Carter presidency and continuing during the 1980s, when Americans became the victims of terrorism in the Middle East, Europe, Latin America, and elsewhere, the American public came to understand the threatening nature of political violence abroad. The first World Trade Center bombing in 1993 and the Oklahoma City bombing in 1995 intensified public worries about further terrorism on U.S. soil. But whereas concerns were high during hostage situations and immediately after bombings and other strikes, fears of further terrorism eventually subsided. As Ronald Hinckley (1992, 92) noted, "The more recent the incident, the highest its salience; the further off the episode, the lower is the perceived importance of terrorism."

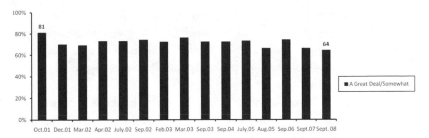

FIGURE 2.4. Concern about more major terrorist attacks

The catastrophic 9/11 strikes marked a turning point, in that the level of public concern about terrorism declined but remained quite high during the years that followed. Moreover, the downward trend was not steadily gradual but had ups and downs as figure 2.4 shows. Understandably, apprehension was at a peak right after 9/11, when four of five Americans were concerned "a great deal" or "somewhat" that more major terrorist attacks would occur. Around the seventh anniversary of the 9/11 attacks, three of five Americans still expressed such concerns—although the number of those answering "a great deal" was significantly smaller and of those choosing "somewhat" larger than in earlier years. Most important, very few people thought that major terrorist attacks were "not likely at all" in the future—4%, the lowest level, right after 9/11, and 13%, the highest, seven years later.

Even though no major terrorist attacks were carried out in the United States long after 9/11, the public seemed unable to forget the events and the risk of further violence in the face of continued reports about terrorist attacks in Iraq or elsewhere that targeted Americans. Moreover, the Bush administration never tired in propagandizing the threat of terrorism and the need to battle it. But whereas a solid majority continued to worry to one degree or the other about terrorism as a major threat, by the summer of 2006 a plurality of Americans, though just a bare one (49%), thought that the Bush administration was using the threat of terrorism and terrorism alerts for political purposes; slightly fewer (45%) thought otherwise.[6] This was an indication that spinning the news—and this issue—had its limits.

Proximity mattered as well. After experiencing first the World Trade Center bombing in 1993 and then the 9/11 attack, a strong majority of New York City residents believed that the risk of another terror attack was greater in their own community than in the country's other cities.

New Yorkers were far more concerned than their fellow Americans else-where that further terror attacks would occur. The psychological impact of 9/11, too, was more severe in New York City than elsewhere according to the conclusions from studies of posttraumatic stress disorders (Shep-pard 2009, 98–100).

In the days and weeks immediately after 9/11 more than half of the American people were "very worried" or "somewhat worried" that they or a member of their family would become a victim of terrorism. While these personal concerns waned during the following years, typically one-third to two-fifths of the public continued to fear that terrorists could harm them or their loved ones. The fact that such concerns increased af-ter major terrorist incidents abroad and after official threat alerts by the administration seemed to affirm the effectiveness of terrorist and coun-terterrorist efforts to manipulate public opinion.

Finally, although the Bush administration obtained public support for the invasion of Iraq (which we examine further in chapter 4), the Ameri-can public did not buy into the administration's claim that the Iraq War was a means to fight terrorists abroad and prevent them from striking the United States. Contrary to the messages issued by the administra-tion's spin machine, more Americans came to believe that the war had increased rather than diminished the threat of terrorism at home.

Different Groups, Different Perceptions

Thus far, we have discussed the threat perceptions of the American pub-lic *at large*, but different subgroups of the population can have differ-ent perceptions and hold different opinions about government policies and their implementation. For example, based on their analysis of opin-ion data spanning half a century, Benjamin Page and Robert Shapiro ob-served that "on a number of issues the young tend to disagree with the old, the rich with the poor, the college educated with grade school graduates, Southerners with Northeasterners, Republicans with Democrats, and blacks with whites" (Page and Shapiro 1992, 318). These differences have been typically depicted as long term and stable, and that was what they largely found: when aggregate public opinion changed, subgroup opinions moved in roughly parallel fashion, with convergence more likely than di-vergence (Page and Shapiro 1992, chap. 7). Our findings were similar—such basic group variations occurred for perceptions of the threat of ter-rorism, along the lines of gender, race, age, education, and partisanship.

Following 9/11, American women were more concerned than men about the further likelihood of terrorist attacks. Surveys conducted in the months immediately following the attacks revealed that "women perceived somewhat higher levels of threat but felt more anxious than men" (Huddy et al. 2005, 599). In the following years, a more distinct gender gap opened with differences varying over time and ranging from 16 percentage points in August 2003 to 5 points in July 2004 and 13 in July 2005.[7] Men led women by the same margins among those who said they were not concerned about future terrorist attacks. According to Darren Davis (2007, 66 and 68), "In general, gender as revealed by psychological studies of posttraumatic stress, is also an important factor in individual reactions to the terrorist attacks, because women were more sociotropically and personally threatened by the terrorist attacks than men were." Here, "sociotropic" refers to *collective* concerns (especially national), in contrast to *self-interested* ones (Kinder and Kiewiet 1979), and to public opinion studies that found gender differences consistent with women's greater protectiveness of society and sensitivity to threats or risks regarding economic welfare, the environment, and collective, personal, and family well-being in general. The greatest gender differences have occurred on issues related to force and violence, although there is also some evidence for diminishing gender differences over time, though varying by issue (see Shapiro and Mahajan 1986).

As for racial differences, African Americans were slightly more concerned than whites about the terrorist threat (differences ranged from 4 to 6 percentage points and were statistically significant overall). Latinos, at least initially, appeared less concerned, but their perceptions converged toward those of whites and blacks as their concern increased noticeably as time went by (see figure 2.5). Our data are generally con-

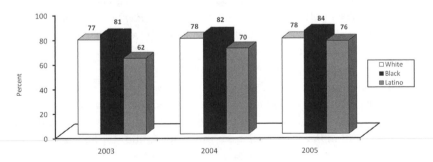

FIGURE 2.5. Concern about terrorist threat, by race

sistent with Davis (2007, 66) who emphasized the black experience
historically and contemporaneously, "African Americans' tendency toward greater stress than other groups," and how "this may create greater
sensitivity to threatening and stressful situations." He found that blacks
and Latinos expressed greater personal threat than whites, but that there
were no significant racial differences pertaining to the terrorism threat
nationally (66, 68).

Americans under 35 years old were more concerned about future terror attacks than those 35 years and older. The age gap actually narrowed
a bit over time from 11 points in the summer of 2003 to 7 points two
years later. It is possible that catastrophic terrorist attacks abroad had
some effect on the threat assessments of young adults and Latinos as
noted above. But overall the age differences appeared stable. According to a survey conducted in August 2003, education did not seem a factor in Americans' concerns about terrorism. But in follow-up polls they
went up a bit among individuals with and without high school degrees
and decreased slightly among those with the highest educational attain-
ment. The gap between those who finished high school and those with
the highest degrees (including postgraduates and professionals) widened
in the following years. Thus in the case of education we see some modest divergences in threat perceptions over time. It is possible that the first
survey was an aberration, deviating from what were more typical differences attributable to the greater overall confidence and sense of well-
being that comes with greater educational achievement. Or being better educated may be associated with exposure to information both about
the terrorist threat but also about efforts to protect the nation from it.

In contrast to Davis (2007, 250n9), we found a persistent and pronounced partisan difference in terrorism threat perceptions. Figure 2.6
presents the data for 10 time points over a five-year period. The differences between self-identified Democrats and Republicans are striking, given that we would normally expect partisan differences to occur
mainly on issues that divide the parties, especially ideological ones, and
not necessarily perceptions of reality—or the reality depicted in the media. In the month after 9/11, 38% of Democrats responded that they worried a "great deal" about more terrorist attacks, compared to 25% of Republicans. This partisan gap remained intact over time. Independents
tended to fall in between, perhaps a bit closer to the Republicans on average. There was one period of convergence in September 2003, as the

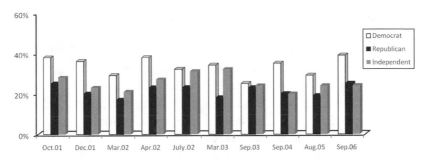

FIGURE 2.6. Concern about terrorist threat, by party ("Great deal")

perception of this threat declined for all groups, perhaps owing to what appeared to be complete victory over Saddam Hussein, whom the Bush administration had tried to link to the terrorism (see chapter 4). While it is possible that the partisan differences we found were attributable to the fact that women and African Americans tend to self-identify as Democrats, the disparities were too large and persistent to be explained fully by this (as Davis [2007, 250n9], finds for personal threat). We had expected partisan differences to be more important on policies we discuss in later chapters where we focus on issues over which partisans might be expected to disagree. But here they emerge apparently because of the increase in partisan polarization that has occurred over the last 30 years. This growing partisanship has been so severe that it has not only led to a great ideological divide among political party leaders and partisans in the mass public on both domestic and foreign policy issues, but has also affected perceptions of facts and realities over which there should normally be little if any disagreement (see Abramowitz and Saunders 2005; Fiorina, Abrams, and Pope 2006; Shapiro and Bloch-Elkon 2006, 2008b; Jacobson 2008, 2010, 2011; Bafumi and Shapiro 2009; Levendusky 2009; Snyder, Shapiro, and Bloch-Elkon 2009; Abramowitz 2010). But in the post-9/11 atmosphere, Republicans were more optimistic in overcoming the terrorist threat because of their great trust in President Bush. The partisan differences regarding threat perception did not widen, so that whatever affected the perceptions of the public as a whole over time, also affected each partisan subgroup about the same.

To sum up, when it came to perceptions of the seriousness of the terrorist threat in post-9/11 America, the differences based on partisanship and gender and, to a lesser extent, race tended to be most pronounced.

Threats and the Dynamics of Public Opinion

After he exploded a bomb in the French National Assembly in 1893, the anarchist Auguste Vaillant justified his deed as the only sure means to be heard and understood. As he explained, "The more they are deaf, the more your voice must thunder out so that they will understand you" (Schmid and de Graaf 1982, 11). In today's information overload, far more than at the end of the 19th century, individuals and groups try get their messages across by resorting to increasingly strident language and—more effective yet—dramatic actions. As one expert noted, "the most difficult task is not getting one's message out, but finding a receptive audience" (Shenk 1997, 102). Public opinion trends after 9/11 show that the public reacted to terrorist threats and government alerts and their amplification in the mass media.

The American public responded understandably to the information it received: Since there were no follow-up attacks in the immediate years after 9/11, it had less reason to fear further terrorist violence. While we need to be cautious in making claims about strong cause and effect relationships, the data are suggestive. As we see in figure 2.7 the line tracking the public's perceptions of terrorism as the most important issue facing the country today reveals that after 9/11 this perception decreased noticeably (we will discuss some of the short-term increases further below). This trend correlates significantly with responses to three questions dealing with concerns about terrorist attacks: great concern about

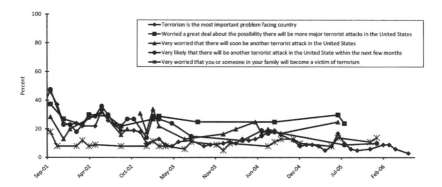

FIGURE 2.7. Concern about terrorist attacks

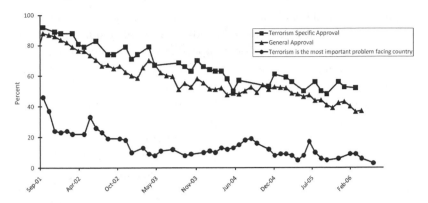

FIGURE 2.8. Presidential approval and terrorism

major terrorist attacks (Pearson's $r = .77, p < .005$), worries about an attack occurring soon ($r = .51, p < .01$), and thinking that an attack will occur in the next few months ($r = .79, p < .001$). Interestingly, the correlation with individuals' personal worries about being a victim of terrorism is much less ($r = .41$, ns).[8] This highlights the difference between terrorism as a collective national issue and as a threat that is not likely to affect individuals directly where they live. As 9/11 and the anthrax scare became more distant history, the terrorist threat as covered in the media became more an overarching national concern and less a personalized one (cf. Davis 2007).

Figure 2.8 shows that public perceptions of terrorism as the most important issue facing the country also tracked significantly with President Bush's general approval rating, ($r = .74, p < .001$) and with his handling of terrorism ($r = .715, p < .001$).[9] This is consistent with the rises and declines of a rally effect in which, in this case, the public tied the president's approval rating to an assessment of the terrorist threat (cf. Heatherington and Nelson 2003). The war on terrorism that President Bush declared kept this issue high on his and the media's agenda. Of course, the causal connection here is weak, if anything, as the long-term decline in approval was ultimately related to the public's dissatisfaction with the Iraq War, the faltering economy, and the declining effectiveness of the White House spin machine. Despite the administration's efforts to convince the public otherwise, during his second term Bush no longer benefited much from any claims of success on the terrorism front (see Jacobson 2008, 2011).

In exploring the dynamics of public opinion, the threat messages from Al Qaeda leaders and the Bush administration, and news coverage of both of them, we focused on responses to survey questions dealing with concern about terrorist attacks over different time horizons, terrorism affecting respondents personally, terrorism as most the important issue facing the country, and President Bush's relevant approval ratings.[10] We examine these data for the 39-month period from October 1, 2001, through December 31, 2004. To avoid confusion over the threats and alerts that were covered by network news and the *actual* threats and alerts by administration officials and the Al Qaeda leadership, we refer in the following discussions to news or media messages that were contained in news coverage and to original or actual statements that were part of speeches or other communications by administration officials or Al Qaeda leaders. We emphasize in our discussion the most notable relationships based on correlations and the limited multiple regression analysis we could do given our fragmentary public opinion data (treating public opinion as the dependent variable and media content and actual statements as independent variables).[11]

At the outset we thought that the volume of threat coverage might relate to public perceptions of terrorism as a major national problem. Since research has demonstrated the agenda-setting function particularly with respect to terrorism (Iyengar and Kinder 1987; Nacos 1996; Norris, Kern, and Just 2003), one would expect that the volume of reported threat messages had a measurable impact on the public's evaluation of the importance of terrorism as the major national problem. Surprisingly, this was not apparent in our case. If anything, it was not the total volume of threat messages that mattered but *who* conveyed such messages. On second thought, this result was less surprising because our measure of the total of threat messages represented only a fraction of the complete public debate on terrorism. And it is the *complete* volume of reporting on terrorism that has been found to affect the public's agenda. So, what did our data suggest? Regarding how the public ranked terrorism as a major national problem, we found that particular media messages and actual threat statements had the strongest relationship. Specifically, messages involving President Bush concerning terrorist threats and alerts were correlated over time with responses to the most important problem question ($r = .63$, $p < .001$). Among all the media variables these messages in television news were related to the public's perceptions. In addition, news messages by or attributed to administration officials alerting the public to specific terrorist threats or describing such threats against the American homeland in general terms had a strong relationship in this case ($r = .83$, $p < .001$; regression coefficient, $b = 2.69$, $p < .001$). There was, also not surprisingly, a correlation ($r = .62$, $p < 001$) between television coverage of what President Bush said about these threats and alerts and the actual statements about them by administration officials.

While these measures decreased over time, there were also some short-term increases along the way. When Bush's and other officials' reactions and comments about terrorist threats were reported in television news, the public was more likely to perceive terrorism as the most important problem the nation faced. This happened at several time points: In June 2002, a high point in the public's threat perception followed several alerts during the previous months, when administration officials initiated a heightened state of concern for railroads and other transit systems and warned of specific threats against the Statue of Liberty and the Brooklyn Bridge. Moreover, in early June Attorney General John Ashcroft made the dramatic announcement that Jose Padilla, a U.S. citizen and Al Qaeda associate, had been arrested before he could acquire and explode a "dirty bomb" in an American city. As television news covered these announcements heavily, the public's view of terrorism as a major problem for the country increased by 11 points. Similarly, two events covered by the press seemed to affect public attitudes: First, the chairman of the 9/11 Commission, Thomas Kean, stated publicly that the 9/11 attacks could have been prevented. Three days later, Secretary of Homeland Security Tom Ridge raised the terrorist threat alert for the upcoming holidays. Finally, in the months before the 2004 presidential elections the public's perception of terrorism as a major problem strengthened steadily, with a high point during the months preceding Election Day and reaching the same level as in November 2002 (when the American-led coalition made progress in the fight against Al Qaeda and the Taliban).Washington's strategically timed threat alerts achieved what they were supposed to.

In the case of the public's concern about additional major terrorist attacks in the United States, sources in the media themselves may have had the only connection to public perceptions. Specifically, we identified TV news anchors, correspondents, and reporters describing the terrorist threat in general terms or reporting on increases in the alert levels ($r = .54$; $b = 1.20$, $p < .01$). This recasts an earlier finding (Page, Sha-

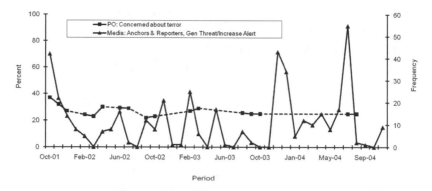

FIGURE 2.9. Concern about more major terror attacks, October 2001–December 2004

piro, and Dempsey 1987; Page and Shapiro 1992) that identified TV news commentary as having the strongest relationship to the public's policy preferences: in this case the professional "voices in the news" collectively appeared to be associated with changes in public attitudes. Figure 2.9 shows a few corresponding high points or small increases over time, when media professionals talked more often about threats or increased levels of alert, and the public became more concerned about terrorist attacks. This happened in October 2001 shortly after 9/11, in the summer of 2002, and around February/March 2003 before the Iraq invasion. As noted in chapter 1, we often have only intermittent public opinion data, as indicated in figure 2.9 and later figures by *broken or dotted lines*, in comparing trends in opinion and news media coverage. More important, in this case and others that we examine, the correlations that we find may be driven by modest changes and high points (and significant correlations [Pearson's *r*], even as great as .9, may result from moderate or small media content and opinion changes).

When poll questions mentioned a particular time frame, asking whether respondents worried that another terrorist attack would occur "*soon*," the actual statements by administration officials, either alerting the public to specific terrorist threats or speaking in more general terms about the threat, were related to public opinion ($r = .49, p < .05$; $b = 1.64, p < .1$). As the public's perceptions went up and down noticeably, a similar general pattern occurred for statements by officials. For example, in June 2002, when there were more official statements about the terrorist threat and increased alert level, the public's level of worry rose by a dozen points compared to the previous poll. Similarly, a large number of threat messages by administration officials in February 2003, only weeks before the Iraq invasion, was followed by a sudden and striking double digit (18-point) increase in the percentage of Americans who were very worried that a terrorist attack would occur soon.

For perceptions of the likelihood of another terrorist attack in United States within a *"few months,"* there was a noticeable relationship between these, the media's coverage of President Bush's statements concerning the terrorist threat ($r = .58, p < .01$), and the actual statements by administration officials alerting the nation to specific threats or speaking in more general terms about the threat of terrorism ($r = .73, p < .001$; $b = 2.86, p < .01$). Figure 2.10 shows the corresponding highs and lows in all three trends. Upticks in public opinion corresponded with increases in actual terror alerts and other threat warnings by the administration and news coverage of such official warnings and alerts.

As to personal concerns, figure 2.11 presents a slightly different picture. Regarding being very worried or worried about becoming a terrorist victim, bin Laden mattered most: specifically, public officials' (including President Bush's) comments on TV about the seriousness of threats from bin Laden or Al Qaeda ($r = .44, p < .05$); news anchors, correspondents, or reporters describing bin Laden's or Al Qaeda's threat communications in general ($r = .46, p < .05$); the actual warnings of more terrorist attacks by bin Laden and his Al Qaeda associates themselves ($r = .44$, $p < .05$); and U.S. officials' actual statements about the threat posed by Al Qaeda ($r = .40, p < .1$; $b = .781, p < .1$). Even as time passed, a relatively high percentage of Americans continued to worry that they personally and their loved ones would be affected by a terrorist attack. There were

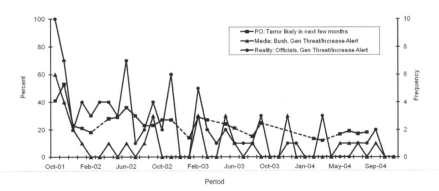

FIGURE 2.10. Likelihood of attack in the next few months, October 2001–December 2004

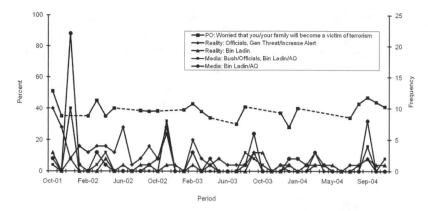

FIGURE 2.11. Worry about becoming a victim of terrorism, October 2001–December 2004

some but not many sharp changes in this trend. In this case, unlike the others we examined, just the mentioning of bin Laden or Al Qaeda in TV news reports, or the appearance or sound of bin Laden or Al Qaeda leaders on videotape or audiotape appeared to matter. Apparently, the architects of the 9/11 attacks continued to have a hold on the public's mind—people remained apprehensive not just about protecting the nation but about their own and their families' security—although the likelihood of any individual being harmed by terrorist attacks was very low. These were very likely emotion-driven responses. When members of the administration, including President Bush, referred to bin Laden by name and this was reported on network news, such references were more numerous than the actual communications by bin Laden or Al Qaeda.

How did all this affect President Bush's approval rating? It appears that both his overall approval ratings and the public's rating of his handling of terrorism were associated in the short term with news coverage of President Bush's statements about the terrorist threat and increases in the alert level (overall approval: $r = .42, p < .05$; approval in handling terrorism: $r = .37, p < .1$) and by administration officials' public statements on this issue (overall approval: $r = .68; p < .01; b = 3.93, p < .01$; approval on terrorism: $r = .64, p < .05; b = 4.03, p < .01$). Even though the general pattern in figure 2.12 was a gradual decrease in both approval ratings, indicative of the effects of increasing dissatisfaction with the president on other fronts as noted above, certain short-term increases in these ratings corresponded with increases in the numbers of administration statements and news reports citing President Bush on the terrorist threat. It seems that as the administration issued terror alerts and otherwise magnified the threat of terrorism, the president's approval ratings benefited. Our finding here is consistent with other research results: based on several time series analyses of terror alerts issued by the Bush administration and presidential approval ratings from February 2001 through May 2004, Rob Willer (2004, 1) found "a consistent, positive relationship between terror warnings and presidential approval."

Further, while it is not surprising that we found a correlation between public perceptions of the terrorist threat and actual or mass-mediated terrorism alerts, this was a one-sided effect. When it came to reporting about the official *lowering* of terrorism alert levels, this news coverage was not prominent—if it occurred at all. One does not have to be a cynic to suspect that pronouncements of a relaxed state of alert for terrorism were not politically beneficial. The 2004 campaign and postelection analyses, as we noted, bore this out.

Hyping the threat of terrorism was part of President Bush's 2004 campaign strategy designed to neutralize the negative perceptions of the Iraq occupation that had gotten bogged down. Ultimately this campaign was successful: exit polls and other survey analyses showed that Bush benefited from voters most concerned with terrorism (Hillygus and Shields 2005; Langer and Cohen 2005). But the propaganda of threat and fear was part and parcel of the administration's post-9/11 politics of terrorism designed to enlist public support for controversial policies adopted in the name of counterterrorism, national crisis, and war.

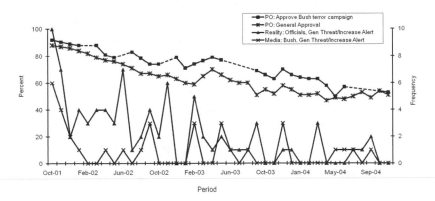

FIGURE 2.12. Terrorism and approval of Bush, October 2001–December 2004

Conclusion: News Media as Government's Big Helpers

True to the media's appetite for sensational and dramatic "breaking news" to engage their audiences, strengthen their ratings, and increase their ad prices, national newscasts devoted ample airtime and prominent placement both to direct threats from Osama bin Laden and his associates on the one hand and to terrorism alerts issued by administration officials on the other. Indeed, network news—and, no doubt, cable TV, radio, and the print media as well—did not simply report but magnified this news. In comparison, the nondramatic and presumably calming news of administration decisions to lower the alert levels went underreported and thus minimized. If anything, the volume and prominence of threat coverage was greater than we had expected at the outset.

These patterns of media attention arguably played into the hands of the Al Qaeda leadership whose communications left no doubt about its goal to keep the threat of terrorism alive in the minds of Americans. President Bush and others in his administration, too, benefited from the prompt and significant coverage of the alerts and threat assessments, thereby reminding the American public why the "war on terrorism" had to be fought. It seemed that the White House did not, in effect, mind the prominent coverage of bin Laden and Al Qaeda threats. Whereas the administration protested against the airing of bin Laden's videotapes by U.S. television outlets shortly after 9/11, no such complaints were filed thereafter. Albeit belatedly, President Bush himself told a White House reporter that he believed "his 2004 re-election victory over Sen. John Kerry was inadvertently aided by Osama bin Laden, who issued a taped diatribe against him the Friday before Americans went to the polls."[12] As the president put it, "I thought it was going to help. I thought it would help remind people that if bin Laden does not want Bush to be president, something must be right with Bush."[13] It was equally or even more likely that bin Laden wanted Bush to be reelected, since the Iraq War continued to be Al Qaeda's most important recruiting tool. Senator Kerry also recognized this; he told an interviewer soon after the election that he lost to President Bush because of the bin Laden video.[14]

After the end of the Cold War, some media scholars expected that the disappearance of the long Cold War consensus would free the media from following presidents' and administration officials' dominance in framing. In contrast, there might have been reasons to expect that the executive branch would still find ways to benefit from the information monopoly or control that it has—or can exert—in *foreign policy and national security*, especially in "crisis" situations. This makes it difficult for critics to compete. They might be co-opted or forbidden from talking (e.g., opposition party members engaged in intelligence "oversight" committee work), or might not want to be proven wrong. There are then no critics or elite debate to cover (Page and Shapiro 1992, chaps. 4, 5, and 8; Page, personal communication; Shapiro and Jacobs 2000). Even if there were a short period in the post–Cold War decade during which the news media were more independent of Washington officials in foreign policy reporting, there was a return to the old reporting patterns after 9/11 with respect to frequent threats by terrorists and government alerts and gloomy threat assessments. Just as during the Cold War and actual post–Cold War military deployments, the news was shaped by sources deemed or "indexed" by the media as most influential inside the administration and among its outside supporters (i.e., experts who tended to be former members of the executive or legislative branches). In the absence of voices in Congress, the news media, and elsewhere who questioned the utility of hyping the threat of terrorism, the administration unleashed an effective propaganda campaign of threat and fear. It was only after President Bush's reelection, that an increasing number of Americans began to suspect political motives behind the strategically timed terror alerts. When the effectiveness of the drum beat of threat waned significantly in President Bush's second term, so did the frequency of official terror alerts.

The attacks of 9/11 themselves and the news of those events, absent opposition voices, fueled the powerful "rally-round-the-flag" that led to the president's sudden and subsequently durable public approval record. The president's own statements about the threat of terrorism and the media's reporting of them appeared to help maintain his robust approval ratings, if not increase them, at a most critical time: It was in the months immediately following the 9/11 attacks, when Bush's public (and elite) approval was at record levels, that the president and his advisers decided on the most far-reaching counterterrorism policies at home and abroad without encountering any strong opposition.

Although declining over time, Americans' concerns about terrorism within the nation's borders remained fairly high after 9/11, and they increased in the short term when the media reported about heightened threats and terrorism alerts. The public's worries about "catastrophic" terrorism in their country persisted, and in the wake of the July 7, 2005, bombings of the London transit system, they were actually more pronounced than in the weeks after the 9/11 attacks.

The public's perception of terrorism as the country's most important problem was related to official government threat alerts and to messages from the main terrorist leaders themselves. But contrary to our expectations, it was not the total volume of "threat" news on television but rather messages conveyed from particular sources that were associated with movements in public opinion. Here, the president and administration officials appeared to have the greatest effect on Americans' collective assessment of terrorism as the nation's top problem. Other public perceptions appeared to be related to messages from different news sources. Media professionals' reporting on terror alerts and threats seemed to track public concerns about major acts of terrorism against the United States occurring *some time in the future*. Americans' worries that terrorism would happen *soon* also appeared to react to actual statements by administration officials—indeed, the administration's official terrorism alerts were covered heavily and were likely to be perceived as signaling imminent attacks. However, bin Laden's actual threats and press coverage of them appeared to be associated with Americans' concerns that they and their families could become the victims of this threatened political violence.

Whereas bin Laden's threat did not win (nor aim for) the sympathies of Americans, President Bush's approval ratings were not hurt by and likely benefited in the short term from the official alerts, threat assessments, and related press coverage. As noted earlier, some administration officials were aware of these effects. After he resigned as secretary of homeland security in early 2005, Tom Ridge told reporters, "There were times when some people were really aggressive about raising it [the color-coded terror alert level], and we said, 'For what?'"[15]

To summarize, Al Qaeda and the Bush administration used the mass media to convey their messages of fear. By overreporting the frequent "fear messages" from the administration, the media contributed to the creation of what one critic called a "culture of hysteria" (Kellner 2005, 28)—a climate of fear that conditioned Americans to rally around the president and his war on terrorism, while keeping possible opponents silent. The press coverage in the months and years after 9/11 was at odds with the concept of news-as-public-good but was consistent with the imperatives of news-as-commodity. More important, this chapter affirms the government's ability—that is, the executive branch's—to affect the news and even to use the media in the way emphasized by both the "indexing" and propaganda or hegemony models of political communication.

CHAPTER THREE

Civil Liberties versus National Security

The cost of freedom is always high, but Americans have always paid it. And one path we shall never choose, and that is the path of surrender, or submission. — John F. Kennedy

On September 12, 2001, the day after the most lethal act in the history of modern terrorism, the *New York Times* published a letter to the editor by a reader from Bethesda who wrote, "The inevitable temptation to change fundamentally the nature of our society, by attacking the civil rights and civil liberties of any individual or group, must be resisted" (Koppel 2001, 26). On the same page, one of the newspaper's editorials warned, "Americans must rethink how to safeguard their country without bartering away the rights and privileges of the free society that we are defending." Similarly, *Times* columnist Anthony Lewis (2001, 27) cautioned that "one danger must above all be avoided: taking steps that in the name of security would compromise America's greatest quality, its open society." In the following week, opinion pieces in the *Times* overwhelmingly supported the upholding of civil liberties. The problem was that during this most critical period the news media, including the *Times*, did not report fully and prominently about the Bush administration's proposed curbs on civil liberties in the name of greater security. And after the administration rushed a massive antiterrorism package through a compliant Congress and the president signed the USA PATRIOT Act into law, the media laid low when it came to reporting about the administration's encroachments on civil liberties and human rights. This led Anthony Lewis to write several years later, after he had left the *Times*,

Coverage of the administration's record on civil liberties since September 11th has, in my judgment, been sadly inadequate. An example: I first heard about the administration's claim that it could indefinitely detain American citizens simply by calling them enemy combatants . . . I saw it in a story a few paragraphs long in The New York Times. I was bewildered. Why wasn't that claim important news?[1]

There was good reason to be bewildered. The cavalier fashion in which the media handled the treatment of captured or suspected terrorists was a case in point. Stuart Taylor, Jr. (2003), for example, wrote that "unlike the 1949 Geneva Convention regarding prisoners of war, the torture convention protects even terrorists and other 'unlawful combatants.' But its definition of torture—intentional infliction of 'severe pain or suffering, whether physical or mental'—leaves room for interpretation." *Newsweek* columnist Jonathan Alter (2001) suggested, "even as we continue to speak out against human-rights violations around the world, we need to keep an open mind about certain measures to fight terrorism, like court-sanctioned psychological interrogation. And we'll have to think about transferring some suspects to our less squeamish allies, even if that's hypocritical. Nobody said this was going to be pretty." In the *Atlantic Monthly*, Mark Bowden (2003) distinguished between hard-core torture and torture "lite" or what he suggested should be called "coercion." With respect to torture lite, he wrote, "Although excruciating for the victim, these tactics leave no permanent marks and do no lasting physical harm." He, too, opted for hypocrisy. "The Bush Administration has adopted exactly the right posture on the matter," he wrote. "Candor and consistency are not always public virtues. Torture is a crime against humanity, but coercion is an issue that is rightly handled with a wink, or even a touch of hypocrisy; it should be banned but also quietly practiced" (Bowden 2003, 76).

In other words, do it but do not admit it and do not get caught. After his article was published, Bowden was interviewed on CNN and NBC's *Today Show*. The hosts did not seem uncomfortable with his views. CNN's Soledad O'Brien started and ended her interview with Bowen by calling his article "fascinating." When opponents of torture did appear on such shows, premised on presenting opposing views, they were typically drawn from human rights/civil liberty organizations and allotted less time to articulate their less provocative arguments.

Some of the leading newspapers took editorial stands against torture. The *Washington Post*, for example, published two such opinion pieces in the two years after 9/11. In one of them, the *Post* stated "there are cer-

tain things democracies don't do, even under duress, and torture is high
on the list" (*Washington Post* 2002). Some editorial pages rejected torture most of the time but accepted it in the context of the post-9/11 "war
on terrorism." Thus, the *Buffalo News* editorialized,

> A recent story in the *Washington Post* makes clear what every American
> must have already suspected regarding the treatment of al-Qaida and Tali-
> ban prisoners. Harsh treatment, perhaps to the point of torture. For the most
> part, we're not losing sleep over that revelation, given the facts of the last
> 15 months. But while aggressive interrogation techniques are both important
> and even, to a point, acceptable, there still must be rules and mechanisms for
> accountability to prevent wholesale torture (*Buffalo News* 2002).

Some of the media's chosen experts were enthusiastic advocates of
wholesale torture and vilified the opponents of this interrogation method.
These voices became more frequent and louder, especially but not only
on the Fox News channel, after the capture of Khalid Sheihk Mohammed, an Al Qaeda operative who organized the 9/11 attacks. Law professor emeritus Henry Mark Holzer (2003, 5J), for example, wrote, "in approving the use of torture—or at least accepting it—they needn't suffer
even a scintilla of moral guilt. Torture of whatever kind, and no matter
how brutal, in defense of human rights and legitimate self-preservation
is not only not immoral; it is a moral imperative."

All in all, advocates of torture, torture lite, coercion, aggressive interrogation, and extraordinary rendition (meaning the "outsourcing" of
torture to states known as notorious human rights violators) were frequently represented and rarely challenged in television and print media
during the time, when the Bush administration implemented what the
Department of Justice's "torture memos" justified. It was only after the
images of Abu Ghraib were publicized in early 2004 that the media paid
more attention to critics of torture and abuse in U.S.-run detention facilities abroad.[2]

Terrorism and the Vulnerability of Liberal Democracies

Liberal democracies are particularly vulnerable to terrorist attack by
individuals and groups because of their commitment to freedom and

openness. One might well have expected the United States to have experienced many more such attacks than it has. Too weak to fight and to defeat the security forces of states, terrorists engage in psychological warfare with two particular goals besides their political objectives: first, they aim to frighten, intimidate, and demoralize a nation's citizenry; second, they hope to push governments to overreact and violate the democratic state's most esteemed values, in particular the rule of law. There is ample evidence that major terrorist events result in high levels of public fear and anxiety. This was particularly true in the wake of 9/11 as described in the previous chapter. Similarly, in reaction to serious terrorist threats, whether domestic or transnational, democratic states tend to curb individual freedoms in the name of preventing further attacks (Wilkinson 2001; Cole and Dempsey 2006; Pious 2006). The United States has experienced foreign threats and reactions and overreactions by decision makers. The Alien and Sedition Acts of 1798, the Espionage Act of 1917, the Sedition Act of 1918, and the internment of Japanese Americans during World War II serve as examples. In this respect, the response of the U.S. government to the attacks on the World Trade Center and the Pentagon was no exception. And Al Qaeda's leaders were aware of this.

Several weeks after those strikes Osama bin Laden told Al Jazeera reporter Taysir Alluni, "So I say that freedom and human rights in America have been sent to the guillotine with no prospect of return, unless these values are quickly reinstated. The government will take the American people and the West in general to a choking life, into an unsupportable hell" (Lawrence 2005, 113). From the perspective of terrorists, the success and failure of their violence are measured less by the number of people killed and maimed than by the psychological impact and the antiterrorism responses in the societies they target. Terrorists win when they persuade the citizens and elites of democracies that "the strengths of these societies—public debate, mutual trust, open borders, and constitutional restraints on executive power—are weaknesses" (Ignatieff 2004). The challenge for democracies is to be able to withstand the pressures from such threats, especially exaggerated ones that lead to violations of civil liberties and rights.

Less than six weeks after the terrorist attacks of September 11, 2001, President George W. Bush signed into law a massive package of antiterrorism provisions that Congress had all but rubber-stamped. In his signing statement the president said, "Today we take an essential step in defeating terrorism while protecting the constitutional rights of all Americans."[3] According to Bush, the USA PATRIOT Act of 2001 had the overwhelming support of Congress, "because it upholds and respects the civil liberties guaranteed by our Constitution."[4] Some constitutional and privacy rights experts, however, concluded later that this hasty response to the 9/11 attacks "violated core constitutional principles" and "reflected an overreaction all too typical in American history" (Cole and Dempsey 2006, 196). Others, however, noted that the choice was between existentially threatening evil and lesser evils, and that "sticking too firmly to the law simply allows terrorists too much leeway to exploit our freedoms. Abandoning the rule of law altogether betrays our most valued institutions. To defeat evil, we may have to traffic in [lesser] evils" (Ignatieff 2004).

The post-9/11 era demonstrated once again that attitudes about trade-offs between collective security and individual liberty are not static but change under different circumstances. As the overview of one constitutional symposium put it,

> The tension between national security and civil liberties fluctuates from normal times to crises; a crisis often forces the reassessment of civil rights and liberties. When people fear their security is threatened, they often are willing to acquiesce in incursions of civil liberties as a perceived trade off to gain a sense of greater personal safety. Conversely, when people feel secure, they are inclined to bridle at even minor constraints on their personal liberties.[5]

In the days, months, and years after 9/11 many Americans feared that another major attack inside the United States would occur in the near future; in effect, they believed that their nation's and their personal security were threatened. As described in chapter 2 these concerns were amplified by frequent threats from Al Qaeda leaders, by warnings issued by the Bush administration, and, most importantly, by the news media's tendency to overcover such threats and alerts.

It was within this atmosphere that President Bush signaled a change in the U.S. government's counterterrorism approach: terrorism would no longer be considered a criminal activity dealt with by law enforcement and the rule of law. Instead, terrorists were regarded as "unlawful combatants" and therefore "not entitled to due process of law or the protection of international conventions regarding the treatment of prisoners of war" (Pious 2006, 7). One day after the attacks on the World Trade Center and the Pentagon, Congress seconded the president's declaration of war against terrorism by authorizing the commander-in-chief to use military force against the 9/11 perpetrators and their supporters.[6] Years later, one scholar concluded that the Bush administration "has relied on this law . . . for almost all actions it takes against those it deems to be terrorist threats, even when there is no al-Qaeda connection" (Pious 2006, 8). As Phillip Bobbitt pointed out,

> There is a virtual universal conviction that the constitutional rights of the People and the powers of the State exist along an axial spectrum. An increase of one means the diminution of the other. On this spectrum we imagine a needle oscillating between two poles, moving toward the pole of the State's power in times of national emergency or toward the pole of the People's liberty in times of tranquility (Bobbitt 2008, 241).

In the climate of fear after 9/11, when Americans were told by their leaders that the nation was at war, the needle moved significantly in the direction of the state's powers.

But while governments have justified the curtailment of civil liberties and the shift from criminal law enforcement to military measures as beneficial to national security, some experts in the field concluded that "on balance, even measured only in terms of effectiveness, there is little evidence that curtailing civil liberties will do more good than harm" (Cole and Dempsey 2006, 196, 197). The later successes of British authorities in foiling terrorist plots and apprehending the plotters were explained by UK officials' willingness to learn "from their mistakes" in the past struggle against the Irish Republican Army, when they relied on military force, and by their subsequent "determination to treat terrorism as crime—*not* as an extraordinary military threat" (Cole 2008, 68). In the process, "the UK has been considerably more restrained and sensitive to rights in its response to terrorism since 9/11 than the United States" (Cole 2008, 68). Whatever the results of curbs on civil liberties, Paul Wilkinson (2001, 115) warned,

> It must be a cardinal principle of a liberal democracy in dealing with the problems of terrorism, however serious these may be, never to be tempted into us-

ing methods which are incompatible with liberal values of humanity, liberty and justice. It is a dangerous illusion to believe one can "protect" liberal democracy by suspending liberal rights and forms of government.

The Press and the Civil Liberties versus Security Debate

Unlike constitutional and privacy rights scholars who discussed and wrote about security-versus-liberty issues and trade-offs after 9/11, the public—even the interested public that read leading newspapers like the *New York Times* and the *Washington Post*—was ill informed about the Bush administration's rights violations in the name of protecting Americans from the next terrorist attack. In the summer of 2004, after the breaking news of torture at Abu Ghraib, Anthony Lewis commented on the post-9/11 arrest of thousands of aliens who had nothing to do with terrorism but who were nevertheless held and mistreated for weeks or months before being deported—typically for visa or immigration violations. The press largely ignored what should have been significant news stories. Citing one example, Lewis wrote, "The secrecy that pervaded the alien sweep—even families were not told where their missing members were—is the sort of thing that usually arouses the press. But with some honorable exceptions, notably a fine series in the *Chicago Tribune*, the detentions were not treated as a major story."[7]

One plausible explanation for the press's failure to inform citizens fully about new problems and issues while watching over government, was simply that reporters, anchors, editors, producers, and others in newsrooms were as shocked and traumatized by the events of 9/11 as the public at large. After all, newsrooms are not hermetically sealed against the prevailing attitudes in the society that they are part of. In addition, members of the news media were well aware of the administration's warning that opponents of counterterrorist measures were unpatriotic and helpful to terrorists. Since the Department of Justice took the lead in pushing for and justifying curbs on civil liberties as an important weapon in the war on terrorism, Attorney General John Ashcroft was especially vocal in attacking critics as being on the side of terrorists. In December 2001, in his testimony before the Senate Judiciary Committee, Ashcroft said, "to those who scare peace-loving people with phantoms of lost liberty, my message is this: your tactics only aid terrorists, for they erode our national unity and diminish our resolve. They give ammunition to America's enemies, and pause to America's friends."[8] This was certainly an attempt to intimidate critics. Finally, the contemporary news media's preference for simple narratives that are well suited for sound-bite reporting worked against providing comprehensive and prominently placed news coverage of the complex legal issues arising from the trade-offs between civil liberties and national security. Add to that the constant vilification of the enemies in America's new war by the president and other sources generously covered by the press, and the result was apathetic reporting that confirmed "the tendency of the press to record rather than critically examine the official pronouncements of government" (Bennett, Lawrence, and Livingston 2007, 9). Regarding coverage of the USA PATRIOT Act, a cursory review of relevant stories publicized in major news outlets concluded,

> Although the new law expanded the federal government's surveillance and intelligence-gathering powers, the news media failed to inform the public fully about the hastily written and adopted legislation's potential impact on civil liberties. Except for mentioning in passing the adoption of the legislation by the U.S. House of Representatives and the U.S. Senate or the president's signing of the bill, the major television networks (ABC, CBS, and NBC) completely ignored the far-reaching legislation. CNN, National Public Radio, and the print media did not do much better in this respect (Nacos 2007a, 149).

Public Opinion on Civil Liberties versus Security Trade-Offs

Traditionally, Americans have been willing to accept curbs on certain civil liberties for the sake of enhanced collective and individual security when they had reason to feel threatened. In the immediate aftermath of the Oklahoma City bombing in April 1995, for example, more survey respondents favored than opposed restrictions on civil liberties in the service of effective counterterrorism. But as time went by the public became less concerned about terrorism and less willing to accept civil liberty curbs. Thus, two years after the Oklahoma City bombing, a solid majority of Americans believed it was not necessary to give up civil liberties in order to fight terrorism.[9] After the 9/11

attacks when the U.S. government adopted extraordinary antiterrorism measures that affected illegal immigrants, legal residents, and even
citizens, Americans were also inclined to give their government more
leeway.

Compelling studies of public attitudes toward the trade-off between
civil liberties and security after 9/11 examined survey data collected
soon after the attacks on the World Trade Center and the Pentagon.
One initial study found that "the greater people's sense of threat, the
lower their support for civil liberties" (see Davis and Silver 2004, 28;
Davis 2007, chap. 4). In addition, however, the degree of trust in government that individuals had also affected their attitudes, in that "the
lower people's trust in government, the less willing they are [and were
after 9/11] to trade off civil liberties for security, regardless of the level
of threat [perception]" (Davis and Silver 2004, 28; Davis 2007; chap. 4;
see also Berinsky 2009, chap. 7). Other researchers compared survey
respondents' attention to the news with their attitudes and opinions: Nisbet and Shanahan (2004) found that people who paid a great amount
of attention to national television news and news on terrorism were far
more fearful of future attacks than those who were less attentive consumers of TV news. Further, those with a high level of fear were significantly more supportive of restrictions on civil liberties than those who
were less fearful. In other words, there were distinct links between news
consumption, perceptions of threat, and opinions toward restrictions on
civil liberties.

While it has been long established that the American public widely
supports constitutionally protected rights and liberties *in the abstract*,
its support for specific rights at specific times depends on whether there
is a credible threat to the nation that might require actions that challenge such civil liberties. The public increasingly favored curbing these
rights (free speech, free assembly, etc.) for particular groups when these
groups posed a threat: most notably communists in the United States
during the early Cold War and others as far back as the Alien and Sedition Acts of 1798, President Abraham Lincoln's actions in the Civil
War, the Palmer Raids against the radical left after World War I, and
the internment of Japanese Americans during World War II. But when
the specific threats subsided or ended, public opinion became less supportive of these restrictions on personal liberties (see Stouffer 1955; Davis 1975; Sullivan, Piereson, and Marcus 1982; Mueller 1988; Page and
Shapiro 1992, chap. 3). Past research, however, did not examine empiri-

cally the role of the mass media in providing the public with information about the status of particular threats to the nation's security and government demands for curbs on civil liberties.

Methodology and Data

For this chapter, unlike the previous one, we retrieved and coded full transcripts of TV network news segments that reported on or mentioned civil liberties and the USA PATRIOT Act in the context of terrorism; the news abstracts often failed to provide all the information required to fulfill our coding requirements.[10] After identifying news sources that were interviewed or mentioned from October 1, 2001, through December 31, 2004, our coders categorized the messages from these sources as positive, negative, or neutral/ambiguous with respect to the government's handling of civil liberty/security measures, proposals, justifications, and so forth. We also took note of any particular government actions and plans designed to restrict particular personal freedoms, such as domestic eavesdropping, the issuance of identification cards, government access to personal records, profiling, and the like.

We collected the relevant public opinion survey data covering Americans' views on civil liberties and/or security, in some instances going beyond the period of our news media analysis. Although the Roper Center's iPOLL contained a total of 3,235 survey questions that included the term "terrorism" in the more than four years from September 11, 2001, to December 31, 2005, there were comparatively few questions about attitudes toward civil liberties and security issues brought on by the terrorist strikes. We retrieved responses to a total of 28 repeated survey questions that were asked twice or more from the iPOLL archive, "Polling the Nations," the Marist College Institute for Public Opinion, and other sources. Unfortunately, in most instances the same question wording was repeated only once or twice. Our analysis therefore focused on five questions that were repeated most often and that dealt with the most important civil liberties versus security issues (see the online appendix for this chapter; available at http://www.press.uchicago.edu/books/nacos/). As in the previous chapter, we also examined the opinions of population subgroups of interest, such as by gender, race, party identification, and other attributes, to find out the extent to which these societal groups varied in their attitudes regarding civil liberties. Last, as in the other chapters, we explored the relationship between television news coverage and the public's perceptions and opinions regarding trade-offs between civil liberties and security.

Modest Substantive Coverage of Civil Liberties Issues

During the weeks, when the Bush administration pushed Congress to adopt in a hurry the most comprehensive antiterrorism package in history, the news media reported sparsely on the substance of the legislation before both houses of Congress. In addressing the legislation, the press focused on the process (e.g., efforts to build bipartisan support in Congress; the attorney general's demand for speedy action); when news items mentioned the content of the legislative package, they were typically limited to enumerating the areas of proposed restrictions. A case in point was the report that ABC News aired on the *World News Tonight* program of October 25, 2001:

> PETER JENNINGS, anchor: At the White House tomorrow, President Bush will sign into law a bill that gives law enforcement sweeping powers of surveillance. The Senate passed the bill today by a vote of 98–1 despite some fierce opposition from civil liberties groups. ABC's Pierre Thomas joins us in Washington tonight. Pierre, the administration got pretty much what they wanted.
>
> PIERRE THOMAS: Peter, the attorney-general said today the government will attempt to get terrorists any way it can.
>
> JOHN ASHCROFT (Attorney General): Let the terrorists among us be warned. We will use every available statute. We will seek every prosecutorial advantage.
>
> THOMAS (Voice-Over): Law enforcement's new powers include making it easier to detain and deport foreign nationals, expanding the power to wiretap telephone conversations, giving the government power to review unopened voice mail, expanding the government's ability to track e-mail and harsher penalties for anyone harboring or financing terrorists. The government's campaign against organized crime in the 1960s is the model for the new Justice Department war on terrorism.
>
> MR. ASHCROFT: Robert Kennedy's Justice Department, it is said, would arrest mobsters for "spitting on the sidewalk" if it would help in the battle against organized crime.

THOMAS: But Peter, critics say terrorist—the government will soon have too much power. And people's civil rights will soon suffer.

JENNINGS: Thank you, Pierre. Indeed, that is an argument.

In the months and years that followed, when this topic was covered, it got little airtime as the following CBS News report of November 19, 2002, illustrates:

SUSAN MCGINNIS, anchor: Opening the door for broader use of wiretap, a federal appeals court gives Attorney-General John Ashcroft a big win and raises some big concerns about personal freedom. Ashcroft had been pushing for more authority to track terrorists through the use of wiretaps. Now he plans a quick push to put them in use. Ashcroft promises a new computer system to get quick court approval for surveillance. It doubles the number of FBI attorneys working with surveillance applications, and it designates one lawyer in each US attorney's office as the point of contact for these cases.

JOHN ASHCROFT (Attorney-General): The court issued an opinion that affirm [sic] President Bush's and Congress' call for greater cooperation and coordination in the war on terror.

MCGINNIS: Civil liberties groups say the ruling violates free speech and due process. Ashcroft claims there is no desire to erode personal freedom.

The *NBC Nightly News* segment of April 19, 2004, followed the same pattern as the previous two reports in that it is short, starts out with a description of the Bush administration's position, provides a member of the administration the opportunity to make a statement, and just mentions critics' concerns:

TOM BROKAW, anchor (Los Angeles): President Bush meantime used a stop in Hershey, Pennsylvania, today to make a case for expanding government powers to root out potential terrorists under the so-called PATRIOT Act. The law, passed after the September 11th attacks, gives law enforcement official broad search and surveillance powers. Some of the act's provisions are due to expire next year. Today, the president tried to get a running start in persuading Congress to renew the bill.

PRESIDENT GEORGE W. BUSH: We must continue to stay on the offense when it comes to chasing these killers down and bringing them to justice, and we will. We've got to be strong and resolute and determined.

BROKAW: But critics say that the PATRIOT Act infringes on civil liberties. Some congressional Republicans as well as Democrats are trying to
amend it.

Even so-called in-depth reports on civil liberties issues after 9/11
received only limited airtime. Thus, when *CBS Evening News* devoted its "Eye on America" feature to examine surveillance practices
(May 16, 2002) and disagreements over the USA PATRIOT Act (October 5, 2004), only 477 and 504 words, respectively, were allotted to these
segments. *NBC Nightly News* dedicated its "IN DEPTH" highlight to air a
450-word report on homeland security and civil liberties (May 8, 2003)
and a 460-word report on the PATRIOT Act (September 10, 2003). And
when ABC's *World News Tonight* reported on the tension between privacy and security (November 25, 2002) and on the PATRIOT Act (July 2,
2003) as part of the program's "A Closer Look" reports, the airtime was
limited to 477 words for the first of these reports and 536 words for the
second.

During the 39-month period we examined, we found 157 relevant
news segments on civil liberties issues that were aired by ABC, CBS,
and NBC News, compared to 373 stories dealing with terrorism threats
and alerts that we discussed in the previous chapter. Of those 157, ABC
News broadcast 40%, NBC News 34%, and CBS News 26%. These news
stories contained 832 separate messages covering various sources' statements and positions on civil liberty issues and on particular aspects of
the security versus civil liberties debate.

It was not President Bush but rather Attorney General Ashcroft who
was most often cited in the news when it came to security and civil liberties. While the president appeared or was cited infrequently in TV newscasts, his attorney general appeared or was cited nearly four times as
often and accounted for 8.5% of all news sources in these types of stories. This reflected Ashcroft's and the Department of Justice's aggressive advocacy of expanded authority for law enforcement and intelligence agencies. Taken together, administration sources had nearly as
large a share (18%) of all sources as they did in the terrorist threat and
alert news. Members of Congress, who rarely made network news with
respect to the threats and alerts, were more often seen, heard, or cited
in the news about civil liberties, comprising more than one-tenth of all
sources. In all, government actors, including members of the administration, Congress, and state and local governments, totaled more than

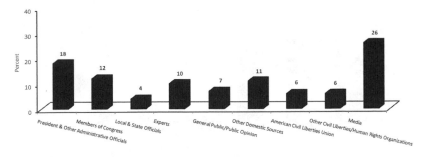

FIGURE 3.1. News: Sources in security/civil liberties news

one-third of all sources and constituted the single largest source category. Representatives of the American Civil Liberties Union (6%) and other civil liberties and human rights groups (6%), as the most outspoken opponents of civil liberties restrictions, totaled 12%, and anchors, correspondents, and reporters combined, about one-fourth of all sources (see figure 3.1).

The pro and con views expressed in television news coverage that addressed post-9/11 policies in the area of civil liberties/security were divided, with 25% of the messages supporting particular government measures other than the PATRIOT Act and 28% opposing them (see figure 3.2). Only 3% of the news messages were ambiguous regarding these policies, whereas 26% expressed the need for an effective balance between providing security and protecting individual freedoms without supporting or opposing particular government measures or proposals. As mentioned above, there was very little reporting on the substance of the original PATRIOT Act that was adopted several weeks after 9/11. In the spring of 2004, the administration began its campaign for the renewal of several provisions of the law that expired after December 31, 2005. By that time, more coverage and attention than before was devoted to opposition voices that arose inside and outside of Congress. This second time period tilted the debate in favor of those who opposed curbs on civil liberties. During the whole 30-month period, 18% of all messages concerned the PATRIOT Act, with 7% supportive, 9% opposed, and 2% ambiguous. It was not unusual for short news reports to air first a neutral description of the issue at hand and then provide President Bush, Attorney General Ashcroft, or other administration officials an opportunity to argue in favor of the government's position; the segments would then have a correspondent or the program's anchor mention that civil

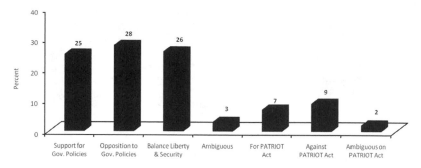

FIGURE 3.2. News: Positions on security/civil liberties

libertarians opposed the measure. While critics ultimately had a slight advantage in the sheer numbers of news messages, members of the administration received more airtime per message and made their case far more often directly in front of cameras and microphones than their opponents. It is noteworthy that more than half of all messages supporting the government's actions dealing with security and civil liberties came from administration sources, and about two-thirds overall from government officials, including congressional and state and local government sources, in addition to those speaking directly for the Bush administration. The American Civil Liberties Union and other civil liberties organizations accounted for about one-third of all messages expressing opposition to restrictions on individual freedoms, followed by members of Congress and experts.

When the networks reported on particular counterterrorism or homeland security proposals and measures, they focused overwhelmingly on restrictions of those freedoms that had the potential to affect many Americans. The more than six in 10 news messages that were devoted to specific curbs on civil liberties and human rights dealt with allowing government agencies to access the personal records of individuals found in the databases of libraries, banks, workplaces, Internet service providers, and the like; followed by the right to eavesdrop on individuals' communications, proposals to issue new identification cards or to use new identification methods, and the practice of "profiling" members of certain groups (see figure 3.3). More of these messages were critical than supportive of domestic eavesdropping and government authority to access personal records, whereas there was far more support than opposition in the cases of new biometric methods and other means to identify foreigners entering the United States and even noncitizens within the country.

Of all the messages addressing civil liberties restrictions, just over a third were devoted to issues of habeas corpus and other legal rights of captured or suspected terrorists, the rights of Americans and foreign nationals detained in U.S. facilities after 9/11, and the legality of torturing or assassinating terrorists or terrorist suspects. News sources taking positions on these issues argued more frequently for granting detainees certain rights and civil liberties, regardless of whether they were swept up in post-9/11 mass arrests across the United States or were "enemy combatants" captured in Afghanistan or elsewhere. As mentioned earlier, the media paid far more attention to critics of inhumane treatment of detainees after the Abu Ghraib scandal broke in the spring of 2004.

In sum, in the over three years after 9/11, the TV news networks infrequently presented their audiences with reports on proposals and laws to protect Americans by restricting various individual liberties. Even when such news features were announced as "in-depth" examinations of important issues, they tended to be rather short. Administration officials, members of Congress, and state and local government leaders were the main news sources. When administration officials were interviewed or cited, they tended to receive more airtime to voice support for new government measures than did critics of these policies. Still, apart from the length of airtime allotted to different news sources, there was a balance between the number of pro and con messages in the debate in the media on security versus civil liberties, with a slight advantage to the critics. This tilt in favor of critics occurred when elite criticism of the Bush administration's conduct of the war on terrorism grew and public trust

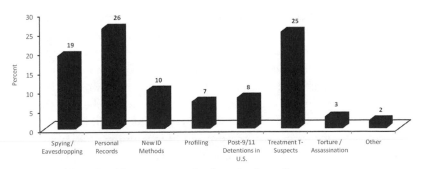

FIGURE 3.3. News: Specific counterterrorism/homeland security measures

in the president's handling of the war against terrorism declined as result of the early ill-fated occupation of in Iraq. The media devoted significantly more attention to potential and actual curbs on Americans' right to privacy in general than to civil liberties and human rights issues affecting detained and alleged terrorists.

The Public and the Balance between Liberty and Security

As noted in the previous chapter, after 9/11 heavy television news viewers were far more fearful of further terrorism in the United States and more supportive of government restrictions on civil liberties than infrequent watchers of TV news (Nisbet and Shanahan 2004). This was hardly surprising since the media magnified any threats and provided a melodramatic narrative that idealized Americans while vilifying the nation's enemies—bin Laden, Al Qaeda, and, by extension, Muslims and Arabs in general. According to Debra Merskin (2005, 375), President Bush contributed to this storyline by applying "words and expressions—us, them, they, evil, those people, demons, wanted: dead or alive" to the enemy. Yet, in one short passage of his address to a Joint Session of the U.S. Congress less than two weeks after 9/11, President Bush spoke about the need to uphold the nation's fundamental democratic values. Directly appealing to fellow Americans, he said,

> I ask you to uphold the values of America and remember why so many have come here. We are in a fight for our principles, and our first responsibility is to live by them. No one should be singled out for unfair treatment or unkind words because of their ethnic background or religious faith.[11]

In reality, the Bush administration and a submissive Congress did not uphold the values of America and instead adopted antiterrorist policies that made for a less liberal state without encountering meaningful opposition. As Ronald Dworkin (2003) noted some two years after 9/11, "Many Americans believe that the Bush administration's security policies are a justified response to the terrorist threat. They believe that the attacks on September 11 require (as it is often put) 'a new balance between liberty and security.'" However, in tune with the administration's overall post-9/11 rhetoric and mass media narrative, it was hardly surprising that issues of balance in this context often came down to "the majority's security and *other* people's rights"—with "others" meaning most of all so-called enemy combatants held in U.S.-run military detention centers (Dworkin 2003).

These attitudinal differences were not limited to the rights of terrorists or alleged terrorists or, rather, the denial of such rights. David Cole (2008, 71) suggested that Americans have "greater sensitivity to privacy than liberty," and that these sentiments "may be attributable to the perception that intrusions on privacy potentially render everyone vulnerable." But while public opinion surveys after 9/11 revealed that the majority of Americans rejected, in general, direct infringements on their own privacy, even in the war on terrorism, they supported such curbs on privacy if such measures mentioned suspected terrorists as the objects of these restrictions. Thus, even immediately after the attacks on the World Trade Center and the Pentagon, seven of 10 Americans opposed the idea of allowing the U.S. government to monitor their own telephone calls and e-mails in order to fight terrorism. Similarly, a majority rejected the suggestion to allow the government to monitor their credit card purchases. A year after 9/11, opposition to such intrusions on privacy had grown even stronger with three of four poll respondents rejecting eavesdropping on phone and e-mail communications and close to two-thirds opposing the monitoring of credit card usage.[12] But when respondents were asked about "increased powers of investigation that law enforcement agencies might use when dealing with people suspected of terrorist activities," Americans overwhelmingly favored such encroachments even when told that this "would also affect our civil liberties." From September 2001 through September 2004, between eight and nine of 10 Americans favored "stronger document and physical security checks for travelers"; close to two-thirds supported "expanded camera surveillance on streets and in public places"; three of five agreed with "law enforcement monitoring Internet discussions in chat rooms and other forums"; and three to four of five supported "closer monitoring of banking and credit card transactions, to trace funding sources."[13]

At times, pollsters seemed helpful to the supporters of far-reaching limits on privacy and civil liberties, when they asked questions like the following, "What about public libraries giving intelligence and law enforcement agents access to the names of people who have borrowed books or other material that might be used in planning a terrorist attack?" Since the question implied that the only targets of such intrusions of privacy were likely terrorists, three of four Americans strongly favored or were willing to accept such measures.[14]

When responding to survey questions about the USA PATRIOT Act that mentioned the law's importance in finding suspected terrorists or preventing further terrorism, a plurality of the public consistently said that the act was about right. While support for the PATRIOT Act declined only a bit, if at all, from the summer of 2003 to December 2005, there was a significant increase during the same period of those who felt that the act "goes too far." One notable shift occurred in "don't know" responses, which declined to merely 4%. The news coverage of the prolonged and contested debate surrounding the renewal of controversial provisions in the PATRIOT Act may have increased the public's awareness.[15]

The American public was divided on the question of racial, religious, or ethnic profiling as a means to identify potential terrorists, according to a survey conducted in June 2002; two months later, however, a solid majority (three of five) said such a measure would go too far.[16] Even so, a majority was adamant in denying suspected terrorists the same rights that detained crime suspects were guaranteed. In the fall of 2002 and 2004, when presented with the statement that "law enforcement officials should have the right to indefinitely detain suspected terrorists," about six of 10 respondents agreed.[17] This suggested that a solid majority of the public supported the Bush administration's refusal to grant suspected terrorists in U.S.-run detention facilities the constitutionally guaranteed right to ask a court to determine the lawfulness of their detention. However, when asked specifically whether the government should be allowed to detain American citizens without review by a judge, the majority of survey respondents said this would go too far.[18] (Eventually, the Supreme Court ruled in a 5–4 decision that detainees at Guantanamo Bay did in fact have the right to habeas corpus and thus the right to challenge their detention in federal court.[19])

The following survey question was asked several times in the years after 9/11: "In order to curb terrorism in this country, do you think it will be necessary for the average person to give up some civil liberties, or not?" While immediately after 9/11 roughly six in 10 Americans answered "yes," this willingness to give up "some," though unspecified, civil liberties weakened in the following months and years (see figure 3.4). By June 2002, the public was divided 46%-46% on this question, and in July

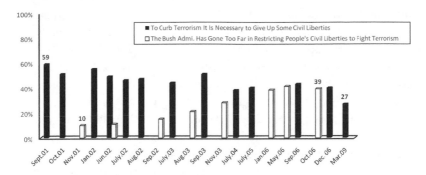

FIGURE 3.4. Public opinion on trade-offs: Liberty vs. security

2003, for the first time since 9/11, more respondents said it was not necessary to give up civil liberties than those willing to do so. In the following years support for curbs on "some civil liberties" declined further as
the opposition grew to solid majorities.[20] There were several slight upticks along the way that followed official terror alerts, major terrorist incidents abroad (e.g., the suicide bombings on London's commuter system), or coincided with anniversaries of 9/11.

As they were faced with the tension between security and civil liberties during a time of perceived national threat, Americans tried to find
some kind of balance in their attitudes; in the process they oscillated between accepting and rejecting "some" restrictions on personal freedom.
This was particularly evident in the way respondents reacted to a choice
in a different question (not shown) of "the authorities taking all necessary steps to prevent further terrorism even at the expense of civil liberties" or "taking such steps without restricting individual freedom." At
first pluralities and then solid majorities opted for the government doing
everything necessary to prevent more terrorism as long as it did so without violating civil liberties.[21] Perhaps more to the point, several weeks after 9/11 only one in 10 respondents felt that the Bush administration had
gone too far in restricting civil liberties in order to fight terrorism, but as
figure 3.4 shows, this criticism became gradually more pronounced and
grew to nearly four in 10 by 2006.

In sum, then, Americans were reluctant to accept restrictions on their
own privacy and on civil liberties in general, but they were willing to allow authorities to violate some of the same rights during the investigation of suspected terrorists and to deny suspects the constitutional guar-
antee to ask federal courts to hear their habeas corpus petitions. Stated

differently, Americans were less likely to accept privacy and other civil
liberties restrictions that they believed would affect them personally and
more likely to support such curbs that they believed to inhibit others,
namely, terrorists, suspected terrorists, and their sympathizers. This assumes implicitly, of course, the ability of the FBI and other government
agencies to distinguish these groups. Most important, actual events (reported in the press) that had the potential of affecting public perceptions
of the threat of terrorism and the overall post-9/11 "us against them"
narrative in the media seemed to explain aberrations in opinion trends
that by and large moved in the direction of putting the brakes on restricting civil liberties.

Subgroup Differences in Opinions

The subgroup opinion data span the period from September 2001 to the
end of 2006. Consistent with Berinsky (2009) and Nisbet and Shanahan
(2004) and based on what we found in our analyses of threat perception,
we expected that partisanship and ideological self-identification (liberal,
moderate, conservative) would reveal substantial opinion differences
when it came to questions of security versus civil liberties. We also expected largely parallel opinion movements over time, as the public as a
whole was influenced by events and new information it received through
the media. Based on trend data before and after 9/11, Berinsky (2009,
chap. 7) found that partisan differences regarding the security/civil liberties trade-off were initially limited, but they grew and fell in line with the
"partisan divisions that mirror the politics of the day" (Berinsky 2009,
166). By and large our data reflect similar trends.

   Again, one survey question central to our analysis asked, "In order to
curb terrorism in this country, do you think it will be necessary for the
average person to give up some civil liberties, or not?" A few days after
9/11, a solid majority of Republicans, Democrats, and Independents responded that it would be necessary to give up some civil liberties. This,
however, did not mean the absence of any partisan divide: Republicans' support for the restriction of some civil liberties was significantly
greater from the outset (12 percentage points more than that of Democrats; 13 points greater than that of Independents). This support gradually declined in all three groups in the following years, but the partisan
gap widened, with only a majority of Republicans seeing the need to give
up civil liberties (see figure 3.5). Respondents who identified themselves

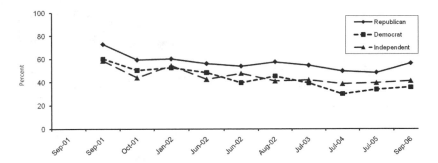

FIGURE 3.5. In order to curb terrorism in this country, do you think it will be necessary for the average person to give up some civil liberties? By party ID ("Yes, it is necessary")

as conservatives favored civil liberty curbs more than did liberals and moderates. Several weeks after 9/11, the gap was 16 points between conservatives (62%) and liberals (46%) and 7 points between conservatives and moderates (55%). These differences did not widen much further, if at all: In September 2006 the ideological differences were 18 points between conservatives and liberals and 10 points between conservatives and moderates.

In the case of racial differences, we can elaborate further on previous research about attitudinal differences and similarities between African Americans and Hispanics on the one hand and whites on the other, based on different group experiences. As Davis and Silver (2004, 31) noted, African Americans have tended to be particularly strong supporters of civil liberties in large part because of "their struggle for civil rights and a distrust of government," whereas "Hispanics may not have as profound a history for civil liberties and civil rights as African Americans, but have also not been fully integrated into American society and show little faith in government." Figure 3.6 shows that during the five years after 9/11 whites were more likely to see the need for restrictions on civil liberties to limit terrorism than were blacks and Hispanics. In a poll taken within days of 9/11, 57% of whites compared to 49% of both blacks and Hispanics thought that civil liberties would have be curbed. By September 2006, a decline had occurred for all three groups, with the gap widening somewhat (to from 8 to 14 points) between whites and the others. The nine other polls between the first and last surveys in this series overall showed a fairly consistent downward trend for white and black Americans regarding the need to give up civil liberties. There

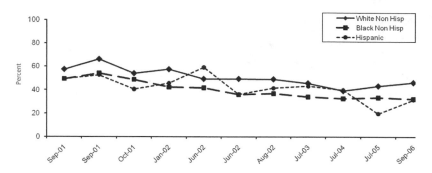

FIGURE 3.6. In order to curb terrorism in this country, do you think it will be necessary for the average person to give up some civil liberties? By race ("Yes, it is necessary")

may have been more fluctuations for Latinos because of the larger sampling errors in their small subsamples. For this issue, the opinions of Latinos appeared more similar to those of African Americans than whites. While Latinos at times may take on the values and perspectives of the dominant group (whites)—which may have occurred for the issues we examine in other chapters—in this case these members of a nonwhite *immigrant* group (broadly defined) may have felt especially vulnerable to restrictions on rights and liberties targeted toward certain foreigners and foreign sympathizers.

Younger Americans under age 35 years were much less willing to give up some civil liberties in order to prevent terrorist acts than were those over 35 years old. This is consistent with the younger age group's lower level of perceived threat of further terrorism (see chapter 2). During the years after 9/11, the differences between the younger versus older age groups were typically around double digits: Immediately after the 9/11 attacks, 44% of those under 35 accepted limits on some civil liberties compared to 59% of those older, a 15-point difference. Five years later, a 13-point gap remained. In between, the difference narrowed twice— presumably in reaction to terrorist attacks abroad and/or official terror alerts. But just as for the public overall and other subgroups, the acceptance of civil liberty restrictions may have diminished over time, because there were no further terrorist attacks in the United States and approval of Washington's handling of the war against terrorism declined.

After 9/11 a majority of men and women were willing to sacrifice civil liberties to help curb terrorism. In past research, women were somewhat more supportive than men of restricting the rights, for example, of communists and others ostensibly threatening the nation, though they were much more likely than men to oppose wiretapping (see Stouffer 1955; Shapiro and Mahajan 1986). But in the first poll after the attacks on the World Trade Center and Pentagon 54% of men and 55% of women saw the need to sacrifice civil liberties. This view declined for both sexes, with no systematic or consistent difference between them. In September 2006, contrary to what past studies would have led us to expect, there was an 8-point gender difference, with 47% of men but only 39% of women supportive of civil liberties restrictions. In between, more often women, but several times men, were more supportive of restrictions. Thus, overall, there was no predictable gender gap.

While partisanship has been a major factor associated with subgroup differences in this and the previous chapter (and it will be again in the next chapters), past research beginning with Samuel Stouffer's seminal work on "tolerance" found that education has been profoundly important in understanding public support for protecting rights and liberties. Indeed, we found that educational levels were related to individuals' attitudes toward the trade-off between civil liberties and security, but not systematically in the way we had anticipated. We had expected the better educated to be most wary of government actions that restricted civil liberties. In some cases they were. For example, when asked in Gallup/ CNN/*USA Today* surveys whether "the PATRIOT Act—goes too far, is about right, or does not go far enough—in restricting people's civil liberties in order to fight terrorism?" those with a college degree were consistently the most likely to say that the PATRIOT Act had gone too far. In February 2004, 33% of college graduates said this, compared to 29% of those with some college, 22% of high school graduates, 12% among those with some high school, and 5% of those with an eighth grade education or less (the figures for November 2003 were 35%, 26%, 20%, 18%, and virtually 0%, respectively).

But some of the responses to the 11 relevant questions for which we had breakdowns by education revealed less consistent results of this sort. The trend data show a lot of similarity overall in terms of parallel opinion changes or opinion convergence over time (Page and Shapiro 1992, chap. 7). In a few cases, individuals with some college education and even postgraduates and those with advanced professional degrees were more likely than those with less education to recognize the need give up some rights and liberties for the sake of combating terrorism (see figure 3.7). This finding was, at first glance, surprising since higher levels

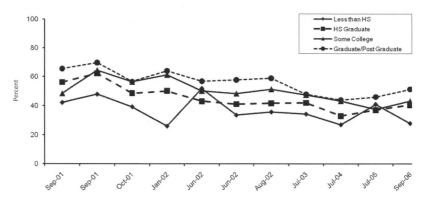

FIGURE 3.7. In order to curb terrorism in this country, do you think it will be necessary for the average person to give up some civil liberties? By education ("Yes, it is necessary")

of education have persistently been associated—for more that 50 years (since such opinions were first measured)—with support for protecting civil liberties; education has arguably led individuals to learn about, understand, and support the nation's constitutionally protected rights and liberties, though this causal process is not fully understood (Stouffer 1955; Davis 1975; Bobo and Licari 1989; Page and Shapiro 1992, chap. 3). On the other hand those who were better educated were more likely to be exposed to breaking news and information about alleged threats—thus learning about the justifications for the restrictions and being persuaded by them (cf. Page and Shapiro 1992; Zaller 1992). Or, after 9/11, they were simply more aware of the reality that people were already being subjected to more security checks that constituted restrictions on what previously had been taken for granted as rights and liberties, so that the better educated were more likely to respond, as shown in figure 3.7, that it was "necessary for the average person to give up some rights and liberties" in order to prevent terrorism.

In this case, the ebb and flow from one poll to the next seemed particularly great among survey respondents without at least a high school degree. According to a survey taken in June 2002, 52% of respondents who had not finished high school supported civil liberties restrictions—a 26-point increase from early January 2002. The same poll revealed that acceptance of restricted civil liberties declined among high school graduates, respondents with some college education, and those with college degrees and further postgraduate education. It is possible that prominent news coverage about the capture of the alleged "dirty bomber" Jose Padilla a few days before this particular survey was conducted threatened the public and affected the survey responses of those with the least education, who had been less attentive to these issues earlier. However, less than two weeks later, the acceptance of civil liberties restrictions among this group dropped by 18 points. Similarly, a few days after the July 2005 suicide attacks in London, 41% of Americans with less than high school education were inclined to give up civil liberties compared to only 27% a year earlier. Except for respondents with some college education who were slightly less willing to give up some rights and liberties than in the previous poll, other educational groups showed slight increases in support for some curbs on their rights.

As we found in the previous chapters, demographic characteristics and partisanship matter in understanding Americans attitudes—in this case toward the trade-off between civil liberties and security. But for this issue, we found no systematic gender differences in opinions, and the results for education also appeared to deviate from those in past research. The magnitude of any subgroup differences aside, we found similar dynamics across groups: changes in concern for protecting civil liberties over several years occurred largely in tandem—as the result of everyone receiving the same information and standards of judgment conveyed through the media (Page and Shapiro 1992, chaps. 7–8).

Dynamics of News Coverage and Public Opinion

As many studies have suggested and as we saw earlier in the case of the threat of terrorism, the volume of news coverage can significantly affect the public's perceptions of the importance of an issue. With respect to civil liberties versus security after 9/11, we found to some extent that when media coverage of this issue increased, the public appeared less willing to allow the government to expand its *specific* investigative powers to prevent future terrorist attacks. Specifically, public perceptions of *particular* methods of surveillance that were directed to identify terrorists but potentially violated every individual's right to privacy were correlated with simply the amount of news coverage of restrictions on civil liberties' and not the particular content of news reports. The overall volume of coverage was less closely related to more *general* attitudes to-

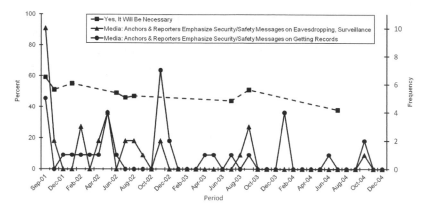

FIGURE 3.8. The necessity to give up civil liberties in order to curb terrorism, October 2001–December 2004

ward civil liberties. The data suggest that particular messages conveyed from different types of news sources were associated over time with public attitudes about the general civil liberties/security trade-off.

Figures 3.8 and 3.9 compare the trends for news reporting on civil liberties with the public's opinions for which we found rough but apparent relationships. The data show that the media's reporting on civil liberties versus security issues decreased noticeably after the initial very general coverage right after the 9/11 attacks, as did the public's willingness to give up civil liberties and to accept violations of basic rights.

Figure 3.8 shows that in response to the question examined earlier— *"In order to curb terrorism in this country, do you think it will be necessary for the average person to give up some civil liberties, or not?"*— the percentage of the public who thought it was "necessary" decreased 22 points from 2001 to 2004 from a high in 2001, when a strong majority believed it was necessary to give up civil liberties in order to fight terrorism. The particular news content appeared to be related to public attitudes. Specifically, statements in the media concerning security or safety that focused on two main topics, domestic eavesdropping (surveillance of communications via Internet, telephone, or other communications) and government agencies' secret access to Americans' medical, bank, and library records had the highest correlation over time with responses to the above survey question ($r = .72$, $p < .05$; $r = .76$, $p < .05$, respectively). Also, messages originating from television news anchors or correspondents appeared to be connected with public perceptions on the general need to curb civil liberties. These relationships were apparent in late 2001, when the press reported extensively on the arrest of the would-be shoe-bomber Richard Reid during a U.S.-bound transatlantic flight and what this revealed about the state of aviation security. Other short-term increases in news reporting and public support for the need to curb civil liberties came on the heels of news about official terror alerts, actual or foiled terrorism, the beginning of the Iraq War, and the failure to capture Saddam Hussein after the fall of Baghdad. From that period onward, the falloff in media attention to security issues, especially involving eavesdropping, led to a public that was less willing to give up civil liberties to avoid future terrorist attacks.

A similar pattern occurred when the survey question was framed in general terms but in a different way: "*Which comes closer to your view—the government should take all steps necessary to prevent additional acts of terrorism in the US (United States) even if it means your basic civil liberties would be violated, or the government should take steps to prevent additional acts of terrorism but not if those steps would violate your basic civil liberties?*" There was an overall drop of 16 points from January 2002, when almost half of the public (47%) thought the United States should take all the steps necessary even if civil liberties were violated, to only 31%, almost two years later, in November 2003. In this case, statements in the media by subcabinet administration officials (including those in the Department of Homeland Security and the Department of Justice) concerning specific domestic security activities

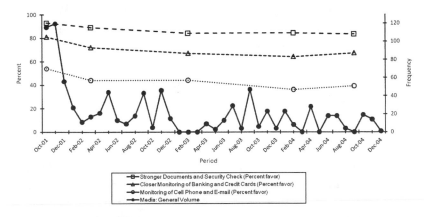

FIGURE 3.9. Favor increased monitoring to prevent terrorism, October 2001–December 2004

such as eavesdropping and surveillance of Internet and phone communication were correlated with the public's positive responses to the above question ($r = .84, p < .05$). The percentage of the public responding that the United States should take all steps even if civil liberties were violated was the greatest the first time it was asked in a January 2002 survey, a few months after 9/11, when news coverage was relatively high; opinion first fell off to 31% in February 2002 as media attention decreased. During the entire period we studied, there were four time points, based on the available data, when our measures of media content and public opinion had coinciding high points.

When we compare trends in news coverage with the public's perceptions of *specific measures* restricting civil liberties, we see in figure 3.9 that the volume of messages concerning civil liberties issues appears to be related roughly to the trend in responses to most of the survey questions: "*Here are some increased powers of investigation that law enforcement agencies might use when dealing with people suspected of terrorist activity, which would also affect our civil liberties. For each please say if you would favor or oppose it . . . Stronger document and physical security checks for travelers?*" As noted earlier, even in the aftermath of 9/11, Americans were reluctant and to a large extent unwilling to support loss of liberty and privacy that affected everyone; but there was significant support for curbing the rights of terrorists, suspected terrorists, and possible supporters of terrorism. The fact that the above question focused first and foremost on suspected terrorists and not on everyone's civil liberties explains the high level of public support for the government's increased investigative powers throughout the period. When the media reported less overall on civil liberties versus security, the public appeared somewhat less supportive of increases in specific investigative powers to protect against future terrorist attacks. To this end, there was a decrease over the years, though not a large one, in those who favored stronger security checks of travelers. But, again, support of such measures remained very high throughout this period. Most important here is that responses to this question were correlated with the volume of media coverage ($r = .90, p < .05$).

In the case of public attitudes concerning "*Closer monitoring of banking and credit cards transactions, to trace funding sources,*" we find a similar pattern: there was a decrease over time among those who favored closer monitoring of such transactions—81% in September 2001, compared to 67% three years later in September 2004. Responses to this question were correlated with the volume of media coverage ($r = .93$, $p < .05$) and also with media reports emphasizing security and safety issues and commenting on eavesdropping and invading personal records ($r = .9, p < .05; r = .96, p < .01$, respectively). The modest decline in public support for closer government monitoring of transactions from October 2001 to March 2002 coincided with a falling off of media reports emphasizing particular security and safety issues.

On the issue of *"Expanded government monitoring of cell phone and e-mail, to intercept communication,"* the overall picture is the similar. In September 2001 more than half of the public, 54%, favored expanding official monitoring of communications, while the percentage decreased steadily over time. By September 2004, exactly three years after 9/11, just over one out of three people were willing to expand monitoring of the above means of communication. In this particular case, in addition to the correlation with the volume of media coverage ($r = .87, p = .055$), there was a comparably strong correlation with media reports concerning security issues, specifically regarding government agencies getting records and personal information on Americans—penetrating bank records, hospital records, and the like ($r = .90, p < .05$). This was obviously a case in which most Americans might fear that investigators could not and would not be able to distinguish between suspected terrorists and completely innocent citizens and residents.

To summarize, then, it appears that the general volume of media reporting on civil liberties issues was not related to the public's general attitudes toward the right balance between security and civil liberties. But news volume, occasionally reinforced by messages emphasizing specific security and safety measures, was associated with public opinion toward closely monitoring the activities of individuals, most of all suspected terrorists.

Last, how did media coverage affect public attitudes toward President Bush's handling of civil liberties? As we saw earlier (see figure 3.4) public criticism of Bush increased in response to the question, *"Do you think the Bush administration—has gone too far, has been about right, or has not gone far enough—in restricting people's civil liberties in order to fight terrorism?"* In the two years from November 2001 to November 2003, there was a sharp increase, almost threefold, of those who thought the administration had gone too far in restricting people's liberties: from only 10% rising to 28% in November 2003. It appears that these results were not related to news reports on this issue. There were no significant

correlations between the public's criticism of Bush on this score and any
media content measures (data not shown)—in contrast to our analysis
of news coverage of the threat of terrorism (chapter 2), in which threat
messages from government officials appeared to produce short-term increases in approval. Americans initially supported efforts to combat terrorism that imposed restrictions on civil liberties, but they became critical of how far the Bush administration was taking the country in that
direction.

Thus there were limits to the public's support for the administration
itself in these actions (Davis 2007)—and limits to the persuasive powers
that administration officials attempted to exert through the media.

Conclusion

Among the ways terrorists intend to harm the democratic nations they
target is to evoke fear that leads to overreactions, which in turn have
other negative consequences. One such consequence is the undermining
of civil liberties, freedom, and political openness in the effort to provide
greater security. The threat of communism after the Bolshevik Revolu-
tion, during the "Red Scare," and later during the McCarthy investigations of the early Cold War increased the American public's apprehension, which then increased support for restricting liberties and rights in
the name of "national security" (see Stouffer 1955; Davis 1975; Mueller
1988; Page and Shapiro 1992, chap. 3). Similarly, in the case of terrorism,
a democratic society will weaken its most fundamental values by acting
in opposition to them in responding to the threat of terrorism (see Davis
2007; Merolla and Zechmeister 2009). This thereby fulfills the goals of
its terrorist enemy. The press can be a force to prevent this, in guarding
democratic values and guarding against government's abuse of power in
attempting to protect the nation. However, news coverage of the terrorist threat, as we saw in chapter 2, fueled the flames of fear that in turn,
as this chapter has shown, led a significant part of the public to go along
with narrowing civil liberties as government increased its monitoring of
the behavior, communications, and records of individuals—most strikingly as it affected suspected terrorists. We found that subgroups differed in their attitudes and that the divisions were strongest along partisan and racial lines.

Several decades ago, in his seminal study of leading news organizations, Herbert J. Gans identified eight values in the news that comported with an underlying "picture of nation and society as it ought to be" (Gans 1979, 39). The admiration and idolization of individualism was one of those inherent values. Based on his content analysis of the news, Gans concluded that "one of the most important enduring news values is the preservation of the individual against the encroachments of nation and society" (Gans 1979, 50). At first glance, it seems that this particular value survived the shock of 9/11 and became a catalyst for some degree of media independence from government and other elite pressures, and it drew attention to government curbs on the rights of individuals. The news we examined gave slightly more emphasis to individual liberties than to support for restrictions for the sake of greater security—although it took a while before critical voices became more frequent and louder in the news. Ultimately, however, news coverage was arguably insufficient to inform the public fully and spur further an ongoing debate that might have challenged the administration's positions. The modest number of pertinent stories, the lack of comprehensive coverage, and the preference for procedural and timing issues rather than substantive reporting might explain the lack of a relationship between the total volume of news about security versus civil liberties and more general public attitudes toward curbs on civil liberties. In the absence of frequent media attention, the public, acting more autonomously, returned to its fundamental support for personal rights and liberties. It is noteworthy, though, that this embrace of liberal values was not extended to detained terrorists or suspected terrorist (cf. Davis 2007; Berinsky 2009, chap. 7; Merolla and Zechmeister 2009).

The data suggest the importance of network news anchors and correspondents whose messages seemed to be associated in the short term with public attitudes toward curbs on its civil liberties. This shows that opportunities exist for newsrooms and news professionals to utilize the slack between business imperatives (news-as-commodity) and journalistic values (news-as-public good) described in chapter 1. News can and in the case of post-9/11 did eventually gain some degree of independence from government and pro-government elites with respect to the security-civil liberties trade-off, especially since the Bush administration did not want to elevate these issues more than necessary. While the press to a limited extent reported on the restrictions of Americans' personal freedom and privacy, there was too little coverage of excessive violations of civil liberties and human rights of particular groups in the

United States and of foreign detainees in U.S.-run prisons abroad when it mattered most.

In his opinion in the Pentagon Papers case, Justice Potter Stewart wrote that in matters of national security the enormous power of the executive is not checked and balanced by the other two branches; therefore, Stewart wrote, "the only effective restraint upon executive policy and power . . . may lie in an enlightened citizenry—in an informed and critical public opinion which alone can protect the values of democratic government. For this reason, it is perhaps here that a press that is alert, aware, and free most vitally serves the basic purpose of the First Amendment. For without an informed and free press there cannot be an enlightened people."[22]

Selling the Iraq War

The Clinton administration was quite fond of this theory that terrorism was either sort of a pickup team, a loose association of terrorists, or it was bin Laden and they did not look hard at the Iraqi government. . . . I think that there may now be some incentive, I hope, for the federal government to take a close look at some of the past terrorist incidents as well as everything they have on this and see whether—if bin Laden was involved, he might have had a Wizard of Oz behind the curtain pulling some levers. — Former CIA director James Woolsey on CBS News, September 11, 2001

In the early morning of September 12, 2001, less than 24 hours after the terrorist attacks on the World Trade Center and the Pentagon, Secretary of Defense Donald Rumsfeld and his deputy Paul Wolfowitz seemed less interested in going after Al Qaeda than taking "advantage of this national tragedy to promote their agenda about Iraq" (Clarke 2004, 30). This was hardly surprising because Wolfowitz, "the intellectual godfather and fiercest advocate for toppling Saddam" (Woodward 2004, 21), and other neoconservatives had pushed for military action against Iraq since the 1991 Gulf War and President George H. W. Bush's decision against conquering Baghdad and toppling Saddam Hussein.

Also on September 12, during a late night working dinner of leading American and British intelligence officials at CIA headquarters in Langley, Virginia, CIA Director George Tenet "gave his [British] guests his word that action against Iraq was off the table. He said that he and Secretary of State Colin Powell agreed on this" (Mayer 2008, 29). Four days after 9/11 and after several highest level meetings in the West Wing and at Camp David, President George W. Bush told National Security Adviser Condoleezza Rice that "the first target of the war on terrorism was going to be Afghanistan" and that Iraq was put off for the time being. But "Rumsfeld was directed to continue working on Iraq war plans" (Woodward 2004, 26).

In the early months of the Bush presidency, there had been "deep divisions and tensions in the war cabinet with [Secretary of State Colin] Powell the moderate negotiator and Rumsfeld the hard-line activist" (Woodward 2004, 23), especially with respect to Iraq. Immediately after 9/11, the hard-liners considered these catastrophic terrorist acts a golden opportunity to attack Iraq, whereas the moderates wanted to go after those responsible for the attacks—Al Qaeda and the Taliban, not Saddam Hussein and the Iraqis.

The supporters of an aggressive Iraq agenda, not the cautious voices inside the administration, got a significant boost in the mainstream media on and after September 11. Within hours of the attacks, former CIA director James Woolsey, one of the more outspoken neoconservatives, utilized his television appearances on ABC News, CBS News, and the PBS *NewsHour with Jim Lehrer* to implicate Iraq as the most likely state sponsor and Saddam Hussein as the possible "Wizard of Oz behind the curtain pulling some levers." Admitting first to ABC News anchor Peter Jennings that he was merely talking about circumstantial evidence, Woolsey spoke in a matter of fact way of contacts between Iraq's government and bin Laden: "it's not impossible that terrorist groups could work together with the government, that—the Iraqi government has been quite closely involved with a number of Sunni terrorist groups and—and on some matters has had contact with bin Laden." In his conversation with CBS News anchor Dan Rather, Woolsey got right to the point in his push to finger Saddam Hussein:

> It's quite possible bin Laden was involved and, indeed, even that his group carried it out, but it strikes me as it did Gary Sick, that there may very well be something else behind it. And one reasonable candidate is Saddam Hussein. The Clinton administration ignored the early ef [*sic*]—efforts of the FBI agent Jim Fox who was in charge of the first World Trade Center investigation in '93. Fox, who's now dead, thought that there was a substantial chance that Ramzi Yousef and the World Trade Center plotters were involved with the Iraqi government, with Iraqi intelligence.

Woolsey mentioned Gary Sick several time, obviously delighted that the Middle East expert had alluded to possible state sponsorship and mentioned Saddam Hussein in an earlier interview with Rather. But when the CBS anchor had pushed his guest to speculate about Iraqi or Iranian involvement, Sick's cautious answer seemed to implicate Iran more than Iraq as the following excerpt from the segment's transcript shows:

> RATHER: I know you don't want to speculate, and neither do I, but it's inevitable . . .
>
> MR. SICK: I know.
>
> RATHER: . . . these questions flow on—that if it was or was not Osama bin Laden, you said it was well financed; it was exceptionally well planned . . .
>
> MR. SICK: Right.
>
> RATHER: . . . a very sophisticated and large operation. If you—if the president asked you what are the chances, Gary Sick, that Saddam Hussein or s— one of the radical Molla [sic] groups in Iran were responsible, would you rule it out?
>
> MR. SICK: Saddam Hussein, today, said that this was the operation of the century, and there was [sic] great celebrations in Baghdad, not in Iran. But you know, if you had to look for a culprit, in terms of organization, structure, money, professionalism—all of the things that go with it, that's one place that you would certainly have to look. And I think that our intelligence services are going to have do a really careful—step back from the—where they've been looking and start looking under some different rocks because I think there's some things going on that we haven't really observed.

But others clearly echoed Woolsey's line. Former U.S. Senator David Boren, for example, mentioned Iraq by name as one among other unnamed state sponsors and a possible link to the terrorist attacks earlier that 9/11 day. Appearing on the *NewsHour with Jim Lehrer*, he said,

> I'd rather not start naming but I think obviously there are states that have reason to have strong feelings—Iraq, for example. We knew back during the Persian Gulf conflict—and that's when we had a lot of intelligence successes because a lot of efforts were broken up to mount terrorist attacks that Saddam Hussein among others was trying to recruit every terrorist organization in the world to serve his purpose. But I think now we're in a situation where we must respond so strongly and send such a very strong signal for the sake not only of our security but the stability and security of the world that nation states that condone terrorism, that harbor terrorists, let alone those that sponsor terrorism will pay a very heavy, heavy price.

Also on 9/11, Fouad Ajami, a Middle East expert, praised "Bush, Cheney, Rumsfeld, [and] my own former dean, Paul Wolfowitz" and spoke of these men's view "that containment of Saddam was a mistake, and they believe that they should now actually finish the job that they didn't do a decade ago."[1]

And four days after 9/11, on September 15, former secretary of state Alexander Haig foreshadowed the neoconservatives' expectations for a quick victory over Iraq when he said on Fox News, "If we decide to take action against Iraq, and that may very well be what we do, it could be done much more quickly and efficiently than the last time, because they were mortally wounded then, and they, they are basically licked. And if we get in there and do it, it'll be quick."[2]

This tough talk of military action, especially when linked to well-known villains like Osama bin Laden and Saddam Hussein, fit perfectly into the media's narrative of America under attack, the nation's new war, parallels to Pearl Harbor and World War II, and the need to unite against dangerous enemies. A case in point was what ABC News anchor Jennings said on the air a few hours after the attack:

> Somebody said looking at the Pentagon this morning that it reminded them of World War II. Clearly, a person too young to remember World War II. As you look at these scenes, you can feel absolutely clear that you are looking at the results of the United States at war with angry and vicious people who will do in the future as they have in the past . . . And so in fairness, without being too carried away with it, we are looking at pictures from a war zone this morning. Not a picture of something that look [sic] like a war zone—looks like an old war zone, but it's a picture of a current war zone in this endless battle between the United States and its enemies.
>
> This is the most serious attack on the US mainland since Pearl Harbor.

In the face of this dominant story line, there was also initially a short moment when the mainstream media seemed determined to report on the disagreement inside the administration with respect to Iraq and perhaps other state sponsors. The day after the attacks, Andrea Mitchell of NBC News reported from the Department of State that "privately, U.S. officials here at the State Department and in other places around Washington are saying that there is no evidence at all that a state, such as Iraq, may have sponsored this."[3] But no one in the administration would elaborate on the record. When a reporter asked during a press briefing, "would you tell me about links between Iraq and Osama bin Laden?" Secretary of State Powell answered, "No, I would not." In a report by Pentagon correspondent Jim Miklazewski, Wolfowitz said, "It's not just simply a matter of capturing people and holding them accountable, but removing the sanctuaries, removing the support system, ending states who sponsor terror—terrorism."[4] It was clear that the deputy secretary of defense was not only talking about the Taliban and Afghanistan but about Saddam Hussein and Iraq as well. Soon, however, the mainstream media fell in line and contributed to the powerful national rally around the president and his responses to the attacks.

Given the often symbiotic relationship between beat reporters in Washington and the officials whom they cover, one would assume that the regular correspondents at the White House, the Departments of State and Defense, and those who covered the intelligence agencies, knew about the internal disagreements regarding the neoconservatives' push for a military move against Saddam Hussein and Iraq well before 9/11. After all, even British authorities were concerned because they "were already well aware of the preoccupation that some of Bush's foreign-policy team had with Iraq [before the attacks]" (Mayer 2008, 29). Further, assuming that newsrooms tend to "index the range of voices and viewpoints in both news and editorials according to the range of views expressed in mainstream government debate about a given topic" (Bennett 1990, 106), the post-9/11 discord over American Iraq policy should have been reflected in the news media. As we noted in chapter 1 and chapter 2, during the Cold War "indexing" was particularly prevalent during foreign policy crises. While one study found only "slight support for indexing" in the coverage of eight foreign crises in the 1990s (Zaller and Chiu 2000), pointing to the emergence of a more independent news media after the end of the Cold War, research on other cases showed that indexing was alive and well in the 1990s (Mermin 1999). Even after the end of the Cold War, then, the mainstream media continued to take their cues from authoritative actors within Washington's political community when foreign policy crises involving the United States unfolded abroad. The indexing pattern was even more prevalent during the period that led up to the invasion of Iraq in 2003.

The Chilling Effect of 9/11 and the Buildup to the Iraq War

To be sure, the events of 9/11 triggered a major crisis with both domestic and international dimensions. It did not take long for the wave of patriotism that was symbolized by the widespread display of American flags, by popular sentiments for revenge as captured by "kick ass" bumper stickers, and by threats against any dissent to what television on-screen banners termed "America's New War" to mute and silence voices critical of any aspect of the "war on terrorism." Most officials inside and outside of government either supported the Bush administration's line or remained silent. Secretary of State Powell was a case in point: as the most respected and trusted member of the administration he agreed to present what eventually turned out to be "cooked" evidence for the existence of weapons of mass destruction (WMD) in Iraq to the UN Security Council. On this occasion, he also linked Iraq explicitly to Al Qaeda and implicitly to 9/11. Powell said, "Iraqi officials deny accusations of ties with al-Qaida. These denials are simply not credible. Last year, an al-Qaida associate bragged that the situation in Iraq was 'good,' that Baghdad could be transited quickly."[5] This presentation provided the American public with the most credible rationale for going to war.

Not only officials like the secretary of state fell in line but there was constant pressure on the rest of the country to do so as well. Asked during a White House press briefing about comedian Bill Maher's joke "that members of our Armed Forces who deal with missiles are cowards, while the armed terrorists who killed 6,000 unarmed are not cowards," press secretary Ari Fleischer not only admonished Maher but issued a broad warning to "all Americans that they need to watch what they say, watch what they do."[6] In view of the administration's and its supporters' frequent charge "that critics were lacking patriotism," Orville Schell (2004, vi) concluded, "Of course, such statements had a chilling effect on reporters, editors, news directors, publishers, and other kinds of media owners. The message coming out of the White House was: 'If you are not with us, you are against us.'"

The result was a tamed mainstream media that acted as the extended arm of pro-war officials and downplayed or excluded opposition voices along the lines of the propaganda or hegemony model of the press. One left-leaning media watchdog organization, Fairness and Accuracy in Reporting (FAIR), examined news coverage of ABC News, CBS News, NBC News, and the PBS *NewsHour with Jim Lehrer* one week before and one week after Powell's UN speech. Of the 393 sources appearing on those broadcasts, 267 were American and 75% of those were present or former government officials. Only one of the sources, Senator Edward Kennedy, opposed a war against Iraq. And, as the report stated,

> When both U.S. and non-U.S. guests were included 76 percent (297 out of 393) were either current or retired officials. Such a predominance of official sources virtually assures that independent and grassroots perspectives will be underrepresented. Of all official sources, 75 percent (222 of 297) were associated with either the U.S. or with governments that support the Bush administration's position on Iraq; only four out of those 222, or 2 percent, of those sources were skeptics or opponents of the war.[7]

While most Washington officials closed ranks behind the president and his team, there were also authoritative domestic and foreign sources that challenged the Bush administration's case against Saddam Hussein and were willing to talk to the press. According to one assessment, "evidence disputing ongoing official claims about the war was often available to the mainstream press in a timely fashion. Yet the recurrent pattern, even years into the conflict, was for the official government line to trump evidence to the contrary in the news produced by the mainstream news outlets reaching the preponderance of the people" (Bennett, Lawrence, and Livingston 2007, 13; see also Western 2005; Krebs and Lobasz 2007; Hayes and Guardino 2010).

When criticized, media circles claimed that there were no credible sources to contradict the Bush administration's case and insistence that Iraq had weapons of mass destruction. However, one media critic noted that "beginning in the summer of 2002, the 'intelligence community' was rent by bitter disputes over how Bush officials were using the data on Iraq. Many journalists knew about this, yet few chose to write about it" (Massing 2004, 25–26). As one of the best analysts of the consensus in the CIA and intelligence services of other countries that Iraq very likely had WMD also observed, administration officials felt compelled to make public statements that went beyond the intelligence evidence (Jervis 2010, and personal communication). When reporters did write stories based on information provided by well-placed sources who challenged the administration's alleged evidence for WMD, they typically saw their reports relegated to the back pages, if they were published at all. More than one year into the Iraq War, the editors of the *New York*

Times apologized to its readers for the newspaper's unbalanced preinvasion coverage; the editors wrote they wished they had been "more aggressive in reexamining claims" by the Bush administration and its supporters.[8] Others in the press followed suit. In examining his own newspaper's prewar coverage, *Washington Post* media critic Howard Kurtz wrote,

> In retrospect, said Executive Editor Leonard Downie Jr., "we were so focused on trying to figure out what the administration was doing that we were not giving the same play to people who said it wouldn't be a good idea to go to war and were questioning the administration's rationale. Not enough of those stories were put on the front page. That was a mistake on my part" (Kurtz 2004, A1).

Belatedly, even a few government officials who were instrumental in selling the war had second thoughts and their own mea culpa moments. After retiring as White House press secretary, Scott McClellan (2008) charged that the Bush administration had manipulated intelligence to justify the war in Iraq. And Col. Lawrence Wilkerson, Secretary of State Powell's close adviser and chief of staff from 2002 to 2005, said that he regretted his involvement in preparing Powell's presentation at the UN. "I wish I had not been involved in it," he said in an interview. "I look back on it, and I still say it was the lowest point in my life."[9]

Methodology and Data

This chapter's research differs from our other chapters in one important respect: in this case earlier published works already took note of the general thrust of the relevant news coverage before the actual invasion of Iraq. About the time we began our research, several media critics, press watchdog organizations, and communication scholars had concluded that the news displayed a strong tilt in favor of pro-war sources and their arguments during the buildup to the Iraq invasion. However, these persuasive accounts were based on selected, qualitative assessments and, in the case of FAIR, on a quantitative analysis of TV news during only two one-week periods.

In contrast, we conducted a systematic quantitative and qualitative content analysis of relevant TV network news during the 18-month period leading up to the invasion of Iraq. We did not examine all Iraq-related news but concentrated on press coverage that dealt specifically with the administration's arguments in favor of confronting Saddam Hussein: namely, the Iraq regime's possession of WMD, its ties to Al Qaeda, and its involvement in the 9/11 attacks. Given the large volume of news stories on Iraq, we did not work with full transcripts but relied again on abstracts from Vanderbilt University's Television News Archive for our content analysis of the major television networks' reports (ABC News, CBS News, and NBC News). We retrieved news segments that contained the terms "Iraq" and/or "weapons of mass destruction," "WMD," "Saddam Hussein," "9/11," "bin Laden," and "Al Qaeda." Sample readings convinced us that these abstracts contained the basic information on the aspects of the news coverage that we had pinpointed as central in the buildup to the war and the initial stages of the U.S. invasion. We retrieved a total of 473 relevant television news story summaries, of which ABC News aired 17%, CBS 44%, and NBC 39%. These segments contained 846 pertinent messages. We also selected a smaller number of full transcripts for our qualitative analysis of stories from the Lexis/Nexis news archives that we saw as particularly important based on readings of the abstracts.

In our coding we identified the domestic and foreign sources in the pertinent news reports. After isolating three broad themes, namely "Iraq and WMD," "Iraq and Al Qaeda," and "bin Laden, Iraq and 9/11," our coders categorized specific messages, such as "WMD exist in Iraq," "No evidence of WMD in Iraq," or "UN weapons inspectors should establish whether or not Iraq has WMD." Along the same lines, they coded different viewpoints toward Iraq and 9/11, Iraq and bin Laden/Al Qaeda, and Iraq's nuclear capabilities.

In addition, we tracked the frequency of four key terms ("bin Laden," "Saddam Hussein," "war on/against *terrorism*," and "war on/against *terror*") in presidential and vice presidential speeches, statements, news releases, etc. from September 11, 2001, through March 31, 2003. For this, we used transcripts available at the White House online archive and from the Lexis/Nexis archive of political transcripts. During the same time period, we also determined the frequency of the four key terms in broadcasts by ABC News, CBS News, and NBC News and also in articles published by the *New York Times*. The rationale here was to probe for possible correlations between the terminology that was used and altered over time by leaders in the White House on the one hand and by the press on the other.

Since research has established various relevant media effects on public opinion, it is hardly surprising that communication scholars assumed that the media's dependence on "official spin" during the buildup to the Iraq War was instrumental in establishing and maintaining strong public support for going to war against Saddam Hussein (Bennett, Lawrence, and Livingston 2007, 43). To examine this, we retrieved from the Roper Center's iPOLL archive data from all available public opinion surveys that ascertained pro and con views toward war with Iraq. We found a total of 62 surveys with responses to identical questions that were asked at least twice and in most of these polls multiple times during the 18-month period that we examined. Our analysis focused on (1) data on public support and opposition to invading Iraq and (2) measures of public attitudes toward various rationales for going to war. In order to explore the depth and durability of public attitudes on the causes for war, we assembled responses to questions in 69 additional polls conducted after the invasion of Iraq until the end of 2006.

We also examined once more opinions as they might vary by demographic characteristics and partisanship, to determine whether different societal groups had similar or different opinions about invading Iraq and removing Saddam Hussein from power.

Last, as in the previous chapters, we explored the relationship between news coverage and public attitudes toward the Iraqi conflict.

Marketing the Iraq War

Although planned and promoted by proxies for many months, the campaign to sell the Iraq War began in earnest in September 2002. For White House Chief of Staff Andrew Card, the selling of the war was no different than the marketing of a candidate for political office. Explaining the timing of the administration's push for a confrontation with Iraq, Card told the *New York Times* in a moment of extraordinary candor, "From a marketing point of view, you don't introduce new products in August."[10] Well aware that serious election campaigns begin traditionally after the end of the summer vacation season and right after Labor Day, the Bush administration rolled out its justification script for invading Iraq in early September 2002, coinciding with the first anniversary of 9/11. Thus, the intense public campaign for another front in the "war on

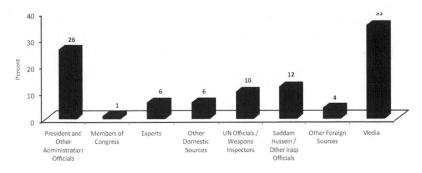

FIGURE 4.1. Sources in pre–Iraq War news

terrorism" unfolded as the nation, led by President Bush, remembered the innocent victims of the 9/11 attacks and was reminded of the further threat of terrorism.

President Bush and Secretary of State Powell were the lead players in the administration's massive media effort to publicize grievances against Iraq and make the case for war (see figure 4.1 for news sources). Bush and Powell combined were the sources of 13% of the 846 network news messages dealing with the administration's justifications for war. Secretary of Defense Donald Rumsfeld and Vice President Richard Cheney combined for a 5% share of them. Taken together, administration officials were the sources of more than one-fourth all relevant messages concerning Iraq and thus a far greater media presence than in any of the issues we studied (see chapters 2, 3, 5, and 6). In contrast, members of Congress were all but invisible sources in this particular type of Iraq-related news with only 1% of pertinent messages attributable to those in the House and Senate. This was far less frequent than for legislators' appearing or cited in television news stories about terrorism related to threats/alerts, civil liberties, and, as we shall see in the next two chapters, prevention or preparedness.

Similarly, all experts combined were the sources for only 6% of the total messages, many of them retired military officers. When such experts and former military leaders were introduced on the air as network news analysts and were obviously hired as such, they were coded as media-based sources. They were particularly prominent on the cable news channels but appeared quite frequently on the three networks we studied as well. According to one account,

The largest contingent [of these military men] was affiliated with Fox News, followed by NBC and CNN, the other networks with 24-hour cable outlets. But analysts from CBS and ABC were included, too. Some recruits, though not on any network payroll, were influential in other ways—either because they were sought out by radio hosts, or because they often published op-ed articles or were quoted in magazines, Web sites and newspapers. At least nine of them have written op-ed articles for The [*New York*] *Times* (Barstow 2008).

While the Pentagon worked closely with most of these expert analysts and, according to Department of Defense documents, referred to them as "'message force multipliers' or 'surrogates' who could be counted on to deliver administration 'themes and messages' to millions of Americans 'in the form of their own opinions'" (Barstow 2008), these retired officers were often featured before, during, and after the invasion, and they largely commented favorably on the coalition forces' strategies and tactics in Iraq.

The descriptions, summaries, and implicit or explicit views of network anchors, correspondents, and news analysts accounted for more messages than any other source category. While the frequency of each of the different sources and their messages is revealing, these percentages do not reflect the prominence in terms of airtime and placement within a news broadcast that various types of sources received. Thus, while more than one of 10 messages came from Iraqi officials and about the same proportion from UN Secretary-General Kofi Annan, other UN officials, and UN weapons inspectors, these sources combined did not receive the airtime that the president and other members of his administration received.

The following report on the *CBS Morning News* of September 12, 2002, is a case in point:

TRACEY SMITH, anchor: One day after leading the nation in prayer and ceremony, President Bush today will tell the United Nations it's time Iraq destroys its weapons of mass destruction. As Bill Plante reports, Mr. Bush made clear his resolve in an address to the nation last night.

PRESIDENT GEORGE W. BUSH: America has entered a great struggle that tests our strength and even more our resolve. Our nation is patient and steadfast. We continue to pursue the terrorists in cities and camps and caves across the Earth. We are joined by a great coalition of nations to rid the world of terror. And we will not allow any terrorist or tyrant to threaten civilization with weapons of mass murder.

BILL PLANT reporting: Mr. Bush did not name the terrorists and tyrants, but he promised a fight to the end.

PRESIDENT BUSH: They are discovering, as others before them, the resolve of a great country and a great democracy. In the ruins of two towers, under a flag unfurled at the Pentagon, at the funerals of the lost, we have made a sacred promise to ourselves and to the world: We will not relent until justice is done and our nation is secure. What our enemies have begun, we will finish.

SMITH: Secretary-General Kofi Annan, speaking prior to the president, will argue the US must act through the United Nations.[11]

While the president appeared in two video clips and was paraphrased and described by the news anchor and correspondent, there was only an 18-word reference to UN Secretary-General Annan at the end of this news report.

Attacked by conservatives in general and the Bush administration in particular as a liberal and even left-wing news organization, CBS News was as compliant a vehicle for the administration's selling of the war as were the other two networks. The above report exemplified the effectiveness of the administration's well-staged and aptly timed roll-out of a marketing campaign that relied on powerful associations between Iraq and 9/11 (or Iraq and bin Laden, or Iraq and Al Qaeda)—most of the time without explicitly indicating such connections. When sources in favor of waging war against Iraq appeared on camera or were paraphrased, they were allotted more time and more prominent placement than ambiguous, cautionary, or outright opposition sources that were often merely mentioned in passing.

To stay with CBS News, after President Bush's UN address earlier in the day, the *CBS Evening News* of September 12, 2002, began with the following lead-in by the ostensibly liberal news anchor Dan Rather:

President Bush told the world today it's time for a showdown and possible war with Saddam Hussein. Standing before the United Nations General Assembly, evoking the ghost of Hitler, the president declared that world peace, and I quote, "must never again be destroyed by the will and wickedness of any man," unquote. One by one, the president ticked off Saddam's transgressions, and one by one he listed the demands that Iraq must meet or face the consequences. Read that: war.

This introduction was followed by several video clips, with the toughest sentences from Bush's UN speech and White House correspondent John Roberts's matter-of-fact characterization of the president's hardline message. Ambiguous, one-sentence statements by UN Secretary Annan and former U.S. ambassador to the United Nations Richard Holbrooke were placed at the end of the 494-word news segment—another example of the lop-sided treatment of news sources.[12]

Not surprisingly, the threat of weapons of mass destruction was the dominant theme in news messages during the buildup phase accounting for more than two-thirds of the message total, with more than an additional 11% devoted specifically to the issue of nuclear weapons in the hands of Iraq (figure 4.2). Thus, 80% of all relevant news messages dealt with WMD. Of the remaining statements, just over half addressed Iraq's relationship with Al Qaeda and/or Osama bin Laden, with 7% of all statements citing Iraq as sponsor of terrorism, and 2% Iraq's role in the attacks of 9/11.

Of all the discernable positions that news sources expressed about the central issue of Iraq's alleged weapons of mass destruction, 39% charged that Iraq had WMD, 42% wanted UN weapons inspectors to establish the facts, and 19% insisted that there was no evidence that Iraq had these weapons. As for nuclear weapons in particular, six of 10 positions taken on this issue were claims that Iraq had such WMD or was close to building them; more than two in 10 expressed uncertainty, and

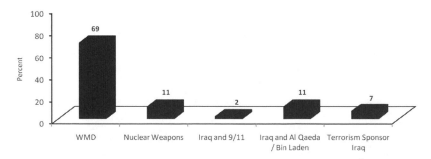

FIGURE 4.2. Subjects of news media messages

only 17% insisted that there was no evidence. Of the numerous messages that addressed Iraq's relationship with Osama bin Laden and/or Al Qaeda, 39% claimed explicitly that such ties existed; 41% implied such a relationship; and only 20% held that there was no evidence for links between Iraq and the group responsible for the 9/11 attacks. The least covered issue was Iraq's role in 9/11, with more than half of these messages implying a role, more than one in 10 claiming explicitly that Iraq was involved in the attacks, and one-third insisting that there was no evidence whatsoever.

In the case of all statements claiming that Iraq possessed weapons of mass destruction, four of 10 were made by or attributed to President Bush (13%), Secretary of State Powell (11%), Secretary of Defense Rumsfeld (10%), and Vice President Cheney (6%). In addition, 15% of the "Iraq-has-WMD" statements were made by media-based sources, mostly former military officers who were specifically introduced as working for ABC, CBS, or NBC News; 5% of the statements came from members of the U.S. military; and 4% from experts, including former military officers who were not identified as working for one of the networks.

While there was no real debate in the media among domestic political actors on the WMD issue, opposing viewpoints were mostly—and most fiercely—expressed by Iraqi officials who made 61% of all statements insisting that Iraq did not possess WMD. UN weapons inspectors and their former colleagues accounted for 15% of the messages claiming that there was no evidence for WMD (compared to 5% who said Iraq had such weapons), experts accounted for 7%, and media-based sources for 6% of such statements. The result was very similar for the issue of nuclear weapons with more than half of all statements in the news accusing Iraq of harboring and/or developing nuclear arms made by members of the Bush administration. Conversely, most messages (60%) denying Iraq's nuclear arsenal and ambition originated with Iraqi officials, 20% with nongovernmental groups (mostly in the antiwar camp), and the remaining 20% with UN weapons inspectors and former inspectors. Two American weapons experts and former UN inspectors, Scott Ritter and David Kay, were among those sought out by the press to speak on this particular issue. They took contrary positions, with Kay reinforcing the Bush administration's accusations during his interviews and appearances on television, while Ritter denied both that Iraq had a substantial WMD arsenal and that it was in the process of developing weapons of mass destruction. As the media pointed out, Ritter was also a prominent figure in the antiwar movement, which may have impeded his influence in the post-9/11 climate.

Most of all, the Bush administration was the driving force in accusing Iraq of having ties to Al Qaeda and/or Osama bin Laden: 81% of all news statements claiming links between Iraq and Al Qaeda came from administration sources. The president's share of these messages was greatest (28%), followed by Secretary of State Powell (19%), Secretary of Defense Rumsfeld (6%), and Vice President Cheney and National Security Adviser Rice (3% each). In this particular case, there was actually a great deal of domestic opposition to the administration's forceful line: 42% of the opposing statements rejecting the administration's claim came from domestic sources (members of Congress, experts, and media personnel); 29% of these statements were made by Iraqi officials; and 12% each by British and other foreign sources.

Except for one cited opinion poll result, network news did not report messages that explicitly connected Iraq to the attacks of 9/11, but 40% of the implicit accusations of an Iraq-9/11 link came from President Bush (20%) and Secretary of Defense Rumsfeld (20%), followed by foreign government officials (20%), members of the American public (20%), and media-based sources (20%). On the other side of this issue, messages opposing the claim of Iraq's involvement in the 9/11 attacks came equally from Iraq officials, media personnel, and domestic sources, namely, from the antiwar movement.

To summarize, television news sources taking positions that represented or agreed with the Bush administration by far outnumbered those of the opposition.

Words Matters: Cues from the White House

In the months after the 9/11 attacks the Bush administration left no doubt that the number one villain and threat to national security was Osama bin Laden. According to the president's and the vice president's public pronouncements and official releases, the Al Qaeda leader was the primary target of U.S. (and coalition) counterterrorism efforts in the "war on terrorism," and bin Laden was mentioned frequently and cited much more often than Iraq's Saddam Hussein. This was obvious in the fall of 2001, when the U.S.-led coalition began its military action in Afghanistan in search of bin Laden and other Al Qaeda and Taliban leaders.

When it became clear that bin Laden and his crew as well as their Taliban allies had fled to hiding places in Pakistan, the White House's public attention to bin Laden declined drastically starting in March 2002, reaching a low point in the fall of that year when the administration's campaign against Saddam Hussein and for war against Iraq went into full swing, and bin Laden was rarely mentioned, if at all, by the president and vice president. September 2002 was the first month since September 2001 in which official statements by Bush and Cheney did not mention Osama bin Laden but referred directly to Saddam Hussein—fully 24 times. This trend continued for the rest of 2002 and became even more lop-sided in the immediate prewar months and weeks.

We were interested in the appearance of the two demonized leaders' names in the president's and vice president's official communications, because we wondered about trends in the news during the period when the mainstream media largely toed the White House's line, with its sources and messages supporting the administration's Iraq policy. The trends in Bush's and Cheney's public attention to bin Laden and Saddam Hussein were reflected in television news reports and in the *New York Times*. The combined data for the three television networks revealed that July 2002 was the first month in which the Iraqi leader was mentioned more often (97 times) than the elusive Al Qaeda leader (69 times). By December 2002 the gap had widened significantly with the name of Saddam Hussein broadcast in the news 375 times and that of bin Laden only 78 times. The *New York Times*, too, reflected the same shift from bin Laden to Hussein. By December 2002, the Saddam Hussein–bin Laden ratio in the *Times* was 192–82, though not quite as drastic a shift as reflected in administration statements and reports by the three television networks. Specifically, we found that the administration's citing of bin Laden and Saddam Hussein correlated significantly over time with the TV networks' references to them ($r = .60$ and $r = .68$, respectively) and the *New York Times'* references ($r = .60$ and $r = .74$, respectively). Since the three broadcast networks and the *New York Times* were very similar in this respect, we report in figure 4.3 the frequency of the two leaders' names used by the highest ranked administration officials and also reported in ABC News broadcasts.

It is hardly surprising that the news reflects such changes when an administration shifts and promotes its new policy focus, especially in foreign policy and national security matters. After all, what top leaders say about important foreign affairs is information that the public should

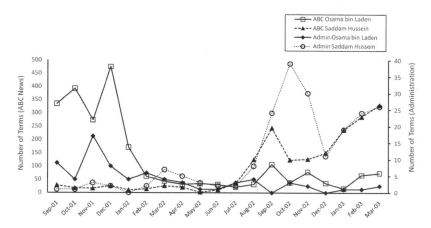

FIGURE 4.3. Saddam Hussein/Osama bin Laden: ABC and administration

know. But the degree to which the news media echoed and amplified leaders in the White House as they dramatically shifted interest from bin Laden (and the war against Al Qaeda and its allies) to Saddam Hussein (and the war against Iraq) indicated that the traditional Cold War crisis-type coverage had apparently survived the end of the Cold War and that the press continued to act as "government's little helper" during this particular period.[13]

In July 2004, more than one year into the Iraq War, linguist Geoffrey Nunberg noted in the *New York Times* that President Bush and others in the administration had shifted from their post-9/11 preference for the term "war against terrorism" and instead spoke increasingly of the "war on terror." Nunberg wrote that "in White House speeches over the past year, those proportions have been reversed. And the shift from 'terrorism' to 'terror' has been equally dramatic in major newspapers, according to a search of several databases" (Nunberg 2004). As far as official communications by President Bush and Vice President Cheney were concerned, we found that the shift from emphasizing "terrorism" (in references to the war against or on terrorism) to speaking more about "terror" (the war on terror or against terror) began in January 2002, when for the first time since September 2001 the word "terror" was used more often than "terrorism" in this context. This trend was more pronounced during the months that followed. In all of 2002, for example, "terror" was mentioned 253 times and "terrorism" 69 times in reference to the post-9/11 "war" in official Bush and Cheney statements. As Nunberg explained, "terror has a broader meaning than terrorism in that unlike 'terrorism,' 'terror' can be applied to states as well as to insurgent groups, as in the President's frequent references to Saddam Hussein's 'terror regime.' Even if Mr. Hussein can't actually be linked to the attacks of Sept. 11, 'terror' seems to connect them etymologically" (Nunberg 2004).

On this count, however, the press did not immediately echo the change in political rhetoric. We found mixed trends with respect to the use of "war on/against terrorism" and "war on/against terror" in White House communications and in the news. When Bush and Cheney used "terror" more frequently at the expense of "terrorism" in the context of the new war, the three TV networks and the *New York Times* did *not* follow suit. However, the gap between the White House's and the media's usage of the two terms narrowed eventually.

Ultimately, we found that there was a substantial correlation between the administration's and the TV networks' ($r = .88$) and the *New York Times'* ($r = .79$) references to both Osama bin Laden and Saddam Hussein over time. We did not, however, find strong statistical correlations for the usage of "terrorism" and "terror" in the context of "war" over the whole period we examined. In this respect, the television networks and the *Times* resisted for a while the administration's effort to shift public discourse to "terror," a term it deemed applicable to Saddam Hussein's and his regime's human right violations, even without his alleged WMD and links to 9/11 and Al Qaeda.[14] Again, given the similarities in the usage trends for the four news organizations, figure 4.4 shows the use

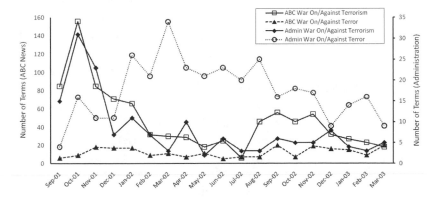

FIGURE 4.4. War on terrorism/terror: ABC and administration

of "terror" versus "terrorism" by the president and vice president and by ABC News.

The Public and the Buildup to the Iraq War

Pollsters take their cues from the news when they decide what questions on current issues to include in their surveys. Since Iraq's government and the country's president Saddam Hussein were implicated by a variety of news sources within hours of the 9/11 strikes, it was hardly surprising that merely two days later, the Harris organization asked poll respondents about the likelihood of Saddam Hussein's personal involvement in the terrorist attacks. Given that nearly all Americans followed the news after the devastating attacks in New York and Washington, it was equally unsurprising that a large majority of the public believed that it was very likely (34%) or somewhat likely (44%) that Iraq's president had a direct role; 9% thought it not very likely, and only 3% did not see a link at all. The following month, 50% of the public believed that Saddam Hussein's was very likely involved—16% more than immediately after 9/11. While responses varied between "very likely" and "somewhat likely," the combined results for the two categories remained at over 70% during the months that followed.[15]

The public also embraced the views of dominant news sources who spoke of links between Saddam Hussein and Al Qaeda and who claimed that Iraq possessed weapons of mass destruction. Before the Iraq invasion began, three of four Americans believed that Iraq's leader was providing assistance to Al Qaeda and that Iraq was harboring Al Qaeda terrorists and "helping them to develop chemical weapons."[16] Since the vast majority of the public also believed that Iraq's ruler was helping Al Qaeda develop chemical weapons, it is hardly surprising that over 90% of Americans polled were convinced that Iraq had weapons of mass destruction or was trying to develop them.[17]

In the second half of September 2002, after the administration rolled out the marketing of the Iraq War, a Fox News poll asked about the topic that came up most often in their conversations with friends and neighbors. Iraq and Saddam Hussein (13%) were mentioned most often, followed by 9/11 (12%), and the economy (9%). Most tellingly, at a time when the administration's and news media's focus had switched from bin Laden and

Afghanistan to Saddam Hussein and Iraq, the masterminds of 9/11 and their Taliban allies were no longer of great interest to Americans.

The die was cast against Saddam Hussein and Iraq in the weeks following 9/11. In October 2001, after letters containing deadly anthrax spores were mailed to well-known media figures in what was feared to be part of a biological terrorism attack, six of 10 Americans thought that Saddam Hussein had his hands in this bioterrorism, with one-third saying it was "very likely" and more than one-fourth believing it was "somewhat likely."[18] In the public's mind, the Iraqi leader was on his way to replacing Osama bin Laden as America's number one enemy. These sentiments were stirred and exploited by the Bush administration and its supporters in the months that followed, as the shifting popularity of the names bin Laden and Saddam Hussein in White House communications attested to.

Since the majority of the public was convinced that Saddam Hussein and his regime were somehow involved in the 9/11 attacks, that they cooperated with Osama bin Laden and Al Qaeda, and that they possessed weapons of mass destruction or were in the process of developing them, there was strong support for going to war against Iraq. This prowar sentiment was already evident shortly after 9/11. Thus, when ABC News asked its survey respondents in early November 2001, less than two months after 9/11, whether they were for or against military action against Iraq to force Saddam Hussein from power, more than three of four (78%) favored and only 17% opposed this action. While fluctuating somewhat over the following months and up to the beginning of the Iraq invasion in March 2003, this public support largely remained well over 60%, dipping only twice under 60% in ABC News/*Washington Post* surveys (on this early support, see also Foyle 2004).[19]

In his speech to the UN General Assembly one day after the first anniversary of 9/11, President Bush said,

We know that Saddam Hussein pursued weapons of mass murder even when inspectors were in his country. Are we to assume that he stopped when they left? The history, the logic, and the facts lead to one conclusion: Saddam Hussein's regime is a grave and gathering danger. To suggest otherwise is to hope against the evidence. To assume this regime's good faith is to bet the lives of millions and the peace of the world in a reckless gamble. And this is a risk we must not take.

The president left no doubt that military action would be taken unless Iraq's leader came clean on the WMD issue and complied with all UN resolutions when he said,

> We will work with the U.N. Security Council for the necessary resolutions. But the purposes of the United States should not be doubted. The Security Council resolutions will be enforced—the just demands of peace and security will be met —or action will be unavoidable. And a regime that has lost its legitimacy will also lose its power.[20]

Coming on the heels of an emotional 9/11 anniversary address to the nation that the president delivered the previous night from Ellis Island with the Statue of Liberty in the background, public support for war increased 12 points from 56% at the end of August to 68% just after Bush's forceful UN speech and his reassuring address to the nation.[21] The same surveys also showed a 13-point jump in the public's approval for Bush's "handling of the situation with Iraq and Saddam Hussein."[22] Thus, shortly after the White House rolled out its heavily covered marketing campaign for a confrontation with Iraq, there was a strong reaction in support of the president's vigorous stand on Iraq.

After Secretary of State Powell's UN presentation of what he described as conclusive evidence of Iraq's WMD program, six in 10 Americans (61%) said they had watched, heard, or read about Powell's UN speech. Of those who watched his presentation, 71% thought that the secretary of state had made a convincing case "for going to war with Iraq," while only 16% of those who had not watched believed so (69% had no opinion).[23] Before Powell's presentation, 54% of the public thought that the Bush administration had presented enough evidence to take military action to remove Saddam Hussein; after the secretary of state's UN appearance, 63% said that enough evidence had been presented, a 9-point increase.[24]

The widely held convictions that Saddam Hussein and Iraq possessed weapons of mass destruction and had links to Al Qaeda and the 9/11 attacks were apparently so deeply ingrained in the public's mind that these attitudes lingered—even in the face of contrary evidence. This was particularly true concerning the alleged WMD. Although no biological, chemical, or nuclear weapons were found during and after the invasion of Iraq, large segments of the American public continued to believe otherwise (figure 4.5). As late as July 2006, more than three years

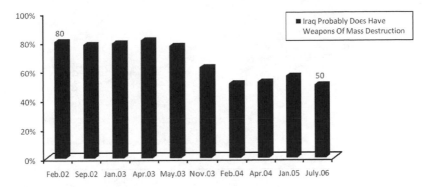

FIGURE 4.5. Public opinion: Iraq and weapons of mass destruction

after the war commenced, 50% of Americans still believed that Iraq had possessed WMD at the time.[25] Only in early 2008 was there a poll indicating that the majority of the public (53%) thought the Bush administration had "deliberately misled" the public by claiming that Iraq had WMD; however, a sizeable minority (42%) continued to believe that the administration had not misled them with respect to Iraq's weapons of mass destruction.[26]

Similarly, the public found the administration's claim that Saddam Hussein and his regime cooperated with Al Qaeda in attacking the United States on September 11, 2001, more credible than the 9/11 Commission's contrary finding. According to a mid-2004 survey, 47% disagreed with the commission's conclusion of Iraq's noninvolvement in the 9/11 attacks, compared to 42% who agreed.[27] More than a year later, the public was still divided on the issue of prewar ties between Iraq/Saddam Hussein and Al Qaeda: 39% continued to believe that such a link existed before the invasion of Iraq, versus 41% responding that such ties did not exist.[28]

In sum, despite evidence to the contrary, a majority or sizeable minority of the public continued to acknowledge the administration's main charges against Iraq as a legitimate target in the war against terrorism— its possession of WMD, cooperation in the 9/11 attacks, and ties to Al Qaeda—in spite of evidence to the contrary. While Americans' faith in their leaders' forthrightness on questions of war and peace may have explained the steady and substantial support for military action against Iraq after 9/11, it was also a testament to the effectiveness of the Bush administration in selling military actions against the threat of existential

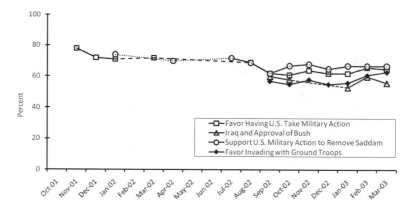

FIGURE 4.6. Public opinion: Iraq and Saddam Hussein's threat, October 2001–March 2003

terror posed by evil-doer Saddam Hussein. Moreover, the news highlighted the administration's charges against Iraq at the expense of expert
views that contradicted the president and his advisers.

Subgroup Differences in Opinions

Figure 4.6 presents opinion trend data showing the substantial and persistent public support for taking military action again Iraq during the period after 9/11 through the invasion in March 2003. But different subgroups of the public at large varied over time in their support for and
opposition to taking military action against Iraq. At times, the data show
similar movements for the subgroups we compare, but there is more visible divergence of opinion—most noticeably and predictably along partisan lines as also found in other policy areas in recent years as we noted
earlier (see Shapiro and Bloch-Elkon 2006; Jacobson 2008, 2011; Bafumi
and Shapiro 2009; Levendusky 2009).

President Bush's address to the nation on the eve of the first 9/11 anniversary and his speech before the United Nations the following morning helped stir the patriotic sentiments and the will to fight the "war on
terror" across various groups. Except for Republicans, who had already
reached a high ceiling in their most solid support, there were significant
changes among other groups in the wake of the president's back-to-back
speeches, both televised live. Thus, following those appearances in September 2002, fully 73% of black respondents said that they favored "military actions against Iraq to force Saddam Hussein from power," their

highest level of support during the whole buildup period. This African American support fell off substantially thereafter as war became more likely. As a group, African Americans responded more positively than any other group when Secretary of State Powell, an African American, made his presentation to the UN Security Council on February 5, 2003, indicting Iraq. In a period of about a week, black support for the war increased 13 points, from 36% a week earlier to 49%. But in general, blacks were consistently less supportive of war than whites and Hispanics, whose pro-war views were quite similar through the early months of the buildup period. However, whereas Hispanics' support for war may have weakened temporarily from 77% in late January 2002 to 59% in early March 2002, that of whites remained at the 75% level before declining a bit somewhat later (figure 4.7).

Gender differences in support for the Iraq War were small during the year after 9/11 with men at most 5 points more supportive than women (cf. Shapiro and Mahajan 1986). During this period their opinion trends were the same, showing sharp drops (17 points for males; 16 points for females) between early March 2002 and late August 2002. After the president's 9/11 anniversary address and UN speech, male and female support reversed direction, by 10 and 16 points, respectively, opening up what was then the largest gender difference up to that time (9 points). In surveys conducted in late 2002 and early 2003, the gap widened to

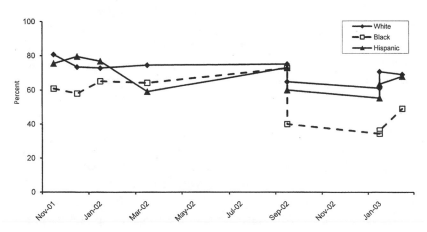

FIGURE 4.7. Having U.S. forces take military action against Iraq to force Saddam Hussein from power? By race ("Favor")

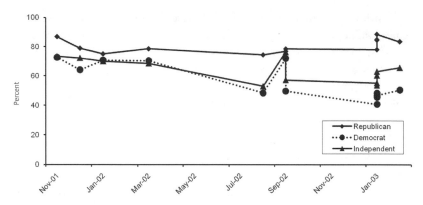

FIGURE 4.8. Having U.S. forces take military action against Iraq to force Saddam Hussein from power? By party ID ("Favor")

between 11 and 16 points. While a majority of both men and women supported the war during the buildup period, support remained greater among men.

Republicans' support for the war was very high in the 18 months before the invasion, with a stunning 87% in the fall of 2001, dropping to only a 74% low in late August 2002 (see figure 4.8). Nearly three of four Democrats and Independents favored the invasion of Iraq in fall 2001, but this support softened in the following months, dropping substantially during the summer of 2002. Democratic support kicked upward by 24 points in September 2002, along with a 23-point increase for Independents coinciding with President Bush's 9/11 anniversary address and UN speech. But whereas a very strong majority of Republicans and a solid majority of Independents favored war throughout the buildup period, only a minority of Democrats supported the invasion beginning in late fall of 2002 though January 2003. By early February 2003, perhaps affected by Secretary of State Powell's UN presentation, a slim majority of Democrats (50.5%) supported war. As expected, the patterns of change were similar among self-identified conservatives, by far the most supportive ideological group, and among moderates and liberals for more than a year after 9/11. By the end of January 2003, there was a 20-point gap between moderates and liberals: 65% of moderates supported the war compared to only 45% of liberals.

Throughout the period we examined, the oldest age group (61 years old and over) was less supportive of war than were all other ages. However, with the exception of January 2003, when only a plurality (47%) of the oldest favored the invasion of Iraq, the majority of older Americans supported going to war throughout the preinvasion period: By early February 2003, 74% of those age 31 to 44 years favored war compared to 66% of those 18 to 30, 64% of those 45 to 60, and 59% of those over 61. Interestingly, the youngest age group was not the most supportive, which deviated, for example, from what was found in the cases of the Vietnam and Korean Wars (Mueller 1985 [1973]).

Even as support for war fell off somewhat at the end of November 2001, a solid majority of those at all education levels supported military action against Iraq. In the case of education, those with some college or more were least supportive during the lead-up to the war, with the largest difference of about 15 points when support among those with less than a high school degree stood at 80%. Thereafter the latter group's support, with some variations due to fluctuations in its measured opinions, was generally the lowest until the invasion of Iraq. Overall, however, the educational differences in opinion were not as pronounced as those due to race and partisanship.

Thus, while there were significant differences at times among the subgroups we have discussed, the majority of nearly all of them, except for blacks, liberals, and possibly Democrats, favored war once the invasion seemed inevitable in early 2003. The Bush administration's selling of the war was a success story.

Dynamics of Public Opinion and News Coverage

In trying to understand further the selling of the war, we looked more closely at the dynamics of public opinion and the short- and long-term flow of media coverage. The volume of news that conveyed the pros and cons of the administration's justifications for going to war (what we will call here "justification messages or coverage") mattered most in explaining short-term opinion changes. Interestingly, we found that when this particular coverage during the buildup period increased, public support for military action declined somewhat at times; that is, more justification messages—whether in support of or opposition to the administration's reasoning—were associated with a falloff in support for war against Iraq. It appeared that this high volume of news implying the likelihood of a coming war against Iraq dampened public enthusiasm somewhat.

On the other hand, more important in the end, overall support for war remained high. As we have described above and as others have argued, it evidently did not take much for the Bush administration to tie Saddam Hussein to bad doings and to gain support for going to war against him (see Kull, Ramsay, and Lewis 2003–4; Althaus and Largio 2004; Gershkoff and Kushner 2005; Shapiro and Bloch-Elkon 2005, 2006; Jacobson 2008, 2010, 2011). Indeed, in response to a question asked in a February 2001 Gallup Poll, just after Bush took office, a 52% majority of the public favored "sending American troops back to the Persian Gulf in order to remove Saddam Hussein from power in Iraq." There has been some debate, however, about how to interpret these results and the seemingly high level of support for going to war against Iraq that persisted in the run-up to the invasion. David Moore (2008) offered persuasive evidence that this support was not definitive support but at most "permissive"; that is, many respondents who said they favored war did not care whether their opinions were followed. So at most, their responses represented a *predisposition* (our word) toward military action that was not firm. Thus political leaders could go either way on war, and the public would go along. But whether a firm opinion or predisposition, a majority of the public, collectively, held to it, and it is important to examine the extent to which these opinions changed in the lead-up to the war. Where we agree with Moore is in his argument that the media's reporting of this high level of "support" for military action against Iraq helped maintain the perception that the public supported the war. Thus, media reporting about stronger public support than might have actually existed may have helped the Bush administration sustain and increase its backing in elite circles, as well as among the public, as the decision was made to invade Iraq.

Figure 4.9 compares the coverage over time of the justification "debate" with the public's opinions, for which there seemed to be the strongest relationship.[29] Most important, again, is that the public's views on military conflict with Iraq were largely steady. The trends suggest some connection to news reports over the years shown, but not an enormous one. The graph focuses on the comparable trends for the two similar questions: The percentages of those who favored "*having U.S. forces take military action against Iraq to force Saddam Hussein from power*" and who supported "*U.S military action to remove Iraqi President Saddam Hussein*" decreased, respectively, from 78% in November 2001 to 65% in March 2003, prior to the invasion, and from 74% who supported it in January 2002 to 67% one year later in January 2003. On this

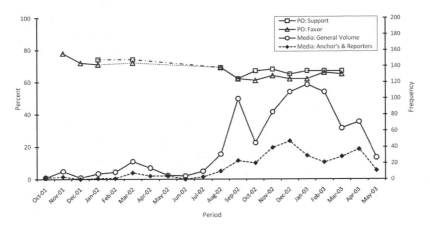

FIGURE 4.9. Military action against Iraq to remove Saddam Hussein, October 2001–May 2003

issue we found that the volume of justification news as well as messages from news anchors or correspondents on television correlated (negatively) with these opinion trends ("favor": $r = -.80$, $p < .01$, for both news content measures; "support": $r = -.72$, $p < .05$; $r = -.70$, $p < .05$, respectively). That is, when this general and particular volume of justification messages went up, the public became less supportive of military actions against Iraq. Conversely, there were also instances in which justification messages decreased and support for war increased. For example, from January 2003 to March 2003, war justification messages from news anchors and correspondents and especially from sources in general decreased while support for the war increased somewhat. Also, as shown earlier in figure 4.6, support for using ground troops to remove Saddam increased from 55% in December 2002 to 63% at the start of the invasion in March. But it was during this period that Secretary of State Colin Powell overshadowed all other news sources when he made his case against Iraq before the Security Council of the United Nations and received extremely positive reactions in the media.

How did it all this affect President Bush's approval rating? A similar pattern appeared here as well (data not shown). For responses to the question *"Do you approve or disapprove of the way Bush is handling . . . policies to deal with the threat posed by Iraq and its leader Saddam Hussein?"*(see the online appendixes; available at http://www.press .uchicago.edu/books/nacos/), approval increased during the period immediately before the invasion, when the volume of justification messages decreased. This approval change was associated with messages from television news anchors and correspondents ($r = -.83$, $p < .10$): When they commented less on war justifications during February 2003 (21 reports compared to 29 a month earlier in January), the president's rating increased to 60% from 53%. At this time, presidential approval and public attitudes toward going to war seemed more affected by Americans' understanding that the invasion of Iraq was inevitable than by mass-mediated discourse about the pros and cons of the administration's justifications.

In the case of the selling of the Iraq War, the short-term dynamics of public opinion that we have described are interesting, but they are a sideshow. The main story is that the justifications for war that were created by the Bush administration helped sustain the public's predispositions, if not enthusiastic support, for military action against Iraq. At most, when this support for war reached its peaks, increased media coverage led more often than not to some reconsideration by the public—although very limited—as the Bush administration attempted to bolster its case for war ahead of the actual invasion. Still, when the president himself and his secretary of state made the case for war in public appearances, Americans listened and for the most part agreed. At crucial moments during the selling of the war period, what the nation's foremost leaders said mattered most of all.

Conclusion

The steady flow of Al Qaeda and Bush administration warnings of further terrorist attacks in the months and years after 9/11 helped maintain an atmosphere in which the mainstream media forfeited their role as watchdog of government. With the backdrop of a climate of fear and the issuance of frequent terrorist threat alerts, which in and of itself can advantage leaders and the foreign policy responses that they might pursue (Merolla and Zechmeister 2009; Gadarian 2010), the president and other administration officials framed and dominated the news coverage of Saddam Hussein's alleged links to terrorism and to the masterminds of the 9/11 attacks. While members of Congress were all but absent from this particular news, the president himself, his secretaries of state and of defense, and the vice president set the agenda along with some other administration officials and their supporters outside of government. While opposition sources were not excluded from TV newscasts altogether, they were overwhelmingly members of the Iraqi government or UN officials with no or little credibility in post-9/11 America.

As for domestic sources who did not run for cover but were willing to publicly challenge the administration's evidence for going to war, "for the most part, those dissenting voices in the US press that did speak out remained buried in the back pages of newspapers or confined to the margins of the media, unamplified through mass outlets in any meaningful way. They were thus denied the respectability that only inclusion in a major media outlet is capable of conferring on new information" (Schell 2004, v).

Another persuasive piece of evidence for the administration's ability to set the media agenda was the way it shifted national attention from Osama bin Laden and Afghanistan to Saddam Hussein and Iraq through careful rhetorical changes in public statements by the president and vice president that readily drew the attention of the press. As the Bush administration switched its focus from Afghanistan and the hunt for bin Laden to Iraq and the overthrow of Saddam Hussein, so did the media.

Our analysis suggests that there was the possibility for a more expansive mass-mediated debate about the need for going to war that might have tempered public support and possibly delayed or even prevented the war. As news coverage of the case for war increased, with news anchors and reporters providing more information about debates at the United Nations and foreign sources that contradicted each of the administration's reasons for going to war, public support for taking military action against Iraq fell off a bit. But in the absence of domestic dissent on the part of opinion leaders, this effect was minimal, short-lived, and inconsequential, as the invasion began and the public rallied in support of the initially successful phase of the U.S. military's occupation of Iraq (see Brody 1991; Jacobson 2008, 2011). A stronger case against the war would have been needed, which neither Democratic leaders, other voices that could get the media's attention, nor the investigative and editorial powers of the press itself could provide. There was no way to overcome the persuasiveness of the Bush administration's arguments, explicit or implicit, for going to war: the existence of weapons of mass destruction in Iraq, Saddam Hussein's connection to Al Qaeda, and what the United States had to do to combat the terrorism threat that became real on September 11, 2001. Like the threat of terrorism that we examined in chapter 2, the Iraq War issue was another classic example of information control by the executive branch suggesting that strong evidence for the indexing theory, privileging members of that branch, can be found in foreign policy and national security.

Ultimately, the Iraq War was a case in which the leading news organizations failed to provide a public forum for a full range of domestic views on Iraq and further scrutiny of its real and alleged threat to American national security. While one would expect a socially responsible press to look for and uncover the facts and truth behind the news it reports and look for opposing viewpoints, in this particular case the major news organizations fell short. Instead, as others noted, "a press system dedicated to telling 'both sides of the story' so often reported only one" (Bennett, Lawrence, and Livingston 2007, 33). This was not mitigated by the fact that the media reported about foreign critics of the U.S. administration's Iraq position, among them Iraqi government officials and Americans and non-Americans at the United Nations. These did not have the same standing, legitimacy, and credibility as homegrown newsmakers in the United States.

Finally, most people in the newsrooms of the mainstream media reacted like most other Americans to the events of 9/11 in how they were shocked, compared the attacks to Pearl Harbor and the United States' entry into WWII, and rallied around the flag. The administration's warning that critics of the president's war on terrorism were siding with the terrorists was intimidating enough to keep the media watchdog muzzled. As one media critic put it,

> It is understandable that governments should want to limit dissent within their own ranks and to avoid embarrassing disclosures. Less understandable, however, is that an independent free press in a "free" country should allow itself to become so paralyzed that it not only failed to investigate thoroughly the rational for war, but also took so little account of the myriad other cautionary voices in the on-line, alternative, and world press (Schell 2004, iv–v).

To put it differently, during the buildup to the Iraq invasion the mainstream media became for the most part a propaganda arm of government.

Preventing Attacks against the Homeland

Somewhere in CIA there was information that two known al Qaeda terrorist had come into the United States. Somewhere in FBI there was information that strange things had been going on at flight schools in the United States. . . . They had specific information about individual terrorists from which one could have deduced what was about to happen. — Richard A. Clarke, 2004[1]

Appearing on NBC a few hours after the 9/11 attacks, retired U.S. Army colonel and military analyst Ken Allard offered a prescient assessment of parallels between the failure to prevent the attack on Pearl Harbor and the terrorist strikes earlier that day. "After the attack on Pearl Harbor, guess what we did? We went back and found out that, yes, the evidence was there. We should have known," he said. "And, again, I think what we're going to see, even in this instance, this Pearl Harbor of the 21st century, is very much the same kind of thing."

Whistle blowers and the 9/11 Commission eventually proved Allard right. Nearly three years after his astute remark, the 9/11 Commission Report (National Commission on Terrorist Attacks upon the United States 2004, 263) observed that the "The September 11 attacks fell into the void between the foreign and domestic threats. The foreign intelligence agencies were watching overseas, alert to foreign threats to U.S. interests there. The domestic agencies were waiting for evidence of a domestic threat from sleeper cells within the United States. No one was looking for a foreign threat to domestic targets." In spite of the persistent failures in inter- and intra-agency cooperation, a Presidential Daily Brief that President George W. Bush received on August 6, 2001, more than a month before 9/11, contained a CIA intelligence assessment under the headline "Bin Laden Determined to Strike the US." The brief warned explicitly that FBI information "indicates patterns of suspicious activity in this country consistent with preparations for hijackings or other types of attacks, including recent surveillance of federal buildings in New York." Yet, President Bush told the National Commission on Terrorist Attacks upon the United States that the August 6 report "was historical in nature" (National Commission on Terrorist Attacks upon the United States 2004, 260). And in her testimony before the same commission, National Security Adviser Condoleezza Rice, too, insisted that the Presidential Daily Brief "did not warn of attacks inside the United States. It was historical information based on old reporting. There was no new threat information. And it did not, in fact, warn of any coming attacks inside the United States."[2]

In contrast to top administration officials' lack of interest in and attention to such warnings before 9/11 (Clarke 2004, chap. 10), the president and his closest advisers declared homeland security their top priority after the attacks on the World Trade Center and the Pentagon. The establishment of the first Office of Homeland Security less than a month after 9/11 and then the Department of Homeland Security in early 2003 was explained by decision makers and understood by the public as the result of the post-9/11 emphasis on preventing terrorism inside the United States and against the nation's aviation and maritime interests. When terrorists struck non-American targets abroad, President Bush and other administration officials assured Americans that their own government was making every effort to protect them from such attacks. Thus, in July 2005, a few days after multiple suicide bombings in London's mass transit system, President Bush told a nervous American public that "to protect the American people, we continue to take extraordinary measures to defend the homeland."[3] Vice President Richard Cheney, appearing on the NBC News program *Meet the Press* on September 10, 2006, told host Tim Russert, "I think we've done a pretty good job of securing the nation against terrorists. . . . I don't know how much better you can do than no attack for the last five years. . . . You've got to give some credence to the notion that maybe somebody did something right."

Others were less satisfied with the state of affairs in homeland security. In October 2002, a bipartisan task force established by the Council on Foreign Relations concluded that America remained "dangerously unprepared" to prevent "a catastrophic terrorist attack on U.S. soil."[4] In late 2005, when the 9/11 Commission released its final grades—predominantly Cs, Ds, and Fs—for the implementation of preventative measures, Commission Chairman Thomas H. Kean warned, "Our leadership has been distracted in this country. Some of the failures are shocking." According to Kean, a former Republican governor of New Jersey, some failures were outright "scandalous"—for example, the fact that "we still allocate scarce Homeland Security dollars on the basis of pork barrel spending and not on risk."[5] Two weeks later, the president opened a press conference in the East Room of the White House with a statement that contained the term "prevent" five times in the context of terrorism.[6] If that was meant to counter the commission's findings, it did not convince security expert Stephen Flynn who criticized Washington's terrorism prevention strategy sharply, when he wrote,

> Rather than address the myriad soft targets within the U.S. border, the White House has defined the war on terrorism as something to be managed by actions beyond our shores. The rallying cry of the Bush administration and its allies on Capitol Hill has been "We must fight terrorists over there so we don't have to fight them here." What this ignores is that terrorists can still come here—and, worse yet, are being made here. . . . The most compelling lesson we should have learned on 9/11 is that our borders are unable to provide a barrier against the modern terrorist threat (Flynn 2007, 4–5).

In late 2008, during a hearing of the Senate Committee on Homeland Security and Governmental Affairs, Republican Senator Susan Collins (R-Maine) complained that "even in our own country, we [have] failed to secure potential biological weapons effectively. Thousands of individuals in the United States have access to dangerous pathogens. Currently, there are about 400 research facilities and nearly 15,000 individuals in the United States authorized to handle the deadly pathogens on what is called the 'select agents list.' Many other research facilities handle less strictly controlled yet still dangerous pathogens, with little or no regulation."[7]

Only a few observers questioned the need for massive prevention measures at home. Arguing that the terrorist threat was overblown by politicians and the security industry, political scientist John Mueller, for example, concluded,

> Current policy puts primary focus on preventing terrorism from happening and on protecting potential terrorist targets, a hopelessly ambitious approach that has led to wasteful expenditures, an often bizarre quest to identify po-

tential targets, endless hand-wringing, and opportunistic looting of the trea-
sury by elements of the terrorism industry (Mueller 2006, 143; see also Lustick 2006).

But the real disagreement was between those who praised and those
who criticized the state of homeland security, not the need for prevention efforts. Ironically, in the years following the 9/11 attacks even officials within the Bush administration oscillated between emphasizing
the effectiveness of their security measures and admitting that nothing
could prevent terrorist acts. That was part of the administration's effort
to keep the fear of terrorism at a high level (see chapter 2) and at the
same time bolster public trust in the success of its "war on terrorism."
Before leaving office in January 2005, Secretary of Homeland Security
Tom Ridge, who had issued frequent terror alerts during his term and
also assured Americans of the government's efforts to protect them from
terrorism, said in interviews that he had "accepted the inevitability of
another attack or attacks" and that it was not a question of "if" but a
matter of "when" attack would occur.[8]

The mixed signals and evaluations of the state of terrorism prevention
inside the United States raise a number of questions: To what extent
did the mass media report on homeland security and the very different
assessments of progress in this area—especially the lack of such progress? To put it differently, how well did the news media inform Americans about the public and private sectors' responsibilities and efforts
to thwart terrorist attacks? What were the predominant news sources
that shaped and perhaps manipulated the information that was reported
about homeland security? Finally, how did Americans perceive the efforts of federal, state, and local governments to protect their lives and
property in the face of the ostensible—and enduring—terrorist threat?
As we saw in chapter 2, public opinion surveys revealed that in the years
after the attacks on the World Trade Center and the Pentagon, Americans worried a great deal about the *threat* of further terrorist acts inside the United States and about their own and their families' safety. Did
this indicate that the public did not have a great deal of trust in government efforts to prevent such attacks, or did it simply result from the
overabundant media coverage of claims about the threat of terrorism by
public officials and by Osama bin Laden and other Al Qaeda leaders?
We examined television news and public opinion data in order to answer
these questions and related ones, including, most important, what this

evidence suggests about the nation's vigilance as time passed since the 9/11 attacks.

The Media and Prevention before 9/11

With few exceptions (Miller 1980, 1982; Nacos 2006, 2007a), there has been a dearth of research that explores systematically how the mass media have covered nonmilitary counterterrorism policies and their implementation, including prevention efforts within the United States and public feelings about homeland security issues. In the years before 9/11, the media paid little attention to information about terrorism prevention (and preparedness as we will see in the next chapter). About three months before the kamikaze attacks on the World Trade Center and the Pentagon, an expert commission appointed by Congress in 1999 wrote in the executive summary of its report,

> Not all terrorists are the same, but the groups most dangerous to the United States share some characteristics not seen 10 or 20 years ago: They operate in the United States as well as abroad. Their funding and logistical networks cross borders, are less dependent on state sponsors, and are harder to disrupt with economic sanctions. They make use of widely available technologies to communicate quickly and securely. Their objectives are more deadly. This changing nature of the terrorist threat raises the stakes in getting American counterterrorist policies and practices right.[9]

Instead of reporting about this eye-opening document and the deficiencies in the antiterrorism and counterterrorism efforts, most news organizations did not deem the commission's findings newsworthy. According to the Lexis/Nexis electronic archives, in the hundreds of newspapers across the United States, only 43 mentioned the commission's report—many of them in a few lines (Nacos 2006, 2007a). For example the *New York Daily News* devoted just two sentences to this report. An editorial in the *Omaha World-Herald* suggested that the National Commission on Terrorism had "envisioned a level of evil more pervasive than common sense and experience suggest actually exists" (*Omaha World-Herald* 2000, 6). The tone of this editorial explained the media's lack of interest: Most news organizations simply did not buy the premise that international terrorism was a major threat and that there was an urgent

need for preventative measures. Another blue-ribbon panel, the U.S.
Commission on National Security in the 21st Century, released a report
in early 2001 with the warning that "the combination of unconventional
weapons proliferation with the persistence of international terrorism will
end the relative invulnerability of the U.S. homeland to catastrophic attack." What the press should have recognized as a wake-up call for heed-
ing pleas for preventative measures received "scant attention" (Alden
2001, 5). The same occurred when CIA Director George Tenet told the
Senate Intelligence Committee of the immediate threat to the United
States posed by the global Al Qaeda network. Looking at the news media's failure to report on these warnings, Kathleen Hall Jamieson and
her colleagues wondered, "Did it matter? Imagine that the press had
made a big deal out of the report and Tenet's testimony. Imagine that
President Bush were asked repeatedly how the United States was preparing. Would the country have been better prepared for September 11?"
(Jamieson, Hardy, and Roemer 2007, 40). However, in the context of our
research, the most important question is whether more *could have* been
done to *prevent* the 9/11 attacks if there had been more overall media attention and scrutiny in this respect. It was only after the events of 9/11
that a few members of the fourth estate recognized the press's failure.
Washington Post columnist Richard Cohen wrote, "We [in the media]—
and I mean most of us—were asleep" (Cohen 2001, A31).

Considering its inattention before 9/11 to what should have been recognized as a potentially nation-shaking policy issue, we wondered at the
outset of our research whether the watchdog press became more inclined
to highlight homeland security in the months and years after September 11, 2001—regardless of Washington officials' attention or inattention
to preventing terrorism in the United States.

Methodology and Data

We define "terrorism prevention" narrowly in this context as prevention
of terrorist incidents inside the United States and as related to aviation,
maritime, and cross-border transportation security. More broadly defined, it would include all kinds of counterterrorist measures from military action abroad, economic sanctions, international agreements, diplo-
macy, etc. But here prevention concerns the securing of vulnerable areas
such as airports, aviation, seaports, a wide range of infrastructure, and

borders. With this definition, we searched the Vanderbilt University Television News Archive for TV networks' news abstracts that contained variations of the terms "prevent," "protect," and/or "secure," in the context
of terrorism or counterterrorism during the 39 months from October 1,
2001, through December 31, 2004. We also reviewed full transcripts
from the online Lexis/Nexis news archive for a qualitative analysis of a
smaller number of especially relevant news stories.

Once more we first identified all news *sources* in the relevant TV network news abstracts. Second, we categorized the content of the news
messages from these sources, coding (1) their evaluations of terrorism
prevention efforts by federal, state, or local governments as positive, negative, or neutral/ambiguous and (2) their references to vulnerable areas
or sites, such as airports, seaports, buildings, bridges, infrastructure,
etc., and also the possible means of attack, such as weapons of mass destruction, missiles, and others.

For our analysis of public opinion, while there were thousands of survey questions related to terrorism and counterterrorism after 9/11, relatively few dealt specifically with public attitudes concerning the government's ability to prevent further terrorist attacks on American soil. We
collected responses to questions, preferably asked by the same survey
organizations and repeated verbatim over time, in order to track short-
and long-term trends. Specifically, we selected poll questions that revealed the public's degree of confidence in, and evaluations of, the government's efforts and ability to prevent terrorist strikes—in the United
States at large, in respondents' own communities, and in the cases of
particularly vulnerable targets. Out of 34 survey questions that were repeatedly asked through the period we studied, we focused mainly on responses to six questions that had the most repetitions or that addressed
central issue areas: confidence in the government's ability to *"prevent
further"* terrorist attacks in the United States; confidence in the government's ability to *"protect"* its citizens from "future" terrorist attacks;
perceptions of whether "the United States is doing all it reasonably can
do to try to prevent further terrorist attacks"; confidence in "airport security"; approval of the way President Bush was handling "policies to
prevent and minimize terrorism at home" and "terrorism and homeland
security"; and general approval of the way President Bush was handling
his job as president (again, when we had more than one time point for responses in one month, we used the monthly average).

Last, bringing in an important related issue, we also collected and analyzed opinion data beyond our main 39-month period in order to probe whether the news coverage of Hurricane Katrina, and the extraordinary mass-mediated debate about the lack of effective preparation for and responses to the devastation that this natural disaster caused, had any measurable effect on Americans' attitudes about their government's ability to *prevent* a different type of catastrophe—terrorist attacks. Although the Katrina debate focused primarily on the inadequate hurricane preparation and performance of emergency responders, a cursory reading of the news coverage revealed that stories about Hurricane Katrina mentioned terrorism quite frequently. For this reason we surmised that the frequent references to terrorism in news coverage of Katrina might have blurred the distinction between "prevention" and "preparedness" and thus affected evaluations of government efforts and capabilities to prevent terrorism. To examine this we used the Lexis/Nexis archive to find the frequency of stories on the three TV networks and also, in this case, in the *New York Times* that mentioned both Hurricane Katrina and terrorism during the period from September 1, 2005, to February 28, 2006. Since the number of African Americans among Katrina's victims in New Orleans was disproportionately high, we were also interested as well in the volume of these stories that mentioned "African American(s)" and/ or "black(s)." The reason for this was that news reporting about the fate of African Americans in New Orleans might have especially affected this racial group's assessments and perceptions of preparedness for *any* disasters, including terrorist acts, compared to the attitudes of whites.

Modest Media Attention to Preventing Terrorism at Home

In the years after 9/11, television network news did not pay as much attention as one would have expected to the state of terrorism prevention as part of homeland security. During the 39 months after 9/11, the combined evening broadcasts of ABC News, CBS News, and NBC News aired only 85 stories specifically dealing with preventing terrorism. In contrast, during the same period the three networks aired fully 373 stories, more than four times as many, that dealt with the *threat* of terrorism. The news segments on terrorism prevention contained a total of 443 messages concerning relevant security measures, issues, or problems, compared to 1,725 messages emphasizing different aspect of the terrorist threat (see chapter 2). About half of the prevention messages in network news were found in NBC News broadcasts, and about one-quarter each in stories aired by CBS News and ABC News. The modest number of such stories was likely the result of the media's day-to-day attention to many other aspects of terrorism and counterterrorism and the newsrooms' preference for dramatic developments or events with shock value such as terrorism alerts and actual or possible military actions

Indeed, most of the reports about preventive measures or evaluations of security measures already in place came on the heels of security breaches, major terrorist strikes abroad, foiled plots, or terror alerts by the Department of Homeland Security as the following three examples illustrate.

(1) On December 23, 2001, ABC News reported on its *World News Tonight* broadcast at length about investigations into would-be shoe-bomber Richard Reid's attempt to blow up an American Airline plane on its flight from Paris to Boston. Reporting from Logan Airport in Boston, Ron Claiborne focused first and foremost on the foiled attempt before mentioning a new airport security measure in the following short exchange:

> CLAIBORNE: At Logan Airport today, there was a new security measure in place: random checks of passengers' shoes.
> MAJOR BRIAN O'HARE (NATIONAL GUARD): The shoes now have to come off of—of the individual. They're visually and manually checked for any type of wires or anything else that may be suspicious.
> CLAIBORNE: Even with tighter security and all four new steps that were announced today, many travelers here said they were badly shaken by what happened aboard American Airlines Flight 63.

While the "four new steps" in airport security that Claiborne mentioned were not spelled out, ABC's aviation correspondent Lisa Stark reported that the Federal Aviation Administration was likely to issue a new security directive and predicted that "you will see more checks of shoes."

(2) In the aftermath of a shooting incident at the El Al ticket counter in the Los Angeles International Airport, correspondent Pete Williams reported on NBC's *Nightly News* (July 5, 2002) about airport security and the fact that in spite of routine passenger screening, "other airport areas, including ticket counters, are generally unprotected, and that's occasionally a problem." A

representative of the "Air Travelers Association" said that more security was
needed in such areas.

(3) Following a story about a new threat by bin Laden and a heightened terror alert
status issued by the Department of Homeland Security at the top of the *CBS
Evening News* on February 11, 2003, correspondent Bob Orr reported on intensified security measures in various parts of the country—for example, stepped
up security at water facilities, power plants, transportation hubs, and in high-
rise buildings, where owners were urged "to secure heating and cooling systems so terrorists cannot use them to spread biological and chemical agents."

Correspondents, reporters, and anchors constituted the most prominent source category in terrorism prevention news, followed by counterterrorism experts and members of the general public. Most surprisingly,
during a time when many Americans were worried about more terrorist attacks at home, the president, the secretary of homeland security,
and other administration officials were not often sources in these stories
(see figure 5.1)—much less frequently than they were in the coverage of
terrorist threats and alerts (chapter 2) or of the buildup to the Iraq War
(chapter 4). On the other hand, members of Congress were nearly as often represented in TV news as were administration officials.

Since terrorists hijacked commercial airliners and flew them into the
World Trade Center and the Pentagon on 9/11, journalists and their news
sources seemed most concerned with efforts to protect the country from
similar attacks. Thus, most of the news about prevention dealt specifically with airport and aviation security, in contrast to the country's need

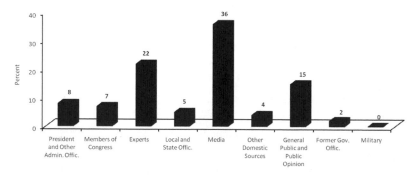

FIGURE 5.1. Sources in terrorism prevention news

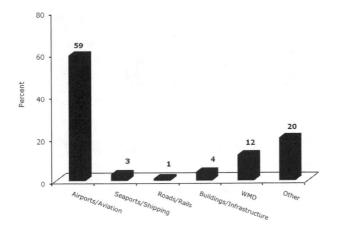

FIGURE 5.2. Areas of evaluation in prevention news

to protect itself from weapons of mass destruction (WMD)—biological
agents most of all and, to a much lesser extent, nuclear and chemical
weapons (figure 5.2). Even less attention was paid to the need to protect other high risk sites, such as major buildings, tunnels, bridges, and
water reservoirs. And although the Madrid train bombings occurred
during the period we studied, only 1% of the news messages were concerned with the security of transit systems or the trucking industry. The
remainder of the relevant coverage, about one-fifth of all the messages,
addressed terrorism prevention in other general terms.

Most news sources did not take supportive or critical positions toward
the prevention efforts by federal, state, and local governments or the private sector. Indeed, over two-thirds of the total messages fell into the
neutral or ambiguous category. But there were significantly more negative than positive evaluations (figure 5.3). In most instances, these pro
and con positions concerned the federal government's homeland security performance, and here there were five times more negative than positive evaluations, with the rest neutral or ambiguous. Though based on
far fewer messages, news sources rated prevention efforts by state and
local governments far more positively than those of the federal government and not negatively at all, with the bulk of the messages, again, neutral or ambiguous. All in all, television news mostly ignored terrorism
prevention efforts, or the lack of them, in the private sector; the few relevant messages were much more critical than positive.

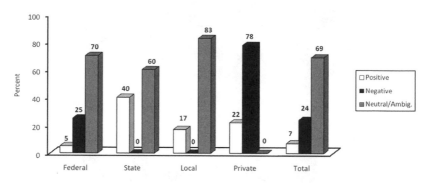

FIGURE 5.3. News message evaluations of prevention efforts

Correspondents, anchors, and others in the media were the most frequent sources who addressed the pluses and minuses in the federal government's prevention policies; they also conveyed a higher proportion
of critical messages than any other source category (38% negative versus 5% positive). Members of Congress were not far behind, with 34%
of their messages critical versus 10% supportive. When members of the
administration addressed questions about homeland security and terrorism, they were a bit more positive (19%) than negative (13%). The fact
that there was criticism on both ends of Pennsylvania Avenue was hardly
surprising, since both the executive and legislative branches were involved in homeland security matters. State-level officials as news sources
did not get involved in these pro and con judgments. When local officials were interviewed or cited in stories about federal terrorism prevention efforts, they gave overwhelmingly positive evaluations (73% of their
messages), but over a quarter of their judgments were negative. Although
other domestic sources, such as representatives of interest groups, were
in large part neutral or ambiguous (63%) in their statements, they also
expressed criticism toward Washington's efforts more than one-fourth
(27%) of the time.

During this period, while there was hardly a newscast that did not
mention or cite President Bush regarding some aspect of terrorism or
counterterrorism, the president, as already noted, was very infrequently
a source in reports about specific homeland security measures. However,
when he made the news about federal, state, or local governments' efforts to protect America from future terrorist acts, the president was the
cheerleader-in-chief with 84% of his messages positive, only 8% critical,
and 8% neutral or ambiguous.

The findings of our content analysis raised the question of whether President Bush's positive statements about terrorism prevention at home countered and perhaps overshadowed the more frequent criticism in the public's mind. If so, the question is whether the impact of the administration's spin on this issue remained steady over time or waned as the public's memory of 9/11 faded and the president's general approval ratings declined.

Public Attitudes toward Homeland Security

Over the years, Americans have shown a fair degree of confidence in their government's ability to prevent terrorism at home. In early 1989, before a major terrorist attack had occurred inside the United States, 46% of the public had a great deal or a good deal of confidence in the government's ability to prevent terrorism in the United States, 38% had a fair amount of confidence, and 16% had no confidence at all. These numbers remained quite steady during the 1990s—in spite of the first World Trade Center bombing in 1993 and the Oklahoma City bombing two years later (Nacos 2006, 274). Strikingly, the public's confidence was rock solid immediately after the attacks of 9/11: On that day two-thirds of Americans (66%) had a great deal or a good amount of trust in the government's ability to prevent future terrorism (see the online appendix; available at http://www.press.uchicago.edu/books/nacos/). This may have been the reaction of a shocked nation showing a stiff upper lip of defiance. But within six months, by March 2002, the percentage with this degree of confidence had dropped 10 points and two months later another 10 points to 46%. In the ensuing years, when the media carried more news about the complexity of homeland security than before 9/11, Americans' trust in the government's capability to protect them from terrorism oscillated somewhat, but it never again came close to the high levels immediately after the 9/11 attack. In August 2005, one month after the four suicide bombings in London's transit system, only two in five Americans (42%) had confidence (a "great deal" or "good amount") in the authorities' ability to prevent terrorism inside the U.S. borders, whereas 58% had only a fair amount (43%) or no confidence at all (15%). It seems that even events, developments, and revelations abroad that were not directly related to security at home affected public attitudes about government's ability to prevent further terror attacks.

When pollsters used different question wordings, there were similar declines of those who had "a great deal" of confidence and increases among those who had "not very much" trust in government in this regard. While no one expects government to "protect" the country from hurricanes making landfall, the multiple failures of the levees and flood walls during Hurricane Katrina in August 2005 evidently had an impact on public attitudes about government's ability to protect Americans from future terrorist attacks. After all, government efforts failed miserably to prevent the catastrophic consequences of the flood in New Orleans and surrounding areas. For a sizeable number of Americans the differences between the prevention of natural and man-made disasters became blurred in the aftermath of Hurricane Katrina: Whereas 69% of the public expressed "a great deal" or "a fair amount" of confidence in government concerning terrorist acts about six weeks before the disaster, 10% fewer Americans (59%) did so in the days after Katrina's devastating landfall.

When asked more specifically about the government's ability to prevent terrorism where they resided, a greater percentage of Americans in the initial years after 9/11 said they were "very confident" or "confident" than "not too confident" or "not confident at all." Over time, however, the percentage of respondents who were confident declined, whereas the percentage less or not at all confident increased. By July 2005, the public was evenly divided on this question, and three months later—and for the first time since 9/11—a clear majority was not too, or not at all, confident that their government could protect them in their own communities. Both the inability of British authorities to prevent the quadruple bombing of the London transit system in early July and the heavily reported post-Katrina nightmare in New Orleans most likely affected public attitudes: when it came to the protection of their own communities from terrorist acts, more Americans came to believe that their government could do no better than the British and the flawed prevention efforts in New Orleans. And there was no rebound in Americans' level of confidence by the summer of 2006.[10]

Similarly, the majority of Americans believed that the United States was doing all it could to prevent further terrorist attacks during the months and years immediately after 9/11, while a minority thought that more should be done (figure 5.4). However, the gap between majority and minority narrowed significantly from fall 2001 to spring 2004. More important, by August 2005 there was a complete reversal in public attitudes

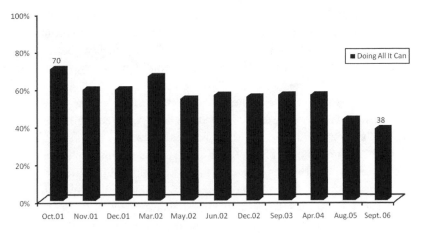

FIGURE 5.4. Public opinion: U.S. doing all it can to prevent future terrorist attacks

as a majority felt that more could be done in terms of prevention. After the hurricane disaster, there was a further decline in the Americans' beliefs that their country was doing all it could to prevent future terrorist attacks, with fewer than four in 10 holding this view.

When asked in 2003 and 2004 whether their country was safer or less safe from terrorism than before 9/11, the public was evenly divided with only a slight edge shifting back and forth between those who thought the United States was much safer and those feeling the country was less safe. But in August 2005, a few weeks after the suicide attacks in London, only 14% felt the United States was much safer than before 9/11.[11]

Terrorist Methods and Targets

In contrast to the majority of New York City residents who remained "not too confident" or "not confident at all" that the government would protect them from terrorists' detonating "dirty bombs," public opinion nationwide in 2002 and 2003 was quite evenly divided. But in subsequent years, the majority of the public also became "not too confident" or "not confident at all" when it came to this. Asked in the summer of 2005 whether they believed that the government was doing enough to prevent terrorists from obtaining a nuclear bomb or material to make one, Americans nationwide were divided: 50% said that the U.S. authorities were not doing enough, and 47% believed that the government was doing enough in this respect. And whereas a plurality or majority were "very confident" or "confident" in the government's ability to protect the water supply from biological and chemical terror attacks, the majority of New York City residents were "not too confident" or "not confident at all."[12]

Finally, except for the immediate aftermath of 9/11, the American public displayed a consistently high degree of confidence in the safety of U.S. airports and aviation. This was hardly surprising during a period when homeland security efforts concentrated primarily on improving preventative measures in the area that had allowed the 9/11 terrorists to carry out their attacks. As noted earlier, the bulk of prevention news coverage, too, was devoted to airport and aviation security.

In contrast, the public was less confident that the government was adequately protecting mass transportation, such as trains and buses, from terrorist acts.[13] Following the suicide bombings of London's transit system in the summer of 2005, a majority believed that not enough was being done by the United States to prevent the detonation of car bombs or explosives carried by suicide bombers.[14]

President Bush and His Administration

Just as President Bush enjoyed high overall approval ratings from 9/11 through the early successes in the Iraq War, he received similarly high grades for taking measures to prevent terrorism. While this specific approval rating declined by a dozen points during 2002 and 2003, it remained impressive. This changed later, however, when approval for his handling of terrorism and homeland security dropped from 65% in February 2004 to 51% in August 2005. The next month, at the height of the controversy over the government's handling of Hurricane Katrina, for the first time slightly more Americans disapproved (48%) than approved (46%) of the president's performance in this area. At this point split on their grading of the president's efforts to prevent terrorism at home, Americans overall had lowered their approval by 19 points and increased their disapproval by 20 points between February 2004 and early September 2005.

When pollsters asked about the public's confidence in the *"Bush administration"* (not "President Bush," the "government," or the "United

States") to prevent further terrorist attacks, they also found a steady and significant decline in confidence.

The heavily reported failures of foreign governments to prevent major terrorist attacks along with the fiasco of the breaking levees in New Orleans may have affected public attitudes toward the ability of their own government to protect them from terrorism. These much reported failures showed that reality did not match the assurances that the president and other administration officials offered with respect to terrorism prevention. This gave more credence to the critics of the administration's efforts to prevent terrorism on the home front.

Partisanship Matters Most

As public confidence in government fell in this area, it declined among all segments of the public, but at times more so for women, African Americans, and self-identified Democrats. From August 2002 through July 2005, women were between 5 and 7 percentage points less confident in the government's ability to protect the area where they live than were men. In October 2005, several weeks after Hurricane Katrina struck New Orleans and other coastal areas, the gender difference stood at 8 points. Whereas men's confidence increased slightly over the following 10 months, women's sank still further: by October 2006 there was a 13-point gender gap, with 50% of men and only 37% women "very confident" or "confident" in the government's ability to protect their communities from terrorist attacks. What explains this difference? Related to our discussion in previous chapters (see also Davis 2007, 66, 68), women tend to be "more personally fearful of victimization than men" (Huddy et al. 2003, 263; on issues of force and violence more generally, see Shapiro and Mahajan 1986), and during the post-9/11 years women were more worried about the threat of terrorist attacks than were men (see chapter 2). Given their higher degree of apprehension, women were probably also more skeptical about terrorism prevention in their own communities.

Differences in opinion were much more pronounced between whites and African Americans, while Latinos' attitudes were quite close to those of whites: From July 2002 to August 2006, their trust in government regarding prevention did not deviate more than 5 percentage

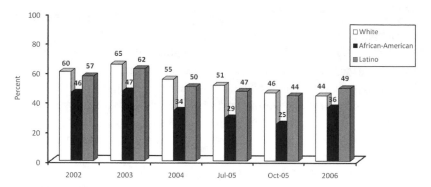

FIGURE 5.5. Confidence in government protection of one's residential area from terrorist attack, by race

points from whites,' whereas African Americans' levels of confidence were significantly lower (8 to 22 percentage points) as figure 5.5 shows. It is possible that the large African American populations in high risk places like New York City, Washington, DC, Chicago, and Los Angeles explain African Americans' greater perception of threat regarding terrorism that we reported in earlier (see chapter 2) and also their lower level of confidence in prevention in their communities. More compelling, however, as we noted in the preceding chapter, is the greater stress that African Americans have experienced, due to past violence against them, discrimination, and alienation (Davis 2007, chap. 8), which would explain their greater sensitivity to perceptions of government inaction in response to threats that might affect them directly. In contrast, as Davis (2007, 168) suggested, "The Latino reaction is not likely to be tied as much to their sense of alienation or discrimination." He cites research in which "differences in the political values among Latinos seem to suggest that, though they often suffer from degrading experiences similar to those of blacks, the political orientations and core values of Latinos— particularly native born Latinos—tend to be more closely aligned with the dominant culture" (de la Garza, Falcon, and Garcia, 1996). As a result, there are circumstances under which Latinos may accept certain values and express attitudes that are more similar to those of whites than of blacks (Davis 2007, 168).

In the case of African Americans, events reinforced their group-specific concerns. In October 2005, about six weeks after Hurricane Katrina struck the Gulf coast, African Americans' trust in the govern-

ment's ability to protect their own communities from terrorist attacks
hit a new low, as figure 5.5 shows. We believe that this low was a reaction
to the fact that African Americans in New Orleans were disproportionately affected by the disaster. This side of the Katrina story was widely
reported by the news media. In September 2005 alone, ABC News, CBS
News, and NBC News combined aired 141 stories that mentioned both
Hurricane Katrina and African Americans or blacks; during the same
period the *New York Times* carried 234 such stories.

However, the gender and racial differences paled in comparison to
opinion differences along partisan lines: Republicans expressed 16 to
33 points more confidence than Democrats and 14 to 19 more than Independents in the government's capability to protect their communities,
during a time period in which Republicans controlled both the executive
and legislative branches of government in Washington (see figure 5.6).[15]
Although pronounced in this case of terrorism prevention, this divide,
as we described in previous chapters, has been part of a trend over the
last few decades in which American politics has become increasingly polarized along partisan and ideological lines (see Abramowitz and Saunders 1998, 2005; Heatherington 2001; Carsey and Layman 2006; Layman, Carsey, and Horowitz 2006; Shapiro and Bloch-Elkon 2006, 2007,
2008b; Jacobson 2008, 2011; Bafumi and Shapiro 2009; Levendusky
2009; Heatherington and Weiler 2009; Abramowitz 2010).

To sum up our findings on public opinion toward homeland security,
in the years after 9/11 Americans became progressively less confident
in the government's ability to prevent terrorist attacks and increasingly
doubtful that the authorities were doing everything possible to prevent

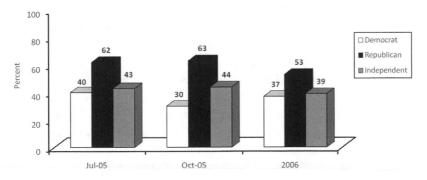

FIGURE 5.6. Confidence in government protection of one's residential area from terrorist
attack, by party ID

the most catastrophic types of attack. This waning trust in the effectiveness of homeland security efforts matched the steady decline in the public's approval of the president's and his administration's handling of terrorism prevention at home.

Public Opinion and News Coverage

In the cases of the threat of terrorism, civil liberties, and the buildup to the Iraq War, public perceptions and reactions appeared responsive to messages and rhetoric in the news from political leaders, media personnel, and other sources. In contrast, what we see in the available data is very different in the case of prevention. First, just as there was far less news about terrorism prevention than about the counterterrorism policies we discussed in the previous chapters, there was also significantly less public opinion data on terrorism prevention over the period we studied. As a result, we are limited in what we can say here about the relationship between public opinion and relevant news reporting because we do not have monthly survey data during periods of brief increases in news coverage concerning prevention. Obviously, the same government officials, news organizations, and pollsters who were highly interested in speaking out, reporting, and polling the public on the threat of terrorism, the reasons for going to war against Iraq, and even the need to curb civil liberties paid much less attention to terrorism prevention or the protection of the public from further attacks. For the Bush administration, as noted earlier, preventing further terrorist strikes at home meant fighting the war against terrorism abroad.

Figure 5.7 compares the trends for sources cited in television reporting on terrorism prevention with public opinion on this issue for which there appear possible relationships. Aside from the high and low points in the numbers of relevant messages from government sources that have some correspondence with public opinion, the numbers of these messages in network news each month are few, and there are often none. The low percentage of the public having a "great deal" of *"confidence in the government preventing acts of terrorism"* is consistent with the low level of attention that government sources including President Bush paid to prevention in their public communications. Public confidence was highest right after 9/11 when government officials' attention to prevention and news coverage of prevention were higher than in subsequent months

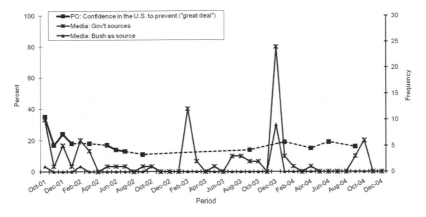

FIGURE 5.7. Confidence in the ability of the U.S. to prevent further terrorist attacks, October 2001–December 2004

and years, but opinion fell off as this attention declined precipitously and pollsters, too, lost interest in asking relevant questions. We have no opinion data in early 2003 when the press cited government officials speaking out more on prevention in the context of the invasion of Iraq. However, the modest increase in public confidence in 2004 occurred after the prominent and extensive coverage of the capture of Saddam Hussein in mid-December 2003. At a time when the majority of Americans believed that Saddam Hussein and Iraq had been directly involved in the 9/11 attacks and had ties to Osama bin Laden's Al Qaeda terrorist organization, seeing the former Iraqi president in prison may well have bolstered Americans' confidence in their government's ability to prevent further terror attacks. It seems that at this point the public bought the administration's argument that the best way to prevent terrorism at home was to fight terrorists and their supporters abroad (cf. Merolla and Zechmeister 2009). Moreover, there was a large increase in early 2004 news reports of Bush and other government sources emphasizing prevention measures, during a period of heightened threat against air travel between Britain and the United States, of reports about the release of a new Osama bin Laden audiotape, and of a multitude of security issues surrounding the period of New Year's Eve celebrations through the Super Bowl. Although the limited and intermittent data allow only a rough statistical analysis, most of the correlations found for the level of public confidence occurred with messages by government sources and by President Bush in particular (r's in the .8 range). These correlations, however, were driven mainly by the trend data from 2001 to 2002, when these measures changed, but not a lot.

We find a similar pattern (data not shown) in the case of changes in positive responses to the question of whether "*the government is doing all it reasonably can to prevent further terrorist attacks*": from October to December 2001, a decline from 71% to 59%. This coincided with a fall-off in administration officials and members of Congress commenting on preventing terrorism and was followed by an increase (to 66%) in March 2002, as more statements about prevention were reported from congressional and other government sources. These changes in the content of television news, again not enormous ones, were correlated with modest shifts in public opinion (*r*'s in the .9 range for government sources). Unfortunately, once more, we have no opinion data to track more fully the effects of the increase in coverage of government sources in early 2003 and 2004.

When we compared trends in news coverage with public confidence in *the ability of government to protect its citizens from future terrorist attacks*, we found that messages involving members of the *general public* on airport or aviation security (i.e., the checking of carry-on luggage, the role of sky marshals, etc.) were correlated with responses to this survey question (*r*'s in the .9 range and about the same for messages involving representatives of interest groups). There was also a correlation, though again involving small changes, between messages addressing security in airports and aviation and levels of public confidence (*r*'s in the .8 range and particularly for messages from media sources). This was probably related to the substantial coverage of airport and aviation security—close to 60% of all messages, as shown in figure 5.2, addressing vulnerable sites relevant to terrorism prevention efforts. These trends moved in tandem briefly in late 2001, when the media reported extensively on the arrest of would-be shoe-bomber Richard Reid. This incident provided an occasion for news organizations to ask questions and report about the state of terrorism prevention in aviation. The peak in prevention news occurred along with a high point in late 2001 in the public's perception that the government was doing a "great deal" (30%) to protect Americans from terrorism. Then, after a decline, there was another uptick in July 2002 when 21% of the public expressed a "great deal" of confidence. This may have been a reaction to news reports of extremely long lines at airport security checkpoints at the beginning of the summer travel season, the first after 9/11. When airline passengers told reporters about superlong waiting times and also said that it is better to be safe after all, this might have reflected and bolstered further the public's positive perception of stricter prevention measures.

Whether considering public attitudes about the government's ability to *prevent* terrorism or *protect* Americans from further terror attacks, it appears that during the years we studied a higher volume of messages about prevention occurred along with increased public confidence, and a lower volume with decreased public trust. Moreover, it was the amount of news coverage for which this pattern occurred and not the positive or negative evaluations of the state of terrorism prevention that the news sources expressed. This may be explained by our finding that the largest number of prevention messages in the news neither lauded nor criticized the performance of the responsible authorities but were neutral or ambiguous.

Was any of this consequential for the public's evaluation of President Bush? It appears that opinion toward Bush's handling of terrorism and homeland security and his overall approval ratings were not affected by reports about prevention. There was no relationship between the decline in approval and our particular media content measures. In contrast to what we found in our analysis of news coverage of the threat of terrorism, where threat messages from government officials and from Bush coincided with short-term increases in approval (see chapter 2), officials' statement concerning prevention did not appear to be related to public opinion in this way—probably because there was not an abundance of such messages.

One further piece of analysis that we did was motivated by the wake-up call that Hurricane Katrina gave to the nation in late August and early September 2005, which bore not only on protecting the nation from the effects of natural disasters but also other catastrophic events, including especially terrorist attacks. Figure 5.8 compares the number of newspaper (*New York Times*) and television network news stories on Katrina, with trends in public confidence in the ability of the U.S. government to protect its citizens from future terrorist attacks. We see some correlation between changes in media coverage of the hurricane catastrophe and public confidence (r's in the $-.9$ range): Public trust in the government's ability to prevent terrorist acts fell off in September 2005 as news stories that mentioned both Katrina and terrorism hit their high-

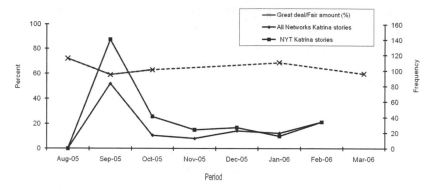

FIGURE 5.8. Confidence in U.S. government to protect from future terrorist attacks, August 2005–March 2006

est level; it then increased somewhat as coverage of Katrina declined in the following months, and dropped off again after an increase in the number of stories on Katrina in February 2006.

As in the case of reports about the plight of Katrina victims in September of 2005, coverage throughout February 2006 contained mostly narrative and visuals critical of the government's handling of the disaster. The news reflected the facts: congressional hearings and reports laid bare the incompetence of public officials in preparing for and responding to Katrina. On February 14, for example, ABC News quoted from a House committee report that concluded, "Our investigation revealed that Katrina was a national failure—an abdication of the most solemn obligation to provide for the common welfare. At every level—individual, corporate, philanthropic, and governmental—we failed to meet the challenge that was Katrina. In this cautionary tale, all the little pigs built houses of straw." The government's Army Corps of Engineers was criticized for failing to assure that New Orleans's levee system would withstand the force of Hurricane Katrina and thereby prevent the devastating flooding of large areas. There were reports about the Federal Trade Commission's investigation into possible price gouging during the catastrophe, negative reactions in New Orleans to President Bush's State of the Union Address, and the six-month anniversary of Katrina at the end of February. In short, the high volume of attention to Katrina that also mentioned terrorism appeared to depress the public's confidence in Washington's ability to prevent terrorist attacks. Indeed, we suspect that news about Katrina, whether it mentioned terrorism or not, may have affected how Americans judged the government's handling of terrorism prevention.

Conclusion

The findings in this chapter are straightforward: Despite President Bush's and other government officials' very frequent warnings of the very real threat of terrorism against the homeland, and despite the media's extensive coverage of this danger, neither the administration and Congress nor the press paid ongoing attention to government and private sector prevention measures—or the lack of them. As a result, in the years after 9/11 the public came to have mixed sentiments about government's ability to prevent terrorist acts, and fewer Americans believed that the government was doing all it should. To the extent that national news coverage served as a measure of the government's efforts to prevent terrorism or to assure the public that it was actively working in the nation's interest in this regard, the Bush administration in particular fell short: it did not inform the public fully and regularly about a most important area of counterterrorism policy, assuming there was a real threat within U.S. borders as President Bush and other government officials repeatedly told the nation. Ironically, by emphasizing the threat and paying less attention to equally or more important prevention matters, the administration may have contributed to the decline of public confidence in its capacity to protect Americans from terrorism. The rare short periods during which administration officials did address prevention issues and initiatives coincided with small upticks in public confidence, whereas long periods of minimal prevention coverage corresponded with somewhat decreasing public trust. It is possible that this downward trend was affected not only by the abundance of mass-mediated threat messages by administration officials (chapter 2) and the scarcity of more assuring prevention messages, but also by the gradual decline in the public's overall trust in the Bush administration's handling of counterterrorism policies and the decline in the president's overall performance rating.

Television news and presumably the rest of the press followed the lead of the top political leaders who paid little attention to the specifics of terrorism prevention. In the wake of the mass media spectacles of the destruction of the World Trade Center and the Pentagon, the Bush administration streamlined its transmission and ritual communications to emphasize the threat of further terrorist attacks and thereby exploited the politics of fear to mobilize public support for the coming war against Iraq and for other controversial measures justified in the name of counterterrorism. During most of the 39 months we examined, the administration's *nonagenda* with respect to terrorism prevention at home became the same for the media as well. Prevention was not a salient issue for Democrats in Congress, who were in the minority in both chambers during this time, nor for other authoritative sources outside the administration. This case suggests the press's failure to exercise its watchdog role in highly important matters of public affairs. There was neither sufficient public information nor the sustained debate in the news media needed to foster "accountability relations between authorities and publics" (Bennett and Serrin 2007, 329). This void allowed the administration to define "the war on terrorism as something to be managed by actions beyond our shores," without addressing "the myriad soft targets within the U.S. border" (Flynn 2007, 4) and how to protect them from terrorist strikes.

According to the indexing model's observation that "sustained debate in the news is usually produced by disagreement among political elites" (Bennett, Lawrence, and Livingston 2007, 132), terrorism prevention policy at home was sparsely covered in the press because authoritative voices did not challenge the administration's low key approach to this issue. If there were exchanges among elites inside and outside of government, they did not make it into the public sphere through the media.

This lack of information obviously did not result from censorship but the choices that newsrooms made while, in sharp contrast, both broadcast and print media reported extensively, frequently, and critically about the devastation that Hurricane Katrina caused and about the public sector's failure to secure the levees—ending in a fiasco—and to prepare an effective emergency response. In this case, the fourth estate set its own agenda and primed the public to evaluate government officials in terms of their policies (or lack thereof) designed to lessen the impact of natural disasters and to prevent terrorism. While post-Katrina news mostly covered *preparedness* and *responses* to such disasters, the media also raised specific questions about breaches in New Orleans's levee system and whether government action could have prevented the breaks that caused the devastating flood. Moreover, there were numerous stories on television and in print news about Katrina that also mentioned terrorism. No wonder that the peak in stories about Katrina and in those that also contained references to terrorism corresponded with falling public confidence in the ability of government to prevent terrorist attacks. Cued by the news and by criticism from Democrats and Republicans in Congress and from state and local governments, the public seemed to recognize that a national government that could not prevent the rupture of levees might not be able to foil terrorist attacks. As we consider further in the next chapter, it took Katrina's horrendous flooding and tortured rescue efforts in New Orleans to shake the news media from their indexing patterns and hegemonic influences to exercise their independence—providing critical reporting along the lines of a socially responsible press—at least in the case of preparedness for disasters.

CHAPTER SIX

Preparing for the Next Attack

The lesson of 9/11 for civilians and first responders can be stated simply: in the new age of terror, they—we—are the primary targets. The losses America suffered that day demonstrated both the gravity of the terrorist threat and the commensurate need to prepare ourselves to meet it. . . . A rededication to preparedness is perhaps the best way to honor the memories of those we lost that day. — The 9/11 Commission Report[1]

The first World Trade Center bombing in 1993, the Oklahoma City bombing in 1995, and, most of all, the 9/11 attacks on the World Trade Center and the Pentagon demonstrated that not all terrorist acts can be prevented—not even by a superpower. However, effective preparedness measures can and do result in meaningful damage reductions in natural and man-made disasters. As Stephen Flynn (2007, 9) noted, "The loss of life and economic fallout that [natural and terrorist] disasters reap will always be magnified by our lack of preparedness to manage the risk actively and to respond effectively when things go wrong" (Flynn 2007, 9). Yet, the catastrophic terrorism of 9/11 did not trigger massive efforts to improve the disaster preparedness on the part of the emergency response community and the public at large. Instead, "overall, the existing government response system is more accurately described as disarrayed, disconnected, uncoordinated, underfunded, and discredited" (Choi 2008, 4). And public opinion surveys revealed "a national state of unpreparedness for emergency events" in the post-9/11 years (Redlener and Berman 2006, 87). As one of the country's foremost security experts put it:

> Why do we remain unprepared for the next terrorist attack or natural disaster? Where are we most vulnerable? How have we allowed our government to be so negligent? Who will keep you and your family safe? Is America living on borrowed time? How can we become a more resilient nation?[2]

   On the fourth anniversary of the 9/11 terrorist attacks and less than two weeks after Hurricane Katrina had devastated New Orleans and other communities along the Gulf of Mexico, the former chair and vice-chair of the 9/11 Commission wrote in an op-ed article: "Katrina raises the question of how prepared we are to respond to another massive terrorist attack that would surely occur without warning. The answer is: not nearly as prepared as we should have been" (Kean and Hamilton 2005). This was not the first time that Thomas H. Kean, a Republican and former governor of New Jersey, and Lee H. Hamilton, a Democrat and former member of the U.S. House of Representatives, had called for greater efforts to beef up the capability of emergency responders to deal effectively with a catastrophic terrorist strike. Based on the 9/11 Commission's finding that the overloaded radio frequencies assigned to New York City's emergency personnel "had led to the unnecessary loss of life" (Kean and Hamilton 2005), they and other members of the bipartisan commission had called for more radio spectrum for emergency responders and a unified command system along with other necessary improvements. But it took Hurricane Katrina and its desperate victims, many of whom waited several days and nights to be rescued, to alert the nation to the stunning weaknesses in local, state, and federal emergency response systems. Unlike hurricanes, terrorist attacks occur without warning and therefore require more immediate and speedier reactions. This crucial difference was not lost on Kean and Hamilton or Senator Joseph Lieberman, the chair of the U.S. Senate's Homeland Security Committee. In a stinging criticism of federal preparedness, Lieberman asserted that Katrina should have been "a lesser challenge to the nation's emergency-management apparatus than the 9/11 attacks: It [the hurricane] was preceded by 72 hours increasingly dire predictions."[3]
   In reality, policymakers—in particular presidents and their partisans in elective offices—seem to have far more reason for supporting and funding disaster relief rather than emergency preparedness. Focusing on natural disasters, research by Andrew Healy and Neil Malhotra (2009, 388) found,

> Voters significantly reward [direct] disaster relief payments, holding the incumbent presidential party accountable for actions taken *after* a disaster. In contrast, voters show no response at all, on average, to preparedness spending, even though investment in preparedness produces a large social benefit.

As a result, federal spending on natural disaster relief has consistently been much greater than funding for preparedness measures. Since quick and effective actions by the most important members of the disaster preparedness and emergency response community (firefighters, police, health care providers, etc.) are crucial during catastrophic events, the limited preparedness funding versus direct relief payments—both before and after 9/11—affected and continues to affect the state of preparedness for terrorist attacks and natural disasters.

Watchdog Press: An Exception, not the Rule

In assessing the early news about Hurricane Katrina and the plight of the many thousands stranded in the Superdome and Morial Convention Center of flooded New Orleans, Lance Bennett, Regina Lawrence, and Steven Livingston (2007, 167) recognized news reporting that deviated from the entrenched coverage patterns of major news organizations: "Whether on radio, TV, or in the papers, journalists were suddenly and surprisingly taking adversarial positions with officials, and even informing those officials about the realities of the situation at hand." In one broadcast, during which he grilled the seemingly clueless head of the Federal Emergency Management Agency, Michael Brown, NBC News anchor Brian Williams said, "tonight, really, my role is viewers' advocate and for the folks here."[4] Taking on the role of reporter and anchor in this particular broadcast, Williams acted as (1) a watchdog of a government that was slow in responding to the disaster and (2) an advocate for the directly affected residents of New Orleans and the American public at large. In this remarkable case the news fulfilled the ideal of a "socially responsible press" that served the public interest—not commercial or other private and special interests. However, in the post-9/11 years the exemplary reporting on the Katrina catastrophe was an exception, not the rule. Most of the time, journalists followed their normal routines and were "constrained by a set of complex institutional relations that lead them to reproduce day after day the opinions and views of establishment figures, especially high government officials" (Schudson 2007, 45). This focus on—that is, indexing of—authoritative sources and their disagreements (or lack of them) occurred for the politics of counterterrorist policies (see chapters 2 and 4), and, as typically was the case, at the expense of attention to less influential actors with opposing views (Bennett, Lawrence and Livingston 2007; Nacos 2007a). On the other hand, when the political establishment—presidents and members of their administrations most of all—fail to speak out sufficiently about certain important national problems and matters of public affairs, significant issues and information will be missing from the media agenda (as in the previous chapter on terrorism prevention). In the words of one proponent of the hegemony theory, "Perhaps, the most common and complete form of distortion is nonreporting" (Parenti 1986, 102; with the broader implications in the seminal arguments on political power and politics of Peter Bachrach and Morton Baratz [1962, 1963] and E. E. Schattschneider [1960]).

One of the most outspoken critics of Washington's failure to adopt a comprehensive preparedness and response policy complained that "our national leaders have shown a decided preference for dealing with our vulnerabilities behind closed doors" (Flynn 2007, 152). At times, government officials may have good reason to remain silent. For example, intelligence about an "imminent" chemical attack on New York City in February 2003 led the New York Police Department to order officers to look out for "improvised weapons" that might be used to release cyanide into the city's subway system. Fortunately, the chemical assault did not occur, reportedly because Al Qaeda's second-in-command, Ayman al-Zawahiri, called the operation off for fear that it might not cause as much damage as the 9/11 attacks. When this incident was revealed more than three years later (Suskind 2006), it was reported that at the time of the behind-the-scenes alert "city hospitals were wrestling with the issue of how to treat anyone exposed to cyanide" and they sought to "increase their stocks of medical antidotes to cyanide and other toxic substances, preparing for any potential mass triage" (Baker and Rashbaum 2006). Had officials—or a leaker—informed the media about a possible cyanide attack, subsequent news reports could have caused a panic in New York City and the greater metropolitan area. Although it never materialized, this nightmare scenario should have convinced Washington officials how important it was to make preparedness for catastrophic terrorism a national priority and to finance this area of counterterrorism adequately. But this did not happen. Instead, "our emergency responders who are straining to keep up with the everyday demand for their services have little to no surge capacity to handle large-scale events" (Flynn 2007, xvi). Moreover, the intended cyanide attack did not convince officials of the need for an intensive campaign to educate the public about what to do in such emergencies.

When decision makers are mostly silent on important policies that do not require secrecy or when they spin the information they make available, a true watchdog press would work hard to investigate and inform the public more fully. However, such vigilance is not the norm but the exception in the contemporary news environment, because aggressive and often costly investigative reporting is not high on the corporate media's priority list. Moreover, many "journalists have sold their souls for access to public officials. . . . As a result, in the nation's capital, the press is often not the 'fourth estate,' it is part of government. And the same tendencies apply in the state house, in city hall, and at corporate headquarters" (Bennett and Serrin 2007, 333). If the men and women in power do not inform citizens about important public matters and the media do not report independently from government, the nation as a whole is the loser.

Terrorism and Preparedness before 9/11

It has been argued that in times of major domestic emergencies the news media, especially radio and television, become "vital arms of government" offering government officials unlimited access to communicate with the public at large (Graber 1997, 135). While officials are especially effective when they can personally appeal to the residents of a region or the nation in immediate danger or at risk, they can also convey their messages indirectly through reporters and others in the media. Following the first World Trade Center bombing in 1993, New York City's television and radio stations repeatedly broadcast important information from public officials and representatives of private companies. Thus, the employees of firms affected by the bomb blast were told not to report to work; motorists learned what streets were closed to all traffic; and everyone was informed of emergency telephone numbers. Similarly, in the hours and days following the Oklahoma City bombing in April 1995, local television, radio, and newspapers served the public interest not only by informing their audiences of the bombing and its aftermath but by also serving as conduits between emergency response specialists and the public in Oklahoma City and beyond. In publicizing and repeating official appeals to citizens not to enter the disaster area and not to interfere with rescue efforts, and to donate blood for the injured in specified places and contribute warm clothing for rescue workers, the media became part of the overall crisis management. When terrorists struck on 9/11, the news outlets once again transmitted important emergency information, such as the closure of all bridges and tunnels to traffic into Manhattan. In New York City especially, Mayor Rudy Giuliani utilized the media repeatedly to attempt to calm New Yorkers and to assure them that the crisis was under control. In short, when it comes to emergency response, the news media are indispensable. Given their centrality in the wake of major disasters, whether man-made or natural, one would also expect newsrooms to be keenly interested in the state of preparedness that determines the effectiveness of disaster response efforts.

However, the press showed little interest in reporting on terrorism preparedness policies and their implementation before 9/11 in spite of the earlier attacks on the World Trade Center in New York and the Alfred P. Murrah Federal Building in Oklahoma City. In the five years from January 1, 1996, through December 2000, the major TV networks (ABC News, CBS News, NBC News, and CNN) and National Public Radio all together aired only 48 stories on preparedness. Most of these reports were about practice drills that simulated worst case scenarios in the wake of catastrophic terrorist attacks (Nacos 2007b, chap. 15). The news was not reassuring. NBC News anchor Tom Brokaw, for example, on one occasion said, "There is a quiet fear among many of the nation's highest ranking law enforcement officers that this country is grossly unprepared for what could be the greatest terrorist threat of all times, that's biological warfare."[5] But in spite of these expressed concerns, television network news did not offer any in-depth reporting on the underlying problems in the politics of emergency preparedness. In the spring of 2001, just months before 9/11, the *Washington Monthly*, a small political magazine, published a lengthy article under the headline, "Weapons of Mass Confusion: How Pork Trumps Preparedness in the Fight against Terrorism." Writer Joshua Green reported that "the billions of dollars spent to prepare for an attack has only created an expensive and uncoordinated mess" (Green 2001, 16). Moreover, Green wrote,

A bidding war in Congress quickly ensued. "There was a rush on Capitol Hill," says a senior researcher in a nonpartisan national security think tank. "There were literally dozens of agencies whispering in lawmakers' ears that their organizations could do the job and, in turn, make that congressman look good for choosing them" (Green 2001, 20).

The politics surrounding highly technical and complex multiagency programs cannot be presented in sound bites or as "*infotainment*" that the corporate media have moved toward in order to please audiences with interesting news instead of presenting important public affairs information. It was not surprising, then, that the television networks and leading newspapers did not have any appetite for in-depth reporting on the politics-as-usual that hindered the country's preparedness for terrorism or other catastrophes.

In view of the mainstream media's poor track record before 9/11 and despite anecdotal evidence that nothing changed fundamentally thereafter, we wondered whether the lethal attacks on the World Trade Center and the Pentagon awakened newsrooms to the need for more effective emergency preparedness—especially during a period of frequent terrorist alerts and warnings by the Bush administration and direct threats by Al Qaeda leaders. As described in previous chapters, the major television networks covered terrorist threats and alerts extensively and prominently after 9/11, but they reported infrequently about prevention and protection against terrorist strikes on American soil. Was this, then, also the case for *preparedness* to respond to such *attacks*? Did news about preparedness this time around resemble the ample coverage of the *threat* of terrorism or the underreporting of efforts to prevent terrorist acts?

Methodology and Data

For this chapter's analysis we coded full transcripts of TV network news that reported about or mentioned preparedness for terrorist attacks on targets inside the United States. Our reading of the available news abstracts indicated that these summaries often failed to provide all the information needed to satisfy our content coding requirements. Besides identifying in this case the sources of news messages, such as the president, the secretary of homeland security, members of Congress, experts, state and local officials, emergency responders, and members of the general public and the media, our coders categorized the types of messages contained in each story as positive, negative, or neutral/ambiguous with respect to the level of preparedness on the part of federal, state, and local governments as well as the private sector. In addition, we identified the likely sites of terrorist assaults and emergency responses, the weapons that terrorists might deploy and that first responders needed to prepare for, as well as the important members of the emergency response community, such as police and fire departments and officials in the public and private health sector.

We also, once more, assembled responses to public opinion survey questions about Americans' views and evaluation of efforts to prepare for more terrorism at home. We selected survey items that revealed the public's evaluation of, and degree of confidence in, the government's preparedness to deal with terrorist attacks in the United States, in respondents' own communities, and in the cases of particularly vulnerable potential targets of terrorism. Of the 26 survey questions found that were repeated verbatim over time (most only twice or three times), we focused mainly on responses to six questions asked most often (citing a few others along the way) about central issues regarding Americans' confidence in their leaders' and institutions' preparedness for further terrorist attacks inside the United States, and regarding their own personal preparations for such emergencies (see the online appendix; available at http://www.press.uchicago.edu/books/nacos/).

Last but not least, we collected data to probe whether the news coverage of Hurricane Katrina and the debate in the mass media about the lack of effective preparation for, and responses to, the devastation caused by this natural disaster had any noticeable consequences for public attitudes toward government's ability to respond adequately to future terrorist attacks. At the outset we thought that the frequent references to terrorism in stories about Katrina would blur the public's distinction between preparedness for natural versus man-made disasters, and this in turn would affect Americans' evaluations of government efforts to prepare adequately for future terrorist strikes. For this reason we examined additional public opinion data on terrorism preparedness beyond the 39-month focus of our overall study.

We also conducted a limited news content analysis to find out whether the coverage of Hurricane Katrina was as critical of the government's handling of the disaster as anecdotal evidence suggested and whether the news about Katrina contained references to terrorism preparedness and to the impact of the Iraq War on the availability of emergency responders—especially the National Guard. To this end we initially examined stories that were exclusively about or mentioned the public sector's preparedness for, or response to, Katrina and also contained the terms "terrorism" or "Iraq." We limited this part of our analysis to the short period from September 1, 2005, to September 15, 2005, and to two television networks (ABC News and NBC News). We, however, also examined the far more extensive coverage in the *New York Times*, because we assumed that print media provided more resources and space to report on questions and issues arising from Katrina. Our coders identified and kept track of all news sources; we also coded messages that (1) were critical or supportive of government disaster preparedness and responses with respect to Katrina and (2) linked experiences before and after Katrina to preparedness for terrorist attacks and to resources devoted to the war in Iraq. Last, we used the Lexis/Nexis archive to find how often stories in the three TV networks mentioned both "Hurricane Katrina" and "terrorism"; or "Hurricane Katrina," "failure," and "FEMA"; or "Hurricane Katrina," "failure," and "response," for the six-month period from September 1, 2005, to February 28, 2006. We were interested in whether the frequency of stories reporting problems in the emergency responses coincided with any waning of public trust in the state of emergency preparedness in the United States.

Because of the large proportion of African Americans among Katrina's victims in New Orleans, we were also interested in the volume of Katrina stories that mentioned "African American(s)" and/or "black(s)" as well. We thought it quite possible that a large number of such stories might have affected African Americans' views of emergency preparedness for disasters in general—including terrorist attacks—more negatively than the perceptions and attitudes of whites.

TV News Paid Little Attention to Preparedness

Less than a month after the 9/11 attacks, the news broke that a man in Florida had inhaled anthrax spores and subsequently died. When letters containing anthrax were mailed to the offices of prominent media figures in New York and to politicians in Washington soon after, news coverage was overwhelming, justifiably, but it was also hyped at the expense of other potentially important and useful public information. The following excerpts from a news segment aired on the *CBS Evening News* on October 10, 2001, at the height of the anthrax scare were typical of this coverage:

> DAN RATHER, anchor: Tonight's Eye on America brings you double-checked facts about the threat, real and imagined, from anthrax. The Bayer Com-

pany said today it is stepping up production of CIPRO, the antibiotic that may treat anthrax in some cases. Many people are clamoring for prescriptions. Is this a good idea? Medical correspondent Elizabeth Kaledin has this and other anthrax information.

ELIZABETH KALEDIN reporting: These microscopic bacteria are looming large in the minds and imaginations of Americans these days. But fear of anthrax is causing an epidemic of misinformation.

DR. LAURA POPPER (Pediatrician): People are terrified. And they feel out of control and they want something to help protect them. Give me one more big breath.

KALEDIN: For doctors like Laura Popper, a New York pediatrician, that means the phones are ringing off the hook.

DR. POPPER: I'm giving no medication at all.

KALEDIN: People are demanding CIPRO, an antibiotic known to fight the deadly bacteria, but she's saying no.

DR. POPPER: To me, it would be the equivalent of saying, "We have a danger. Let's give everybody a gun."

KALEDIN: Stockpiling antibiotics won't help. Doctors say the drugs are only effective if used immediately after exposure. Misusing them could weaken their effectiveness. Other people are turning to gas masks for protection, but some say gas masks are a waste of money.

MR. KEITH HOLTERMANN (Bioterrorism Expert): Gas masks absolutely are not helpful. It is the kind of situation that unless you have it on 24 hours a day, seven days a week—because, again, you have to have it on when the event occurs.

Far from fulfilling the promise of Dan Rather's lead—"Debunking the myths and finding out the truth about anthrax"—this story and others like it may have increased their audiences' anxieties but not their knowledge of how to prepare for bioterrorism. About four months later, on February 5, 2002, *NBC Nightly News* opened a 386-word report with the following exchange:

TOM BROKAW, anchor: Now to the war on terror here at home. After proposing a huge increase in spending on bioterrorism yesterday, the president reinforced his message today. He traveled to a Pittsburgh medical center that is part of an early warning system against biological attacks. NBC's David Gregory from the White House tonight. David, what's the latest there?

DAVID GREGORY reporting: Tom, a strong warning from the president tonight. He says America must be prepared to fight a war against bioterrorism, but experts say we are not ready.

Images of horror. A new British TV film called "Silent Weapon" depicts the panic following a smallpox attack in New York, the work of a lone terrorist. The threat is real. Actual drills simulating such a localized outbreak have produced grim results. The disease could spread around the world, experts say, killing at least 100,000 people. Public health officials say the anthrax crisis last October exposed dangerous weaknesses.

DR. MARGARET HAMBURG (Nuclear Threat Initiative): We're behind the eight ball. We are not adequately prepared to address the threat of naturally occurring disease, let alone the threat of an intentional introduction of a biological agent.

The rest of this newscast and most other reports on the state of preparedness for terrorist acts were not more reassuring. Announced as providing "a closer look at terror attacks," a 522-word story on ABC's *World News Tonight with Peter Jennings* on May 16, 2003, began with the following sentences:

FIREFIGHTER, MALE: There's one live one. A lot of dead ones that we pulled out over there.

PIERRE THOMAS, ABC NEWS (Voice-Over): A thousand people would have died in Chicago's mock biological attack. Chicago hospitals were about to run out of medical supplies and beds. In Seattle, more than 100 would have been injured after a dirty or radiological bomb went off. Communications between emergency agencies were pushed to the limit. Streets and highways were clogged, making it difficult to get residents to safety. Homeland Security Secretary, Tom Ridge, oversaw the exercise.

TOM RIDGE, SECRETARY OF HOMELAND SECURITY: We'll have to go back and take a look at whether or not we got all the assets we needed to either site as quickly as we possibly could.

PIERRE THOMAS (Off Camera): Most of the experts we talked to agree that drills are necessary to force different agencies to work together. But many question how good a barometer this was, since everyone knew what was going to happen two years in advance.

Yet, although the media were obviously aware of severe problems in first responders' readiness for terrorist emergencies, television news did not pay much attention to preparedness after the 9/11 attacks. During the 39-month period we examined, ABC News, CBS News, and NBC News aired in all only 81 stories specifically about emergency responders' readiness for terrorist attacks at home. These segments contained a total of 653 preparedness-related messages. In contrast, during the same period the three networks aired a total of 373 stories that dealt with the *threat* of terrorism, with fully 1,725 relevant messages (chapter 2), and did not highlight the urgent need to prepare better for terrorist attacks. Just over half of the messages about preparedness were contained in NBC News broadcasts and one-quarter each in stories aired on CBS News and ABC News. The modest number of such news segments was probably the result of the press's much greater attention to other aspects of counterterrorism and the newsrooms' preference for more dramatic and shock-filled events and developments—terrorist threats and alerts and actual or possible military actions in the "war on terrorism."

Although one of the president's several roles includes that of the nation's protector-in-chief, President George W. Bush did not initiate a public debate about the importance of preparedness nor did he appear as a frequent source in the news about this important policy matter. More surprisingly, this was also true for the secretary of homeland security, whose department included the Federal Emergency Management Agency (FEMA), the bureaucracy charged with preparing for and responding to major natural and man-made disasters. In the 39 months after 9/11 that we examined, President Bush and Homeland Security Secretary Tom Ridge combined comprised only 3% of all sources in stories that covered or touched on terrorism preparedness; taken together, administration officials, including Bush and Ridge, constituted only 5% of all relevant sources and were in fact cited or interviewed no more often than members of Congress (see figure 6.1). Local officials were identified somewhat more often as news sources than were members of the Bush administration and Congress, and they far exceeded state officials. Beyond media personnel (anchors, correspondents, and news readers) who were the dominant sources, security experts were the next largest group followed by first responders, such as officials of police and fire departments as well as officials or representatives of the public health and private health sectors. Finally, members of the general public were infrequently sought out by network reporters to express their views on preparedness. This contrasted sharply with newscasts covering terrorism prevention, in which ordinary Americans were frequently given the

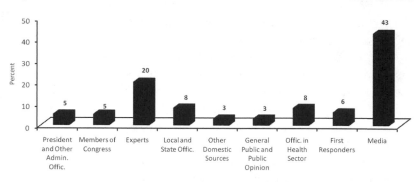

FIGURE 6.1. Sources in terrorism preparedness news

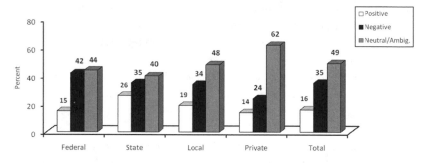

FIGURE 6.2. Evaluations of preparedness efforts in the news

opportunity to express their observations and opinions, especially with respect to airport security (chapter 5).

When news sources spoke about preparedness, 44% of their messages concerned the federal government, 7% state governments, 23% local governments, and 26% the private sector, such as hospitals and pharmaceutical companies. Taken together, about half of these messages were neutral or ambiguous, 35% were critical (negative), and 16% were supportive (positive) of measures or policies designed to promote preparedness. Moreover, negative evaluations were significantly more numerous than positive ones for all levels of government and for the private sector as well (figure 6.2).

Nearly one half (48%) of all these messages addressed the public and private sectors' readiness to respond to the use of weapons of mass destruction in future terrorist attacks, most of all biological or chemical agents, including the intentional spreading of the deadly small pox virus (see figure 6.3). Eighteen percent of the pertinent coverage dealt with preparedness generally ("other"), and 5% with responses to terrorist attacks on buildings, bridges, and other infrastructure. Only 3% of the media messages addressed preparedness for attacks on airports, aviation, seaports, and railways; this differed sharply from TV news coverage of the *prevention* of terrorist attacks in which more than 60% of all messages were devoted to these particular areas of vulnerability (see chapter 5).

As noted above, the president, the secretary of homeland security, and other members of the administration were infrequent sources in preparedness news; but when they appeared or were cited in broadcasts, they were upbeat and expressed confidence in the state of the nation's readiness. Fully 71% of President Bush's and 61% of Secretary Ridge's messages explicitly supported the public and private sector's preparedness efforts, with the rest falling into the neutral or ambiguous category. Not surprisingly, there were no critical assessments at all from the White House, the Department of Homeland Security, and other administration officials. Members of Congress were evenly split in their supportive (21%) and critical (21%) assessments. The most questioning sources were experts, with 45% of their evaluations of preparedness falling into the negative category followed by first responders, such as police and fire department officials (44%); media-based sources, such as correspondents and anchors (38%); and representatives of the public and private health sectors (28%). In the case of media personnel, only 5% of their evaluations were positive—by far the lowest proportion of all sources. By comparison, 24% of the evaluations by health sector officials, 17% of first

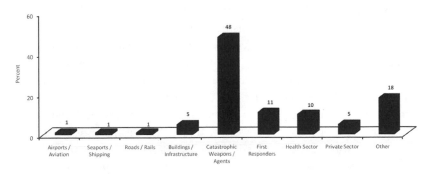

FIGURE 6.3. Areas of preparedness/first responders in the news

responders, and 15% of experts were positive. But aside from their neutral or ambiguous statements, all of these sources expressed more criticism than approval. Without the president and his administration making much effort to initiate and keep alive a debate about preparedness, critics of the public and private sector's performances were more vocal in the media debate than those who spoke out in favor of the state of preparedness.

The limited news attention during the post-9/11 years may have played a role in voters' disinterest in disaster preparedness policies. Indeed, Healy and Malhotra (2009, 389) suggest that various newsroom imperatives "may lead journalists to publicize dramatic relief efforts after newsworthy disasters take place, while not discussing more pedestrian preparedness efforts" and that in this way "citizens may be primed to consider relief spending when evaluating government performance," while giving short shrift to the funding of preparedness initiatives.

Katrina and Preparedness

Given its catastrophic consequences, Katrina deserved the media attention it received during the days, weeks, and months after the hurricane's landfall. In the first half of September 2005, the three news organizations we examined carried a total of 151 stories that mentioned preparedness or responses to disasters in the context of both Hurricane Katrina and future terrorist attacks or to Katrina and the Iraq War. During the short period we examined, the *New York Times* carried more such stories (62) and significantly more news messages (258) than ABC News (36 stories with 134 messages) and NBC News (53 stories, 131 messages). The more extensive coverage in the *Times* was not surprising, given that newspaper articles typically contain considerably more narrative than television news stories. Media personnel comprised 33% of all sources in this coverage, but taken together government officials—namely, President Bush (7%), other administration officials (9%), members of Congress (11%), and state and local officials (11%)—totaled 38% of all sources and appeared more frequently in the news than any other source category. Eleven percent of the sources were ordinary Americans, mostly victims of Katrina, while experts constituted only 4%. This was a striking departure from the distribution of sources in the news about terrorism preparedness, described above.

The media's evaluations of the public sector's preparedness and response in the case of the Katrina catastrophe were mostly directed at the federal government and much less toward local authorities during the period we studied. These evaluations were far more critical in that 11% gave the federal government's *disaster* preparedness negative grades and only 3% approved Washington's performance; 2% of these messages criticized and none approved state and local level preparedness. Still, overwhelmingly, most messages did not take pro or con positions. Far more criticism was directed at the federal government's *immediate* emergency *response after the hurricane struck*, with half (49%) of all evaluations critical and 10% approving of Washington's performance. Six percent of these messages specifically criticized President Bush's and only 5% approved his handling of the disaster. While state and local governments along the Gulf coast escaped criticism of their *emergency preparedness* measures, they did receive some blame for inadequate *emergency response*: on this count, 5% of all evaluations were critical of the relevant state governments and 4% of the governments of local jurisdictions that were struck by the Katrina, compared to fewer than 1% supportive messages for both. But this was a far cry from the massive disapproval of Washington's response to Katrina.

In a separate analysis of news messages that contained the terms "Katrina" and "terrorism" or "Iraq," we found that slightly more than half of them (51%) simply mentioned terrorism without offering a particular view or judgment regarding preparedness for such attacks. However, in 14% of these messages the federal government's preparedness for terrorist disasters was questioned based on the lack of preparation for Katrina; there was not a single statement supporting Washington in this respect. Similarly, 7.5% of these messages questioned the federal government's ability to respond effectively to terrorist attacks based on its agencies' responses to the hurricane disaster. Again, no voices in these news stories expressed confidence in the federal government's ability to respond to terrorism in the context of Katrina. Finally, 13% of the news messages named the war in Iraq as the reason for the shortage of emergency responders in the case of Katrina, while 7.5% denied such a connection.

In short, the coverage of Hurricane Katrina in the first half of September 2005 was not only far more negative than positive with respect to disaster preparedness and response, but it also questioned the federal government's preparedness for a terrorist attack based on its poor handling of the Katrina crisis. In addition, it linked the shortage of emer-

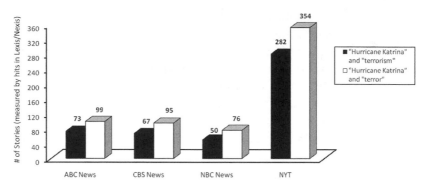

FIGURE 6.4. News coverage of Hurricane Katrina and terrorism, September 2005–February 2006

gency responders to the deployment of National Guard units and reservists to fight the "war on terrorism" in Iraq. There were some differences in the coverage of the three news organizations: The *New York Times'* coverage was more critical than reporting by ABC News, and far more critical than NBC News.

As mentioned above, the news media continued to pay attention to Katrina far beyond the initial days and weeks after the hurricane struck. For this reason we searched for terrorism and counterterrorism related words in stories about Katrina during the six-month period from September 1, 2005, to February 28, 2006 (and in some cases to the end of August). As figure 6.4 shows, during this period the three TV networks aired a large number of stories that contained the terms "Hurricane Katrina" and "terrorism" or "terror" (this search also retrieved "terrorist" and "terrorists"), led by ABC News with a total of 172 such news segments, CBS News with 162, and NBC News with 126 stories. But the network coverage paled in this respect compared to the 636 news items in the *New York Times* that contained the above terms. While some of the stories retrieved in the "Hurricane Katrina and terror" category were exclusively about the terror felt by Katrina victims, all of those in the "Hurricane Katrina and terrorism" category linked some aspect of preparedness for and/or response to Katrina with readiness for terrorist acts—or the lack thereof.

To sum up, contrary to the television networks' infrequent coverage of terrorism preparedness in the 39 months following 9/11, broadcast and print media paid a great deal of attention to issues of emergency response *after* Hurricane Katrina struck and the lack of preparedness *before* the disaster. The pictures of desperate hurricane victims, who were stranded on the roofs of their houses or suffered intolerable conditions in emergency shelters, provided compelling human interest news of the sort that the media, especially television, thrive on. A significant number of these stories linked the lack of effective emergency response measures to the state of terrorism preparedness and the shortage of emergency responders from the ranks of National Guard units and reservists due to the war in Iraq. Since the federal government was the prime target of criticism, the president and administration officials had no choice but to participate in the post-Katrina debate in the media—if only for damage control. Thus, it was not 9/11 but a devastating hurricane that directed the attention of the media, the American public, and government officials to the importance of effective disaster preparedness—if only for several months.

Preparedness and the Public

We found in previous chapters that news organizations and polling feed off each other in that the media agenda is closely related to what questions are asked in polls. By reporting these survey results, the media make public opinion a dimension of the issues they cover. Again, this is not surprising since most polls about public policy and politics are conducted or commissioned by news organizations and typically by partnerships of TV networks and print media organizations (e.g., ABC News and the *Washington Post*, NBC News and the *Wall Street Journal*, CBS News and the *New York Times*). The scarcity of surveys with repeated opinion about terrorism *prevention* during the years we studied (chapter 5) was even more pronounced for the issue of *preparedness*.

Although the most prominent theme in news coverage of terrorism preparedness was the need to be ready for catastrophic biological and chemical weapons attacks, few survey questions about this were repeated over long time periods. The inclusion of such questions by pollsters seemed to coincide with short-term reporting about particular incidents and threats, most notably the anthrax-laden letters in the fall of 2001. For these questions, as often happens in survey research, the number of response choices offered affected respondents' answers. When asked in November 2002 and August 2003 about the government's ability to handle chemical or biological terrorist attacks, majorities of 51% and 57% of respondents, respectively, chose "very prepared" or "somewhat prepared," but when given fewer response options in September 2002, only 21% of respondents said that the United States was adequately prepared (see online appendix; available at http://www.press.uchicago.edu/books/nacos/). The public's trust in the ability of the health care sector to respond effectively to biological, chemical, or nuclear attacks declined from a solid 53% who were "very confident" or "confident" in August 2002 to 39% several weeks before Katrina to merely 28% in July 2006.

In spite of media reports about the possibility of attacks in the United States by terrorists reacting to the Iraq invasion in March 2003, close to two-thirds of Americans told pollsters that the United States was adequately prepared to deal with another terrorist attack. In July 2005, 58% of the public still believed that the country was "very prepared" or "prepared" for future terror strikes. However, by October 2005, with the experiences of the flawed emergency response to Hurricane Katrina fresh in mind, only 42% believed this, with the majority (56%) saying the United States was "not very prepared" or "not prepared at all." As the memories of Katrina appeared to fade at least somewhat, public trust in the nation's terrorism preparedness recovered, and by August 2006 the public was evenly split on these questions.

Significant to begin with, people's skepticism remained with respect to the overall emergency response capability that they perceived in their own communities. When asked before Hurricane Katrina in August 2003, July 2004, and July 2005, 54%, 49%, and 46% of survey respondents, respectively, did not deem their localities adequately prepared for terrorist attacks. In the post-Katrina period, the public's trust declined markedly: by October 2005 and August 2006 fewer than one-third of Americans perceived their own communities' preparedness for terrorism to be adequate, while solid majorities responded that it was not (see figure 6.5).

While most Americans were willing to offer their perception of the state of the United States' preparedness, with generally fewer than 10% saying they were "unsure" or "did not know," surveys in July 2004, July 2005, and October 2005 revealed that about three of four respondents said they were "not very familiar" or "not familiar at all" with the emergency or evacuation plans in their own communities in the event of a terrorist attack. And after Hurricane Katrina, two of three Americans felt

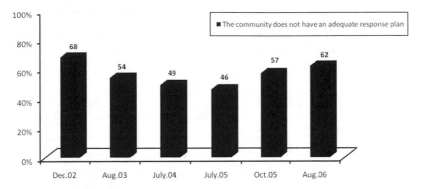

FIGURE 6.5. Public opinion: Terrorist attack and community emergency response plan

personally "not very prepared" or "not prepared at all" for a terrorist attack in their immediate surroundings.

Preparedness and Presidential Performance

As we noted earlier, the news media's sparse coverage of terrorism preparedness in the years after 9/11 was matched by most pollsters' not asking and repeating questions about this issue. It is not surprising, then, that the public was not asked over time to evaluate the president's handling of terrorism preparedness. In August, September, and October 2005, pollsters asked respondents whether they approved or disapproved of the way George W. Bush was handling terrorism and homeland security. Perhaps perceiving that this question encompassed all aspects of offensive and defensive measures in the "war on terrorism" and thus homeland security in a wider sense, respondents may have reacted to the preparedness fiasco in the case of Katrina. This would explain why the president's approval in this context declined, albeit modestly, from 51% in early August 2005 before Katrina to 48% afterward in September 2005 and to 45% in October 2005 (see online appendix; available at http://www.press.uchicago.edu/books/nacos/).

In the poll data discussed above, we found much greater declines in the public's confidence in national and local terrorism preparedness after October 2005, very likely the result of the media's sustained attention to the hurricane debacle. Since pollsters did not repeat the above question about presidential performance after the survey in October, we can only speculate how the public might have evaluated the president regarding terrorism and homeland security a year or more after Katrina.

Demography Matters

We consider once more the similarities and differences in opinions and perceptions among population subgroups, especially along gender, race, and partisan lines.[6] Even before Hurricane Katrina, women were less confident than men that the United States was adequately prepared for terrorist attacks. In July 2005, 62% of men and 55% of women thought their country was "very prepared" or "prepared," but three months later, after Katrina struck, these percentages dropped to 45% versus 38%. By August 2006, both the confidence of men and women climbed back somewhat to 54% and 45%, respectively, with the gender difference at 9 percentage points and both sexes still perceiving the nation as less prepared than a year earlier. African Americans were much less confident of the country's preparedness for further terrorism than whites and Latinos (figure 6.6). In July 2005, before Katrina, only 49% of blacks expressed confidence in preparedness for terrorism in the United States, compared to 56% of Latinos and 60% of whites. In October 2005, shortly after Katrina, the polls showed a sharp decline of confidence in all three groups. By August 2006, African Americans' confidence remained at a low 37%; it recovered to 50% for whites, and increased to a 65% high for Latinos. These gender and racial differences were, overall, consistent with what we found for threat perceptions and prevention of terrorist at-

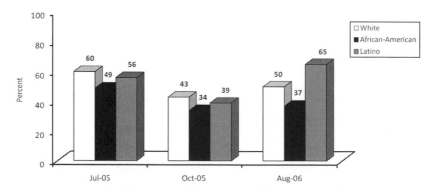

FIGURE 6.6. U.S. prepared for future terrorist attack, by race

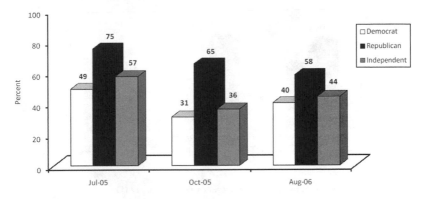

FIGURE 6.7. U.S. prepared for future terrorist attack, by party ID

tacks, revealing greater wariness on the part of women and blacks, as gender and racial subgroups' opinions moved in parallel. The one exception were Latinos in August 2006, perhaps due to sampling variation for the small number of Latinos surveyed, but also, possibly, as described in the previous chapter, reflecting attitudes that are closer to the dominant group, whites, than to African Americans.

Again we found the most pronounced differences regarding the nation's preparedness between Republican party identifiers who were the most confident and Democrats who were the least, with Independents' attitudes falling in between but closer to the Democrats' attitudes. Less than two months before Katrina, 75% of Republicans, 57% of Independents, and 49% of Democrats expressed confidence in the nation's state of preparedness for terrorism; this confidence dropped to 31% for Democrats, 65% among Republicans, and 36% for Independents. By August 2006, these opinions converged somewhat, but Republicans still remained significantly more confident than Independents and Democrats (figure 6.7).

Similarly, in July 2005, as shown in figure 6.8, 47% of Republicans but only 36% of Independents and 30% of Democrats thought that *their own communities* had adequate emergency plans for terrorist attacks in place. In October 2005, several weeks after Katrina struck, there was no noticeable change except among Independents: 48% of Republicans thought their local preparedness was adequate, 28% of Democrats, and 28% of Independents (an 8-point decline). However, by August 2006 there was an overall convergence: Republicans' confidence in their lo-

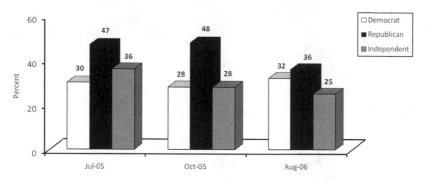

FIGURE 6.8. Community has adequate emergency plan, by party ID

cal jurisdictions' emergency plans had dropped to 36% and that of Independents to 25%, with Democrats holding steady near their 30% pre-
Katrina level. Still, Republicans remained more confident in this respect
than Democrats and Independents.

In the cases of race and gender we found a similar convergence as
whites and men in particular became less optimistic about their own
communities' emergency plans. From July 2003 through August 2006,
there was generally a gender difference of 4 to 7 percentage points when
respondents were asked whether their own communities' emergency
preparations for terrorist acts were adequate. In the week after Hurricane Katrina, by October 2005, the differences closed fully with 31% of
men and 32% of women perceiving local preparedness as adequate. And
repeating the pattern we saw in the previous chapter, from July 2003
through October 2005, African Americans consistently expressed less
trust in the adequacy of their own communities' preparations for terrorism than did whites and Latinos (see figure 6.9). By August 2006, however, we see that the three racial groups converged at the same low level
of confidence, with African Americans at 32%, whites 31%, and Latinos 30% (with corresponding large percentages lacking confidence: 61%
among whites and African Americans and 65% for Latinos).

Last, when survey respondents were asked whether they were *personally* prepared for a terrorist attack in their community, there was a substantial gender difference. Before Katrina, in July 2005, this gap stood
at 18 points, with 45% of men reporting that they themselves were "prepared" or "very prepared," compared to only 27% of women expressing
this view. A few weeks after the hurricane men's and women's percep-

tions of their own preparedness had not changed (not at all for women and an insignificant 2 points for men). By August 2006, after months of frequent news coverage of the pre- and post-Katrina debacle, the gender difference narrowed to 8 points. Less than two months before Katrina struck, whites (38%) were more confident than African Americans (29%) and Latinos (23%) that they personally were very prepared or prepared for terrorism in the area where they lived. But, as many victims of Hurricane Katrina were black, African Americans' evaluations of their own preparedness dropped to 20% in October 2005 and remained at 23% in August 2006. In contrast, Latinos' confidence increased to 33% and 37%, respectively, during this period. By August 2006, about the same percentage of Latinos as of whites (34%) perceived themselves as prepared. It is plausible that the news media's ample coverage of African American victims of Katrina contributed to or sustained black Americans' lack of confidence in both the nation's collective preparedness and their own personal readiness for terrorist strikes.

Two months before Katrina and then less than six weeks after the killer hurricane made landfall, 45% and 47% of Republicans, respectively, believed that they were personally prepared or very prepared for terrorist attacks in their communities, compared to much smaller percentages of Democrats (28% and 27%, respectively) and Independents (36% and 36%). But these partisan differences shrank during the following 10 months for Republicans versus Democrats, and nearly disappeared for Republicans versus Independents: by August 2006, 39% of Republicans, 28% of Democrats, and 37% of Independents viewed their own preparedness positively.

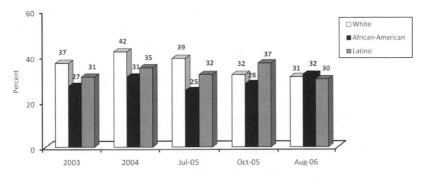

FIGURE 6.9. Community has adequate emergency plan, by race

Overall, there were recurring differences in attitudes and perceptions by race, gender, and partisanship, but there was also noticeable convergence as the attitudes of men, whites, and Republicans approached those of women, blacks, and Democrats, respectively, after Hurricane Katrina struck—especially concerning perceptions of their personal and their communities' preparedness for terrorism.

Public Opinion and News Coverage

In examining the relationship over time between public opinion and news media coverage, what we found in the case of preparedness was different from what we described in the previous chapters. When it came to preparedness news and polls, there was less that we could say with confidence because of the lack of data to compare over time.

Based on the limited data, in addition to what we have described above, public perceptions regarding government's ability to prepare for another terrorist attack were heavily influenced by news reports of the way the government handled—or, rather, mishandled—Hurricane Katrina.

We also found some correspondences between media coverage of preparedness and related opinions that were not at all affected by Katrina-related news. Prior to 2005, the percentage of the public who had *confidence in the health care system's preparedness* decreased significantly from 53% in 2002 to 39% in 2004. This decline occurred along with different peaks in media coverage related to this particular issue near the September anniversaries of the 9/11 attacks and after the start of the Iraq War in March 2003. A drop in public confidence to 46% after the Iraq invasion followed a sharp increase in overall media coverage, including especially the volume of messages (normally averaging 10 or fewer each month) coming from media-based sources—reporters and news anchors. This increase in coverage, to more than 80 messages, was also associated with a decline in public confidence in the nation's preparedness for future terrorist attacks. Interestingly, the public's reactions were less affected concerning the *adequacy of their local community's emergency response plan*, showing only a slight decrease, from 54% in 2003 to 49% in 2004, of those believing that their community planning was *inadequate*. As discussed earlier, these attitudes changed significantly following the Katrina disaster. When the press, both the print and broadcast media (which showed the same reporting patterns), reported on the Katrina response fiasco, the American public became more critical toward literally all aspects of government's emergency response capability in case of future terrorist attacks. These declines in public confidence were particularly pronounced after news stories that mentioned both "failure" and "response" to Katrina hit their highest level in the weeks immediately following the hurricane catastrophe. For example, from July 2005, shortly before Katrina, through September 2005, confidence in the nation's health care systems sank from 39% to 28%. Opinion changes that occurred during the year after Katrina moved in a direction explicable in terms of news coverage of the failures in the federal government's response to the hurricane. Thus, a major peak in media reporting occurred in February 2006, when congressional hearings probed the preparedness and response problems before and after Katrina.

And what effect did all this have on the public's evaluations of President Bush? It is not surprising to see in figure 6.10 that the percentage of the public approving the president's handling of Katrina decreased steadily through the year following the disaster. It started at 54% at the end of August 2005 and then dropped to a low of 28% in early 2006, at a time when a peak in television news coverage emphasized the "failure" of the government's response. After this low, Bush's rating increased a bit but still stayed relatively low through the year at around 36%. It appears that the public's views toward Bush's handling of terrorism and homeland security (and perhaps his overall approval rating; see the general appendix online, available at http://www.press.uchicago.edu/books/

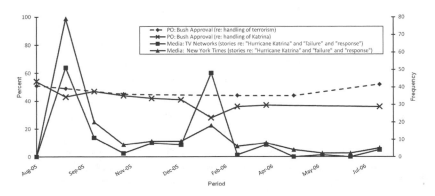

FIGURE 6.10. Terrorism and Katrina: Bush approval and stories citing "Hurricane Katrina," "failure," and "response," August 2005–August 2006

nacos/) were affected by Katrina. The public's approval of Bush's handling of terrorism dropped somewhat after Katrina, from 51% in August 2005 to 45% in November 2005—remaining at the same lower level for nearly a year until recovering to 52% in August 2006. It should be noted here that other aspects of counterterrorism enter into the assessment of a president's handling of terrorism. Overall, then, the high volume of news about Hurricane Katrina that focused on the government's ineffective response to it depressed public confidence in Washington's preparedness for terrorist attacks. News about Katrina, whether it mentioned terrorism or not, affected Americans' evaluations of how well prepared the public sector was to respond effectively to terrorist attacks—similar to what we saw in the last chapter regarding the prevention of future terrorism in the United States.

Media and Government: Little Attention to Preparedness

The 9/11 terrorist attacks and even more so the aftermath of Hurricane Katrina emphasized the need for the nation to be ready to respond to the devastation caused by natural and man-made disasters. Because it is unlikely that preventive efforts can reach the point at which acts of terrorism will not occur or will fail, countries at risk must be well prepared to respond to large-scale terrorist attacks. As this chapter has shown, there was a striking lack of attention to the state of such preparedness in public debate as reported in the press after 9/11—just as there was little interest during the preceding years in grappling politically with this policy area. Even after the catastrophic attacks on the World Trade Center and the Pentagon, officials at all levels of government, including those overseeing emergency management agencies, had little to say in public about the state of preparedness and first response. Although administration officials issued many terror alerts and warned of the likelihood of more terrorist attacks at home, members of the public remained largely clueless as to what they should and could do when the color-coded alert level was raised. This, then, was another case of news indexing, in that the media followed the lead of those whom they usually consider authoritative actors, and it was these sources whose lack of public attention to terrorism preparedness mattered. Although experts and the 9/11 Commission gathered and publicized evidence of severe problems in the nation's emergency response systems, especially inadequate and incompatible communications equipment and lack of coordination among various agencies, the overall news coverage reflected less the inattention to knowledgeable critics than the passivity of the Bush administration and Congress—including the lack of conflict at and between both ends of Pennsylvania Avenue. The scarcity of independent reporting on this issue indicated that, in the absence of decision makers' interest in a very important public policy area, the press failed to bring related issues to the public's attention.

This all changed fundamentally with the government's failure to respond to Hurricane Katrina. By reporting and broadcasting dramatic reports of residents stranded on the roofs of their flooded houses and in overcrowded emergency shelters, the media told the shocking story of the feebleness of America's preparedness for major disasters. The images of the victims of Katrina juxtaposed with those of incompetent officials from the Department of Homeland Security—including FEMA—and state and local agencies, undermined the public's trust in the national and local governments' ability to respond to catastrophic events. By logical extension, critics both inside and outside the news media wondered about what would happen in the case of terrorist attacks that—unlike hurricanes—would hit without warning. How prepared was government at all levels—federal, state, and local? Sources cited by the press and news media professionals themselves raised this question.

However, it did not take long for the media and public officials to return preparedness to the backburner. Three months after the Katrina disaster, when the members of the 9/11 Commission issued their final report card on the implementation of their recommendations, they gave policymakers two failing grades along with two unsatisfactory and one satisfactory assessment for preparedness and response. They were particularly critical of the failure to "provide adequate radio spectrum for first responders, a situation that had plagued the 9/11 rescue efforts in the World Trade Towers and prevented effective coordination and communication among first responders during the Hurricane Katrina disaster in New Orleans and elsewhere along the Gulf coast four years later."[7] Of the 18 stories about the commission's dismal report in various ABC, CBS, and NBC News broadcasts, most were very short and did not mention anything about problems in the preparedness of first responders but rather highlighted flaws in efforts to prevent terrorism in the first place. And of the eight news segments that did refer to problems in the nation's readiness, only three focused prominently on the most serious radio communication issue. ABC's *World News Tonight*, for example, aired the following passage within 640-word story on the 9/11 Commission's report card:

THOMAS KEAN (Chairman, 9/11 Commission): There's some things the administration isn't doing, things the Congress isn't doing.

MARTHA RADDATZ (ABC News, Voice-Over): One glaring example, emergency communications. A major failure during 9/11. A major failure during Katrina. Police, firefighters and medical personnel in large cities are still unable to communicate reliably in a crisis.

CHIEF MARY ANN VIVERETTE (President, International Association of Chiefs of Police): This is a major problem across the country. And the chiefs are upset about it.

MARTHA RADDATZ (Voice-Over): Why the holdup? The 9/11 commission says part of the problem is that broadcasters have not set aside part of the radio spectrum for emergency personnel, keeping it instead for commercial broadcasts.

LEE HAMILTON (Vice Chairman, 9/11 Commission): And so, there's strong interest to prevent that or to slow it from happening.

MARTHA RADDATZ (Voice-Over): There is legislation pending that would resolve that. But even if it passes, it won't take effect until 2009.[8]

By spring 2007, Senators Joe Lieberman and Susan Collins wrote a letter to the secretary of homeland security, Michael Chertoff, expressing disappointment that the Department of Homeland Security had not moved forward quickly to improve its interoperability communications program, and they warned that without a strategic approach and firm leadership first responders would continue to be imperiled because of an inability to communicate effectively during an emergency or disaster.[9]

Even after Congress legislated and President Bush signed into law measures to improve disaster communication, "major weaknesses" remained because of inefficient implementation by governmental agencies. As one of the 9/11 Commission members, Jamie Gorelick, explained during a TV interview in December 2005,

You know, we have short memories. And the interest has faded. We've gone on to other issues. And when, and when American citizens don't pressure their government, frankly, the government isn't as responsive as it needs to be. You could see that in the aftermath of Katrina. You know? We assume that our government would be able to do what it needed to do. And it, it, and it didn't do it.[10]

As public opinion data showed, in the absence of an ongoing debate in the mass media about preparedness issues, Americans' confidence in their government's efforts in this particular area of counterterrorism was not great during the post-9/11 years and well before the stunning (and heavily reported) failures in the overall emergency response to Hurricane Katrina. With the lack of pertinent news and information, the public seemed to conclude—correctly—that terrorism preparedness was not high on the government's agenda.

Yet, while massive media attention to insufficient preparedness for disasters, such as Hurricane Katrina, heightens the public's awareness of the need for improvements in first responders' readiness and produces more critical attitudes toward government failure in this respect, Healy and Malhotra (2009, 402) suspect that such effects "may be temporary," since all in all "voters respond only to relief spending that consists of direct payments to individuals [after catastrophes occur]." In other words, since neither decision makers nor the media are credited for paying attention to and closing gaps in disaster preparedness, they do not vigilantly attend to problems in this area.

CHAPTER SEVEN

Mass-Mediated Politics
of Counterterrorism

We will not be driven by fear into an age of unreason, if we dig deep in our history and
our doctrine, and remember that we are not descended from fearful men—not from men
who feared to write, to speak, to associate and to defend causes that were, for the moment,
unpopular. — Edward R. Murrow[1]

Talking about the failed bombing attempt aboard a Northwest airliner on Christmas Day 2009, former New York City mayor and
presidential candidate Rudy Giuliani said during a TV appearance on
ABC's *Good Morning America*, "We had no domestic attacks under
Bush. We've had one under Obama."[2] Discussing the deadly shooting
at Fort Hood in November 2009, Dana Perino, White House press secretary during part of the George W. Bush presidency, said on Fox News'
Sean Hannity Show, "We did not have a terrorist attack on our country during President Bush's term."[3] While neither of the hosts, George
Stephanopoulos of ABC News and Sean Hannity of Fox News, immediately set the record straight, these and similar statements demonstrated
that spin has its limits.[4] In this case the critics responded quickly, and the
public was not hoodwinked. Even for less surreal claims than 9/11 not
taking place on President Bush's watch, reality can and does trump the
pseudo- or media reality that Walter Lippmann ([1922]) described. John
Zaller (1998) observed this in his research on public opinion trends during the Clinton-Lewinsky scandal—that the public could see through the
bickering and attempted political manipulation and make its own sense
of the situation. In examining post-9/11 counterterrorism policies and
the marketing of those policies by the Bush administration we, too, found
evidence for the old saying that you can fool all the people some of the
time, and some of the people all the time, but you can't fool all the peo-

ple all the time. The Bush administration's well-calibrated spin machine could not maintain indefinitely public support for the president and his counterterrorism policies, through strategically timed threat alerts to increase the nation's fear of imminent terrorist attacks. Yet, the administration's public relations campaign worked effectively for a long time during which major policy decisions were made.

Most important, our research revealed that in the months and even years following the 9/11 terrorist attacks, officials in Washington—especially the president and members of his administration—were able to set the media agenda when that was their intention. As long as these political elites held news conferences, gave speeches, granted interviews, and otherwise went public, the television networks provided them with frequent and prominent coverage to make their case and in fact dominate the news. Conversely, when the president and his advisers were not particularly interested in publicly explaining, promoting, or defending counterterrorism policies, other sources were likely to get access to the media—albeit invariably without receiving the prominent treatment that high-ranking administration officials enjoyed. For two of the five issues we studied (terrorist threats and alerts in chapter 2 and the Bush administration's justifications for going to war against Iraq in chapter 4), President Bush and others in his administration were very active and prominently covered newsmakers: they provided more than one-fourth and one-fifth, respectively, of all policy-specific messages in the news and the largest share apart from the typically dominant media professionals, such as anchors, correspondents, and, more recently paid network analysts (see table 7.1). Typically retired military officers, intelligence experts, or other former administration officials, these hired analysts tended to be in touch with and echo the views of their former colleagues at the Pentagon, the CIA, and in other departments and agencies.

In both of these cases, the TV networks presented or "indexed" (Bennett 1990; Mermin 1999) the news to a large extent according to the fairly narrow range of views expressed by members of Washington's elite circles as news sources. Newscasts also contained viewpoints expressed by foreign sources (i.e., in the case of the threat of terrorism by Osama bin Laden and other Al Qaeda leaders; in the case of the Iraq War, by UN weapons inspectors, members of the Iraqi government, and officials of other countries and international organizations). It might well be that foreigners have minimal if any influence on American news audiences when it comes to foreign policy and international crises. Accordingly, some

TABLE 7.1. **News messages by domestic sources on terrorism (percentage)**

	Threat	Civil liberties	Build-up Iraq	Prevention	Preparedness
President/administration	21	18	26	8	5
Members of Congress	5	12	1	7	5
Experts	16	10	6	22	20
Local/state officials	8	4	. . .	5	8
Other domestic	9	23	6	6	17
Public/public opinion	9	7	. . .	15	3
Media	33	26	35	36	43

Source: Authors.
Note: Percentage of total sources (because foreign sources are not included in the table, the listed sources do not add up to 100% in all cases).

analysts disregarded these sources altogether in examining the mass media in foreign policy debates. In his study of news coverage of U.S. interventions after the Vietnam War, for example, Mermin explained:

> The focus of the analysis is on critical viewpoints not attributed to foreign sources. This is because foreign critics of U.S. foreign policy do not have much credibility to an American audience. Foreign critics, as a rule, do not phrase arguments in terms that speak to American interests or concerns and often argue in ways that are bound to strike Americans as outrageous, irrational, or simply bizarre (Mermin 1999, 13).

The threat of transnational terrorism is an exception to this rule. As we described in chapter 2, news reports of Osama bin Laden's frequently expressed threats of further attacks inside the United States affected the American public in one respect: these reports increased Americans' fears that they themselves or members of their family could become victims of terrorism. Obviously, then, when bin Laden's threats were reported by the news media, the public deemed these messages to be "outrageous," but nevertheless credible.

More notably, by paying a great deal of attention to America's enemies-in-chief, first Osama bin Laden and later Saddam Hussein, the news media reminded the public of the evil antagonists in a melodrama that glorified the moral virtues of the protagonists: a unified nation and its leader George W. Bush in their quest for retribution and any actions to protect themselves. President Bush and his advisers and bin Laden and Al Qaeda utilized ritual communication to draw like-minded people closer together and, at the same time, employed demagoguery to divide the virtuous in-group from an evil out-group (Carey 1992; 1998; Roberts-Miller 2005). As one student of demagoguery noted,

> Demagogues polarize a complicated (and often frightening) situation by presenting only two options: their policy, and some obviously stupid, impractical, or shameful one. They almost always insist that "those who are not with us are against us" so that the polarized policy situation also becomes a polarized identity situation (Roberts-Miller 2005, 462).

By framing 9/11 within hours after the attacks as a story about good versus evil, the news media provided a stage for protagonists and antagonists to act their parts in this continuing melodrama of polarizing propaganda. In the hours following the catastrophic events to midnight that day, the term "evil" was mentioned 16 times on the nonstop television specials of ABC, CBS, and NBC News. During the same span of 14 hours or so, news anchors of the three networks and their guests cited Afghanistan 43 times and Iraq 15 times in their discussions about possible state involvement in the terrorist strikes. As for the Bush administration's push for the implementation of its policies in response to 9/11, this storyline was more than helpful in that "state action was characterized as both necessary and good; therefore political debate over state action became simultaneously unnecessary and immoral" (Anker 2005). In such a climate, any questioning of frequent terror alerts, curbs on civil liberties, or the justifications for going to war against Iraq was deemed un-American.

With regard to the planned, announced, or enacted restrictions on civil liberties in the name of greater security, we found that President Bush and other administration officials appeared somewhat less often in television network news than in the terrorist threat and Iraq War cases. The reason was obvious: The USA PATRIOT Act that gave the government greater power to encroach on citizens' civil liberties in the name of greater security was adopted by Congress without meaningful opposition and signed into law by the president a few weeks after 9/11. Beyond that, the administration apparently saw no reason to keep issues about civil liberties and security on the front burner; instead, illegal eavesdropping and other violations occurred in secret (but were exposed much later). The administration displayed a laid-back public relations attitude with respect to terrorism prevention and preparedness issues (see table 7.1).

Throughout the period we studied, the administration showed relatively little interest in informing the public about prevention and preparedness. For these issues, experts and other domestic actors followed media professionals as the most frequent news sources in what we found to be moderate or sparse coverage. However, when the president and other administration officials spoke about these areas of homeland security, they received more prominent coverage in terms of their placement within broadcasts and their allotted airtime.

It was only a result of the grossly inadequate preparations for, and responses to, Hurricane Katrina in late August/early September 2005 that news reporters and commentators, officials outside the administration, and the public itself engaged in a lively debate about the failed policies bearing on both natural and man-made disasters. This forced administration officials to participate in this debate.

Because presidents need to enlist public and elite support for what they deem important policies and objectives—especially in foreign affairs and national security—they and their advisers must use the media to appeal to the nation (Kernell 2007). In the process they put their policy priorities high on the news agenda. It was hardly surprising that after 9/11 the president and administration officials launched public relations campaigns on two international security issues: to heighten the terrorist threat posed by Al Qaeda and the danger of WMD in the hands of Saddam Hussein. As table 7.2 shows, these two issues received significant attention in the number of news segments devoted to them: 373 for the threat of terrorism and 473 dealing with the reasons for invading Iraq.[5] From the administration's perspective, publicizing the terrorist threat and Iraq's starring role was intended to assure a fearful public's support for the administration's counterterrorism policies at home and abroad. From the media's perspective, the continuing terrorist threat and the potential war against Iraq were issues far more likely to captivate news audiences than the complexities of formulating and implementing domestic counterterrorism measures.

In contrast to the administration's success at keeping the threat of terrorism and charges against Saddam Hussein alive in the news, there was no comparable government effort to debate and wrestle with civil liberties issues; the result was only moderate news coverage (157 segments). Even less occurred for the issues of terrorism prevention (85 news segments) and preparedness for attacks (81 segments) during the 39 months we examined.

TABLE 7.2. **Number of TV news segments and messages**

	Segments	Messages
Threat	373	1,725
Civil liberties	157	852
Build-up Iraq*	473	846
Prevention	85	443
Preparedness	81	653

Source: Authors.
*While the total threat, civil liberties, prevention, and preparedness segments and messages constitute the data for 39 months after 9/11, those of the Iraq build-up period cover 18 months up to the actual invasion.

In all, we found evidence that the news media's "self-imposed dependence on officially sanctioned information" affected the volume of reporting and the selection of news sources; or, to put it differently, "in most matters of public policy, the news agenda itself is set by those in power" (Bennett, Lawrence, and Livingston 2007, 9, 54). When administration officials provided ample "new" information about the threat of terrorism or reasons for going to war against Iraq, they elevated these concerns on the media agenda; when they took less initiative in a debate, there was more modest news coverage (in the case of civil liberties); and when they laid low, there was much less media attention (prevention and preparedness). In short, the five issues we studied demonstrated the power of government officials, especially the president and members of his administration, to control the media agenda.

The stark exception to this was the tragedy of Hurricane Katrina that triggered an impassioned and overwhelming debate in the media on the dismal state of America's preparedness for natural and man-made catastrophes. Here we found that the news media—especially and most visibly TV news—departed strikingly from the symbiotic relationship between the press and government officials to reclaim their watchdog role by reporting extensively and compassionately on the human suffering in the aftermath of Katrina. Live broadcasts about the lack of or slow emergency responses in New Orleans and elsewhere along the Gulf coast, about clueless leaders in the Federal Emergency Management Administration and the Department of Homeland Security, and about a president who flew over the region on his way back from a vacation at his Texas ranch produced a mighty chorus of administration critics eager to make their case in the press. To their credit, media professionals, members of

Congress, and officials in the emergency response community extended the debate about preparedness and prevention issues beyond hurricanes and other natural disasters to include terrorism. Thus, it took a devastating hurricane, a press that acted in the public interest, and critical voices inside and outside of government to elevate preparedness and emergency responses to terrorism, as well as its prevention, upward on the media agenda. One should not forget, however, that Hurricane Katrina struck about four years after 9/11, when the rally-'round-the-president was no longer as strong as in the previous months and years. Had Katrina occurred two or three years earlier, the press and critical voices in the Congress and elsewhere might have been far less outspoken.

To restate more broadly, we found that news coverage of the terrorist threat and the Bush administration's justifications for going to war against Iraq was indexed to dominant administration sources and that this facilitated state propaganda as anticipated by the hegemony model of media behavior. As we suggested at the end chapters 2 and 4, these two issues unfolded as classic cases of information control by the executive branch that has its greatest advantage in the areas of foreign policy and national security. While the press provided ample access for Osama bin Laden and his mission to spread fear, its pattern of news coverage was most helpful to President Bush, the avenger in the good-versus-evil melodrama.

In the cases of terrorism prevention and preparedness and to a lesser extent the issue of civil liberties versus national security, the indexing of the news was apparently affected by the lack of disagreement among and news-seeking by authoritative sources. Without much interest on the part of decision makers, the media did not independently initiate relevant news investigations. Instead, these were more or less cases of the media taking cues from a mostly inactive White House, consistent with the hegemony model.

Contrast this to the issues raised by Hurricane Katrina, when TV news anchors and reporters acted independently as their critical reports became flashpoints for the public and for the Bush administration and other governmental actors. The press acted independently from its usual elite level sources and awakened decision makers and the public to the flaws in the country's disaster preparedness and prevention policies. This was a case of news as public good in stark contrast to the follow-the-leader(s) coverage pattern in the other issues we examined.

Our research confirmed that there is a strong relationship between the volume of news coverage of particular issues and events and the questions asked in public opinion polls. While this is not surprising since most polls are conducted by survey partnerships involving major news outlets, we still found striking the degree of correspondence between the volume of particular media coverage and the number of questions asked in national surveys on closely or somewhat related issues. At the same time as the press amply covered the terrorist threat and Iraq-related issues, pollsters frequently asked and repeated related questions. There were far fewer polls about the state of terrorism prevention and preparedness, which mirrored the more limited news coverage of these issues. The case of civil liberties fell in between, with less coverage and survey data than for the terrorist threat and Iraq War issues, but considerably more news and relevant polling than for prevention and preparedness. And last, the massive media coverage of Hurricane Katrina and revelations about the defective state of emergency readiness and about how the flooding of New Orleans could have been avoided by the timely improvement of the city's inadequate levee system were matched by public opinion polling that probed disaster prevention and preparedness.

Subgroup Opinions

Not surprisingly we confirmed that "group characteristics can clearly make a difference in how people see the political world" (Erikson and Tedin 2001, 205). When it comes to the public's perceptions of counterterrorist policies, recent research revealed, as had past studies during periods of different threats, that demographic as well as other characteristics of individuals were related to support for restricting civil liberties (see Stouffer 1955; Sullivan, Piereson, and Marcus 1982; Nisbet and Shanahan 2004; Davis 2007). Across the issues we examined, partisanship consistently accounted for the most striking differences in the public's attitudes about counterterrorism policies. Since President George W. Bush and the Republicans were in control of the executive and legislative branch during the post-9/11 period we studied, it was not surprising that Republicans were significantly more satisfied with and supportive of the government's handling of terrorism prevention and preparedness, civil liberties, and the buildup to the Iraq War in 2003 than were Independents and much more so than Democrats. Moreover, partisan differences in particular often widened, deviating from the pattern of in-tandem changes or "parallel publics" that typically occurred in the past and that indicated that the same influences—(benignly) shared standards of judgment or (more cynically) processes of manipulation— were at work across most segments of the public (Page and Shapiro 1992, chap. 7; cf. Zaller 1992).

While not quite as conspicuous, there were notable differences with respect to gender and race. Women were far more worried about further terrorism inside the United States than men, and they were less confi- dent that the government would be able to prevent further acts of terror- ism and less confident that the nation and their own communities were adequately prepared to respond to terrorist strikes. Women were all along less supportive of military action against Iraq and the removal of Saddam Hussein than were men, but this difference widened in the fall of 2002. In early March 2003, when it was clear that the invasion was im- minent, women's support for war was 13 points lower than men's. There were only minor and inconsistent differences when it came to govern- ment restrictions of civil liberties, but in September 2006, men's support for such limits was 8 points greater than women's—in the opposite direc- tion found in past studies (Stouffer 1955; Shapiro and Mahajan 1986).

African Americans were significantly more concerned about future terrorist attacks than Hispanics and somewhat more than whites. They were far more skeptical than whites and Hispanics of the government's ability to protect their communities from terrorist attack and had far less confidence in the state of preparedness. As the likelihood of the in- vasion of Iraq grew in the fall of 2002, African Americans' support for military action plummeted, but it later rose after Secretary of State Co- lin Powell, an African American, made a strong case for going to war in a much publicized appearance before the UN Security Council. Very likely because African Americans' most fundamental rights were vio- lated for hundreds of years, they were significantly less supportive than whites (and somewhat less supportive than Latinos) when it came to gov- ernment restricting civil liberties (Davis 2007).

The role of education was not fully as expected in the case of sup- port for protecting civil liberties in the face of a threat to the nation (cf. Stouffer 1955; Davis 1975; Page and Shapiro 1992). Perhaps due to quicker and greater exposure to ostensibly credible information con- cerning the nation's immediate vulnerability, more of the better edu- cated than others were persuaded of the need (at least in the short term) to be watchful in ways that could limit freedoms and liberties.

The Media and Public Opinion: Foreign Policy Dimensions

In her compelling examination of the contemporary media's preference for violent news and the presentation of violence as entertainment, Sissela Bok reminded us that throughout history violence has always had a particular attraction to human beings but that today's "media violence" has been brought by television (and, most recently, the Internet) into the homes of far larger audiences than the eyewitnesses of old (Bok 1998).[6] Terrorist acts, like crime, war, and destructive disasters, are not simply reported once but are rebroadcast "over and over again until they become burned into the mind's eye (Bok 1998, 4). The attacks of 9/11 were certainly among the highest ranked violent events on the "mayhem index," so to speak, and this assured President Bush and his administration, Osama bin Laden and other Al Qaeda leaders, and the media themselves that they would have a highly attentive audience. While 9/11 was a media event that called for news as public good, it was equally compelling for offering news as commodity. How did the public react to the abundance of terrorism- and counterterrorism-related media coverage in some cases and moderate or scant attention in others?

While research has shown that there is a strong relationship between the total volume and placement of news and the public's issue priorities according to opinion polls (e.g., Iyengar and Kinder 1987), one would not necessarily expect this dominant effect for media coverage of terrorist *threats* since this news comprised only part of the total attention to different aspects of terrorism and counterterrorism in the years after 9/11. We found, however, that warnings and alerts by President Bush and his administration were related to the following: the public's perceptions of terrorism as a major problem facing the nation; Americans' concerns about the likelihood of further terrorism on American soil; and the president's terrorism-specific (and perhaps general) approval rating over the short term. Messages coming from news anchors and reporters, in particular, seemed to be related to Americans' worries about terrorism occurring within six months, whereas messages coming directly from Osama bin Laden and Al Qaeda were associated with increases in individuals' concerns that they or their loved ones could become victims of terrorist strikes. The correlations over time between threat messages and the public's concerns and fears were the strongest correspondences we found between news content and public opinion in this particular case (chapter 2).

The volume of reports about the pros and cons of the administration's accusations against Iraq was high during the buildup to the invasion in March 2003, which we think helped keep steady the opinion of the majority that was predisposed to support going to war. At the same time, however, we found different and somewhat counterintuitive *short-term* dynamics with respect to news coverage and public attitudes toward taking military action: when the number of messages in the news about Iraq's WMD and its Al Qaeda and 9/11 connections decreased, and the same occurred for messages attributable to news professionals, public support for going to war increased; when these messages increased, public support decreased. While one would expect that news about Iraq's alleged WMD capabilities and alleged ties to 9/11 and Al Qaeda would move the public toward support for war against Iraq and the forceful removal of Saddam Hussein, it is possible that this kind of "fear-inducing information stimulates questions which have either violent or non-violent answers" (Grimm 2009, 17). Since fear-inducing news in this particular case was closely related to 9/11, to the threat of more terrorism, and to the global war against terrorism, it is possible that higher volumes of such news resulted in a loss of aggression in an apprehensive news audience; and then attitudes swung back toward more aggressive sentiments and support for war when these fear-inducing messages decreased.

It has been argued that it is important "to distinguish between fear and the cognitive perception of personal and national risk because they have different effects, even though they are related." More specifically, "fear reduces support for U.S. military intervention overseas . . . , whereas perceptions of risk increase it" (Huddy et al. 2003, 259; cf. Merolla and Zechmeister 2009). We suggest that the fear factor might have affected public attitudes toward war during the buildup period to the Iraq invasion and that the overall increase in the volume of news messages might have increased fear and anxiety more than risk perceptions.

It is difficult, however, to distinguish between the public's fear and perceptions of risk based on responses to opinion poll questions about perceptions of threat. Also, there is a trade-off between the risk of not taking action against Iraq and the risk associated with going to war (cf. Jacobs and Shapiro [2000], on the media's framing of issues and on the effect of uncertainty and risk aversion more generally). We wondered, nevertheless, whether and how public perceptions in the aggregate about the likelihood of more terrorist strikes in the years after 9/11 may have been related to collective opinion toward going to war against Iraq.

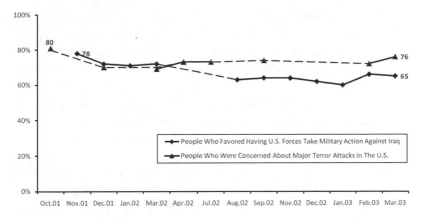

FIGURE 7.1. Threat of terror attacks and support for military action against Iraq

When we compare trends in public concerns about further terrorism in the United States and public support for taking military action against Iraq before the actual invasion occurred (see figure 7.1; dashed lines for intermittent data), we find that the trend lines move in similar directions. Relatively speaking, when the public's concerns about another major terrorist attack at home were lower, support for military action was lower; when public concerns were higher, support for war was greater as well. This suggests that aggregate support for going to war against Iraq behaved similarly to the public's perception of the risk or likelihood of major terrorist attacks. Moreover, since news about terrorism alerts and warnings were related to the public's perception of threat (chapter 2), taken together these data suggest connections among this media coverage, threat perceptions, and the public's attitudes toward military action against Iraq.

Media and Public Opinion Dynamics:
Domestic Policy Dimensions

David Cole's suggestion (2008, 71) that Americans are more eager to protect their own right to privacy than safeguard civil liberties in the abstract was born out by public opinion polls after 9/11: when pollsters asked about the need, in general, to restrict liberties in order to fight terrorists or terrorism, more respondents supported restrictions on civil

liberties than when they were asked about specific measures that could
limit the average person's privacy (e.g., surveillance of phone or e-mail
communications). We discerned similar distinctions in comparing news
coverage and public opinion trends. Most of all, the volume of messages
in the media about actual or proposed measures to curb civil liberties
appeared to be related to public attitudes toward those restrictions that
were likely to affect the average person and threatened people's right to
privacy. Specifically, the increased volume of such *general* messages was
related to reduced public support for eavesdropping and other *specific*
restrictions that amounted to invasion of privacy. News messages from
particular sources, most notably by administration officials in various
departments and agencies, were associated with increased public support for *general* curbs on civil liberties in the name of security, while the
volume of these messages from all sources were somewhat less related to
this support.

Anthony Lewis characterized the overall post-9/11 news coverage of
civil liberties restrictions as "sadly inadequate," and he especially criticized news organizations for not paying much attention to the unlawful,
extended detainment of foreigners who were swept up after the terror
attacks.[7] The watchdog role of the press that the Founding Fathers envisioned and that provided the rationale for freedom of the press in the
first place would have required more than simply reporting arguments
for and against violating civil liberties, human rights, and the right to
privacy, but also speaking out in support of these fundamental rights—
for U.S. citizens, noncitizens, and even suspected and actual terrorists.

Instead, the comparatively limited volume of news coverage about
civil liberties and security may have left room for the fear factor, magnified and amplified by the overcoverage of terrorism alerts and warnings, to influence public attitudes. One study conducted more than three
years after 9/11 found that those Americans with high levels of fear of a
terrorist attack were significantly more supportive of government limits
on certain civil liberties (i.e., monitoring of the Internet; detaining terrorists indefinitely; outlawing un-American activities) than were others
with less fear (Nisbet and Shanahan 2004, 4; for other individual level
studies, see Davis 2007; Berinsky 2009; Merolla and Zechmeister 2009).
When we compare opinion trends over the period we studied for the percentage of people who were worried that they themselves or their loved
ones could become victims of terrorism with the percentage willing to

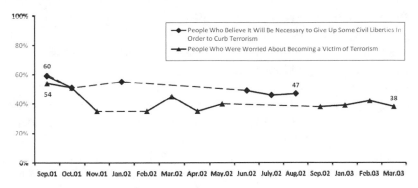

FIGURE 7.2. Civil liberties and worry about becoming a victim of terrorism

give up some civil liberties to curb terrorism, we too found some correspondence (see figure 7.2; dashes for intermittent data): Decreasing fear
levels appear to occur with less acceptance of curbs on civil liberties.
Since Osama bin Laden's threats conveyed through the media were associated with more Americans worrying that they or their families could
become victims of terrorism (see chapter 2), this is an important finding in that it underscores the motivation and ability of the world's most
notorious terrorist leader to use the media to manipulate the public of
a targeted country. It seems that when *personal* fear of becoming a victim of terrorism increases, support for limiting civil liberties follows. As
bin Laden's communications over the years have revealed, this has been
what he and other Al Qaeda leaders (and traditionally terrorists in general) have sought (Lawrence 2005).

When it comes to terrorism prevention and preparedness in the context of homeland security, the news media's lack of attention to these important policy issues was striking, as was the modest number of opinion
polls questions that were asked about them. Obviously, the news media
followed the lead of government officials who were far more active in
spreading the word about the threat of terrorism and in justifying military action against Iraq than informing and educating the public about
measures at home to prevent and prepare for terrorism. This was particularly troubling in the case of preparedness for such emergency situations, since the best possible response to a major disaster depends not
only on well-trained first responders but also on citizens who know what
to expect and what to do in such an event.

Propaganda and Press Responsibility

Since the term "propaganda" has negative connotations and is closely
tied to the propaganda apparatus in Hitler's Germany and other dictato-
rial or authoritarian regimes, most people would not use this "p"-word to
describe their own leaders' efforts to manipulate public perceptions and
opinions. As two students of propaganda once put it, "the goal of modern
propaganda is not to inform and enlighten but rather to move the masses
toward a desired position or point of view" (Pratkanis and Aronson 1991,
13). This is what President George W. Bush, his administration, and his
supporters in Congress and elsewhere attempted to do. Just as terrorists have tended to follow up their attacks (or what has been called "propaganda of the deed") by issuing messages that threaten and intimidate
targeted societies, leaders in the attacked and threatened countries, too,
have tended to resort to "propaganda of fear" to sell their counterterrorism agenda or what they claim must be done in order to prevent further
attacks. In the process, those who have attempted to sell fear by commit-
ting and threatening political violence against civilians—terrorism—and
those who have tried to do the same in the name of counterterrorism have
engaged in ritual communication and in the familiar demonizing narrative of good versus evil, the good guys against the evil-doers.

In the early months and years after 9/11 when the Bush administration asked for and Congress rubber-stamped important counterterrorism laws, when the president and his closest advisers made secret decisions that supported gross violations of human rights and civil liberties,
and when intelligence information was distorted or "cooked" in order
to justify and obtain congressional authorization for the Iraq invasion,
the press was too intimidated to discharge its responsibility as a watchdog monitoring government on behalf of the people. Thus, the administration's propaganda of fear, abetted by Al Qaeda's frequent publicized
threats, helped maintain a crisis atmosphere and strong support for the
president and his counterterrorism policies. To the extent that officials
and political leaders opposed those policies, they remained silent for the
most part. Without authoritative opposing sources to turn to, the media
behaved as more of a lapdog than watchdog. In the few cases of reporting in the watchdog mode, there was no follow-up involving the press's
traditional herd mentality in news coverage. For example, in late 2002
Dana Priest reported in the *Washington Post* about the brutal treatment
of detainees in U.S.-run prisons in Afghanistan and the CIA's practice

of "rendering" them to other countries with histories of human rights violations and torture. One anonymous U.S. official was quoted as saying,
"We don't kick the [expletive] out of them. We send them to other countries so they can kick the [expletive] out of them" (Priest and Gelman
2001, 1). But in the absence of immediate and frequent follow-ups in the
rest of the news media, there was no outcry, no outrage among members
of the political establishment or among the interested public.

Media Politics and the Limits of Spin

Given the media's agenda-setting capacity and their ability to frame issues, we wondered whether reporting that conformed with the expectations of American journalism's longstanding ethic would have contributed to a different outcome for the counterterrorism responses after
9/11. The media fell short on all three of the fundamental obligations
that are stated in the "Statement of Principles" of the American Society of Newspaper Editors, the trailblazer in the establishment of nationwide press ethics. According to these principles, "The American press
was made free not just to inform or just to serve as a forum for debate
but also to bring an independent scrutiny to bear on the forces of power
in the society, including the conduct of official power at all levels of
government."[8] In the period after 9/11 that we examined, the media did
not inform the public fully about the most important events, developments, issues, and problems concerning counterterrorism; they did not
provide a forum for real debate; and they did not scrutinize the selling of
fear and the so-called war on terrorism. When the press rediscovered its
bite, it was too late in that the Iraq War had long begun, violations of human rights and civil liberties had occurred, and improvements in important areas of terrorism prevention and preparedness were lacking. But as
more critics of the administration in Congress and elsewhere spoke out
and the press reported more independently, the effectiveness of the administration's public relations messages weakened; a growing number of
Americans used available information and their own judgment as a reality check. In short, reality eventually proved stronger than the pseudo-
world of existential threat and the administration's messages of fear and
"shock and awe" retribution.

    John Zaller (1998, 186) defines media politics as "the attempt to gov-
ern on the basis of words and images that diffuse through the mass me-

dia. This communication—whether in the form of presidential speeches, press conferences, TV ads, media frenzies, spin, or ordinary news— creates a sort of virtual reality whose effects are arguably quite real and important." But he also noted that the results of media politics need to be examined in each particular case "because sometimes the effects are real and lasting and other times they are not" (Zaller 1998, 187). Looking at the Bush administration's selling of the most important aspects of its counterterrorist policies, we found that media politics created a pseudo- or virtual reality in the public mind that lasted for many months after 9/11. As time went by, however, reality made headway and became eventually stronger than the pseudo-reality of the administration's marketing efforts; the results were growing public disapproval, for identifiable reasons, of George W. Bush's performance as president, and doubts about his counterterrorism policies (see Jacobson 2008, 2011).

The New Communication Landscape

When the 9/11 attacks occurred, when the Iraq War commenced, and when the images of horror at the Abu Ghraib prison were publicized, the mass media and communication landscape in the United States and around the world looked very different than it did later at the end of the first decade of the 21st century. These past events predated the speedy proliferation of electronic social networks, popular and influential blogs, and other Internet outlets for information and for debate that expanded the marketplace of ideas. The opposite trend occurred in the traditional news media, particularly in the newspaper sector. Toward the close of that decade and during the most severe economic slump since the Great Depression, there was hardly a month without another newspaper becoming increasingly insolvent, closing foreign and/or domestic offices, switching to electronic-only editions, decimating their newsrooms, or going out of business. Since the young adult generation and increasingly middle-aged Americans as well obtain less and less information about public affairs from the print media and rely increasingly on the Internet and late-night entertainment programs, such as *The Daily Show* and *The Colbert Report*, the audience for newspapers and news magazines will continue to shrink.

In an article on the plight of newspapers, Albert Hunt wrote in early 2009, "Maybe when the economy rebounds, newspapers will get a bounce, too, although the structural problems predated the financial crisis. And there will be costly casualties in the interim. That may not matter much for a vibrant economy. It matters a lot for a vibrant democracy" (Hunt 2009).

To be sure, a robust press can provide an indispensable, extra-constitutional check on the formal branches of government. Elite newspapers, specifically, have traditionally taken the lead in reporting independently and conducting investigative reporting to uncover important information and lay bare abuses of power, corruption, and other wrongdoing on the part of government or other sectors of society. However, they along with television and radio broadcast networks fell short on these counts in the years immediately after 9/11. This begs the question of whether a blogosphere as it exists today could and would have made a difference in the post-9/11 years—by offering a diversity of views, promoting vigorous public debate, and questioning the government's counterterrorism responses. Could bloggers have ferreted out more information and knowledgeable critics regarding the terrorist threat after 9/11 and the case for invading Iraq? When a presidential administration has such solid information control? They will surely face an uphill struggle to penetrate the truth. Moving forward, we would like to believe that there will be influential bloggers who are less reluctant to scrutinize leaders during actual or perceived crises, and who will have increasing opportunity to grab the attention of the traditional media, the political establishment, and the public. Such a blogosphere could help weaken the virtual reality of media politics and strengthen the public's ability to recognize actual reality.

If there were any doubts about the growing importance of blogs and Internet-based social networks and sources, these diminished when, during his second prime time news conference in 2009, President Barack Obama called on the correspondent of a popular blog (Sam Stein of the Huffington Post) to ask a question, and shortly thereafter the president conducted a town-hall meeting on the Internet.

Today, as in the past, newspapers remain the predominant news-gatherers. Alex Jones, the director of the Shorenstein Center on the Press, Politics, and Public Policy at Harvard University, estimated that about 85% of today's news (in 2009) is generated by newspaper personnel.[9] Bloggers typically are not reporters who gather news or conduct investigations; instead they work with, expand upon, comment on, and interpret information provided in large part by newspapers and other traditional media organizations. One exception has been Josh Marshall's TPM (Talking Points Memo), a blog that has presented original reporting and through its muckraking unit has conducted investigative reporting. And in spring 2009, the Huffington Post, one of the most popular and influential blogs, announced that it would finance a team of investigative journalists in collaboration with the Atlantic Philanthropies and other contributors to the Huffington Post Investigative Fund. Arianna Huffington, the founder and editor-in-chief of the Huffington Post, explained that "she and the donors were concerned that layoffs at newspapers were hurting investigative journalism at a time when the nation's institutions need to be watched closely" (Associated Press 2009). One major report on *The Reconstruction of American Journalism* (Downie and Schudson 2009, 72–97) also argued and offered proposals regarding "What needs to be done to support independent reporting" and, we hope, continuing vigorous journalism.

By and large, at the moment, the old and the new media continue to feed off each other, because, for the most part, they perform distinct functions. While this may change in the future, for now the best bulwark against unfettered manipulation by government, or terrorist, leaders may well be the blogosphere's—or its future successor's—free-ranging marketplace of ideas that the old media cannot ignore.

President Obama

Underselling Fear?

We know that the aim of those who try to carry out these attacks is to force us to live in fear, and thereby amplifying the effects of their attacks—even those that fail. But as Americans, and as a nation, we will not be terrorized. We will not cower in fear. We will not be intimidated. We will be vigilant. We will work together. And we will protect and defend the country we love to ensure a safe and prosperous future for our people. That's what I intend to do as President and that's what we will do as a nation. — President Obama, after a failed car bombing in New York City's Times Square

In early February 2009, less than two weeks after Barack Obama was sworn in as the 44th president of the United States, former Vice President Richard Cheney warned in an interview of the high probability of "a 9/11-type event where the terrorists are armed with something much more dangerous than an airline ticket and a box cutter—a nuclear weapon or a biological agent of some kind."[1] When deployed in the center of an American city, Cheney predicted, "That's the one that would involve the deaths of perhaps hundreds of thousands of people, and the one you have to spend a hell of a lot of time guarding against."[2] In the years following 9/11 and particularly during President Bush's first term, the administration's regular drumbeat of warnings and alerts kept America's fear of further terrorism alive and helped avert opposition to its counterterrorism policies. In the waning weeks of the Bush administration and immediately after the changing of the guard at the White House, Cheney and a growing chorus of his supporters relaunched a campaign that hyped the likelihood of catastrophic terrorism at home in order to defend the Bush administration's controversial post-9/11 record and to attack critics of those policies. Most of all, Cheney took shots at President Obama's announced policy changes (i.e., the ban of torture, the closing of the Guantanamo detention facilities) as "in fact, rais[ing] the risk to the American people of another attack."[3] In addition, Cheney and other former administration officials and supporters of Bush's counter-terrorism policies began a publicity campaign to defend the controversial aspects of post-9/11 actions, such as eavesdropping without court warrants and other violations of Americans' civil liberties; torture of terrorists and unlawful combatants; extraordinary rendition through kidnapping of noncitizens to foreign states, already well known as human rights violators; and the long discredited justifications for going to war against Iraq. All of this echoed the saying of baseball wit Yogi Berra, that it was "déjà vu all over again." The same could be said of Osama bin Laden, who released an audiotape after remaining silent for 10 long months. Obviously referring to Obama's upcoming inauguration, the Al Qaeda boss warned that "Bush leaves his successor with the worst inheritance . . . two long guerrilla wars and no options. He either withdraws and faces military defeat, or carries on and drowns his nation in financial trouble."[4]

How did this the new wave of propaganda of fear affect the political climate around President Obama's counterterrorism policies?

In an effort to defuse the post-9/11 demagoguery of hate and apprehension, the administration moved away from using the terms "war on terror" or "war on terrorism" that the previous administration had repeated and exploited. The incoming secretary of homeland security, Janet Napolitano, was among the high-ranking administration officials who instead spoke of "man caused disasters" in general. This rhetorical shift was decried by alarmists as a dangerous denial of terrorism as an existential threat. Peter King, the ranking member of the Homeland Security Committee of the U.S. House of Representative, complained after Napolitano's first testimony before the committee that "he was struck that Napolitano's prepared remarks did not include terrorism, Sept. 11, new threats" and that "this can't be the evil we don't speak about. Any testimony on homeland security should be centered around the threat of terrorism and what we're doing to combat it."[5] Such critics would not think of using the "t"-word and suggest counterterrorism policies when right-wing extremists of the neo-Nazi/antigovernment variety or antiabortion fanatics killed people in premeditated acts of political violence.[6]

On the one hand, these criticisms were part of the continued and expanding partisan conflict and polarization, in which Republicans attacked the Obama administration and Democrats in Congress on every

possible front. On the other, the "war on terrorism" in particular became a relentless fight for Republicans against President Obama and his
counterterrorism policies because of the Democrats' vulnerability, especially since the Carter administration, if not earlier, on national security issues (see Holsti 2004). This was blatant politics, not just irony, because Obama followed his predecessor's lead on actual policies in many
respects—albeit not in rhetoric. To begin with, Obama not only continued to fight the two wars he inherited but decided in favor of a significant
(30,000) troop surge in Afghanistan. Yet, while the National Security
Council pondered plans for the most promising strategy to succeed in
Afghanistan, former Vice President Cheney again led the choir of knee-
jerk and persistent Obama critics charging the president with "dithering" instead of just doing "what it takes to win."[7] At the left end of the
ideological spectrum, progressives who had been Obama's strongest supporters during the 2008 campaign were upset about the significant troop
buildup in Afghanistan as well as other decisions, such as the Justice Department's efforts to deny victims of illegal eavesdropping and extraordinary rendition their day in court.

As we noted in chapter 7, for defenders and revisionists of the Bush
administration's counterterrorism performance the attacks of 9/11 were
struck from the record or attributed to what was described as ineffective
policies during the Clinton presidency. Similarly, these critics' had selective memories in comparing the presidents' responses to the near attacks
that occurred. Republicans lost no time in attacking President Obama
and his administration after Umar Farouk Abdulmutallab, a passenger on Northwest Airlines Flight 253 from Amsterdam to Detroit, tried
to detonate pentaerythritol tetranitrate, a powerful plastic explosive he
had hidden in his underpants. Representative Peter King and others criticized the president for not addressing the nation immediately after the
failed attempt on Christmas Day. It is far from clear that this would have
been the right public response. This would have added to the media hype
and rewarded any masterminds of the latest terrorist plot with the highest levels of attention that they have continually sought. After all, the
attempt failed. More important, President Obama's public statement
three days after the incident provided a full account of what had happened. This contrasted sharply with how President Bush reacted after
the would-be shoe bomber, Richard Reid, tried to down a U.S.-bound
airliner in December 2001, less than four months after 9/11. It took the
vacationing Bush six days before he mentioned the incident—and then

only in passing. When some media outlets pointed belatedly to this discrepancy between the two presidents' reactions to very similar terrorist misses, it was probably too late to jog fully the public's and elites' memories.

As to avoiding such an incident on Christmas Day in the first place, just as there was an opportunity for the Bush administration to prevent the 9/11 attacks, if intelligence on some of the hijackers and FBI agents' field reports had been coordinated and analyzed in time, the available information about the Christmas Day bomber (especially his father's alarm at and direct report to the U.S. embassy in Nigeria of his son's embracing of the jihadi cause and traveling overseas without checking luggage) should have been enough to follow the example of UK authorities who stopped him from entering their country. If there was reason to criticize the Obama administration, it should have been for its failure to revamp the coordination of various security and intelligence systems that were put in place by the Bush administration.

And then there was the failed attempt to explode a car bomb at busy Times Square in New York City on May 1, 2010. When asked during an appearance on Fox News whether the failed bombing attempt could be seen as a victory, the former governor of New York, George Pataki, said, "I don't think you call it victory. I think victory would be being able to prevent these before they get to that point where you have a loaded van in Times Square. I think it's more a question of lucky."[8] Although it took law enforcement less than 54 hours to arrest Faisal Shahzad, a U.S. citizen and native of Pakistan, aboard an Emirates flight to Dubai on a runway at Kennedy International Airport, Republicans were quick to question and criticize the administration's handling of the incident. They claimed that the administration was more interested in protecting the rights of terrorists than the security of Americans; they suggested that the accused bomber Shahzad should not be granted Miranda rights—although he was a U.S. citizen. Senator John McCain, for example, said, "When we detain terrorism suspects, our top priority should be finding out what intelligence they have that could prevent future attacks and save American lives. Our priority should not be telling them they have a right to remain silent" (Baker 2010). It did not matter that the enforcement agencies reported about the arrested bomber's willingness, if not eagerness, to reveal important information. Representative King, again, was among those who wanted Shahzad classified as an enemy combatant, not a civilian. Ignoring civil liberties issues, he argued that "in these kinds of cases, the first preference should be a military commission because you can get more information" (Baker 2010). Nor did it matter that would-be shoe-bomber Reid, a foreign national, had been read his Miranda rights soon after his arrest and had been tried by a civilian court in Boston, not by a military tribunal. Five days after the Times Square bombing, Senator Joseph Lieberman proposed legislation in the Senate that would strip those Americans affiliated with a foreign terrorist group of their U.S. citizenship and presumably give way to treating them as unlawful combatants.

For still others, the Times Square incident was a welcome opportunity to attack President Obama's overall approach to defeat terrorism. House Minority Whip Eric Cantor (R-Virginia) "blasted Obama for ditching a 'proven U.S. national security strategy' by embracing 'a naïve moral relativism in which the United States bears much responsibility for the problems we face around the world.'"[9]

In today's highly competitive media environment, news thrives more than ever on conflict, all-out political infighting, drama, and outrageous sound bites. However erroneous, irrational, and inflammatory, initial accusations thrown out into the political arena tend to be more extensively and more prominently covered than responses based on fact and record. This tends to be true for much of the mainstream media's news but far more so for the 24/7 offerings on the "all news" cable networks and the growing number of blogs devoted to politics. Add to this the media's fascination with and extraordinary attention to the "Tea Party" movement and its stalwart supporters—former vice presidential candidate Sarah Palin and Representative Michele Bachmann, among others—leading the relentless anti-Obama campaign.

Contrary to President George W. Bush who enjoyed bipartisan elite consensus on his counterterrorism policies for a prolonged period after 9/11, his successor was confronted by a hostile out-party from the very beginning. "For Obama," as reported by Jonathan Alter (2010), "this was the greatest surprise of 2009. '[It wasn't that] I thought my political outreach and charm would immediately end partisan politics,' the president said. 'I just thought that there would be enough of a sense of urgency that at least for the first year there would be an interest in governing. And you just didn't see that'" (Alter 2010, 129).

There was a change in one respect: During the Bush presidency the administration hyped the terrorism threat as a means to bolster support for its war on terror; in contrast, during the early Obama pres-

idency, former administration officials such as Dick Cheney and their
supporters in Congress and in the old and new media, continued to sell
fear by overblowing the threat of terrorism. This continued pressure left
its mark on decisions in the Obama administration. Thus four days after the Times Square incident, when the no-Miranda-rights-for-terrorists
debate heated up, U.S. Attorney General Eric Holder announced that
the Obama administration would work with Congress on a relaxation of
Miranda rights when dealing with the arrest and detention of suspected
terrorists. In fact, there was no need to make exceptions during extreme
emergencies, because the current legal requirement allowed the police
to question persons under arrest without reading the Miranda warning
when this was deemed necessary for public safety. Similarly, while President Obama's first executive order prohibited coercive interrogation
methods, he left in place the equally controversial extraordinary rendition program that came down to an outsourcing of torture to countries
with a tradition of gross human rights violations. Moreover, officials in
Obama's Justice Department followed the example of their predeces-
sors in advancing a sweeping view of executive secrecy powers as they invoked "state secrets" in their refusal to testify in trials and thereby force
the dismissal of court actions initiated by victims of extraordinary rendi-
tions and torture, as well as illegal eavesdropping.[10]

We wondered whether and how this affected the news consuming
public, as found in opinion polls, and how this compared to the findings,
themes, and conclusions of our study. While the Obama administration
somewhat changed the context and focus of counterterrorism politics,
the same questions and issues that we raised remained.

Less than three weeks after President Obama's inauguration, there
was a significant partisan divide in the public's evaluation of the new
president's handling of the threat of terrorism. According to a Pew Research Center poll, while a majority of Democrats (66%) and Independents (51%) approved of his performance, only 26% of Republicans did
so. About a year later, in early January 2010, that already low level of Republican approval remained while that of Independents decreased by 4
points and approval among Democrats increased by 8 points to 74%. The
48-point partisan difference (26% to 74%) echoed the already wide and
increasing partisan conflict revealed by the nearly 70-point Democratic-
Republican difference (84% to 15%) in Obama's overall approval rating, up from 54 points (88% to 34%) in February 2009. It was already
clear that the new president was also going to have a difficult time be-

ing a "uniter" rather than the "divider," as his predecessor had aspired—
and failed—to be, and this wide partisan chasm continued through 2010
in all polling of presidential approval (see Jacobson 2011, and opinion
tracking done at pollster.com). Not surprisingly, then, in January 2010,
a plurality of Democrats (47%) felt that, compared with Bush's policies,
Obama's agenda made the United States safer vis-à-vis terrorism (versus 6% less safe), while the same plurality of Republicans (46%) believed
that the country was less safe (versus 8% safer); Independents were divided (22%-22%) on this issue, with a majority (51%) seeing no difference. At that same time, a large minority of Republicans (43%) and Democrats (41%) and the majority of Independents (51%) told pollsters that
there was no difference concerning the two administrations.[11] A September 2010 ABC News/Washington Post poll found that approximately
the same 48% of all partisan groups said the country was safer now than
it was before 9/11, with Republican responses down fully 34 percentage
points and Independents down 17 points from two years earlier, and no
change among Democrats.

The persistent attacks on the Obama administration's insistence on
human and civil rights for terrorists and alleged terrorists, including the
closing of the Guantanamo detention facilities, trying 9/11 mastermind
Khalid Sheihk Mohammed in a Manhattan Federal Court, and granting
the Christmas Day bomber Miranda rights affected Republicans, Democrats, and Independents alike: A clear majority of the American public (58%) in January 2010 felt that the government's antiterrorism efforts
had not gone far enough to protect the country—an 18-point jump from
November 2009, when 40% gave that response as part of a largely gradual downward trend since 2004; in contrast, only 27% of the public felt
that the government had gone too far in restricting civil liberties—compared to 36% two months earlier, after trending modestly upward until
then. Most notably, the increase in those seeing antiterrorism efforts as
not going far enough was greater among Democrats and Independents
(a 20 percentage point increase) than among Republicans (11 points), so
that the partisan gap between Republicans and like-minded Democrats
and Independents narrowed from 22 points in November 2009 (57% to
35%) to 13 in January 2010 (68% to 55%).[12]

While the public's overall evaluation of Obama's performance in handling terrorism remained largely steady (in the 50%–57% range in the
Pew Research Center polls, not particularly high) during the first year
of his administration, it seemed that his track record in fighting terror-

ism at home and abroad was affected negatively by the attacks on the administration's policies resonating through the news media. What is important in this case, compared to the Bush administration's post-9/11 years, is that the press was needed less in a watchdog role because of the strong—indeed, strident—conflict among the political leaders of both parties that played itself out in the media. That said, reality, too, figured into public perceptions. In 2009 and 2010 there was no dispute, as evidence cumulated about actual or foiled attacks by individuals or cells associated with Al Qaeda—in most cases, like-minded lone assailants or small groups. Thus, while a total of 12 such acts occurred in the seven years after 9/11 through the end of 2008, involving persons born in the United States or immigrants from abroad, there were 8 in 2009 alone.[13] In short, the combination of these actual and failed instances of terrorism, and the Republicans' unrelenting anti-Obama rhetoric, informed the public about policy issues concerning terrorism and counterterrorism at home and abroad.[14]

How do these issues compare to those covered in the chapters of this book? What has changed? We would like to think that some learning had occurred, in that if any relevant issues, problems, or facts did *not* come out of the competition and conflict among political leaders, an independent press would fill in the gap. This is something to watch in the years ahead. The prospect, however, was still dim (at this writing in September 2010) during the first two years of the Obama presidency. The lessons from Hurricane Katrina were not fully learned, near the Louisiana coast once more, in the response to the massive explosion at an oil rig that killed 11 workers and produced an extraordinary oil spill disaster, wreaking havoc on the Gulf of Mexico and its shores. What did not change were the questions that such catastrophes continue to raise broadly regarding efforts to prevent them and to be prepared for them if and when they occur. As the nation observed the ninth anniversary of 9/11 amidst a divisive public debate (during a conflict-ridden midterm election year) about the establishment of an Islamic community center some two-and-a-half blocks from "Ground Zero," the site of the former World Trade Center, the terrorist threat remained very real. Yet, just as the threat was overblown since the catastrophic attacks of 9/11, "the nation's politics remain[ed] in thrall to the specter of terrorism"—even as "government [over]reactions to terrorism often impose[d] greater costs on the societies attacked than terror attacks themselves" and did "the work of terrorism" (Friedman, Harper, and Preble 2010, 1). Moreover, selling fear either by the Bush administration or the opponents of the Obama administration had not resulted in the most effective prevention and preparedness policies.

Thus, more than eight-and-a-half years after 9/11, Irwin Redlener, the director of the National Center for Disaster Preparedness at Columbia University, had no doubt about the lack of adequate preparedness for catastrophic terrorism and other disasters. In the spring of 2010, Redlener said, "There's not a single city that's done anything that remotely approaches what needs to be done to prepare. We just engage in random acts of preparedness" (Paumgarten 2010). This was hardly reassuring.

Notes

Chapter One

1. The video of the conversation is available on YouTube at http://search .yahoo.com/search?p=Rather+on+Letterman+and+9%2F11&toggle=1&cop =mss&ei=UTF-8&fr=yfp-t-701.

2. The surveys were conducted by the Gallup Organization, September 7–10, 2001, and September 21–22, 2001. After the Afghanistan War began in early October, presidential approval increased another 2 percentage points to 92% according to an ABC News survey carried out October 8–9, 2001.

3. The "Statement of Principles" is available at the American Society of Newspaper Editors' Web site at http://www.asne.org/index.cfm?ID=888, accessed June 2, 2009.

4. In describing the concentration of power in the hands of large media corporations, White wrote, "Power, said Karl Marx over a century ago, is control over the means of production; that phrase, said Arthur Schlesinger, Jr., recently should be changed—power in America today is control of the means of communication."

5. Searching iPOLL on "terror!" (where "!" is a 'wildcard" that allows for any letters after "terror"), the corresponding numbers are 976 and 6,718, respectively.

6. Anthony Lewis, for example, voiced his criticism in a speech at a conference on "Weapons of Mass Destruction, National Security, and a Free Press" at the Benjamin N. Cardozo School of Law at Yeshiva University. The transcript of his remarks was published in the *Nieman Reports* 58, no. 2 (Summer 2004).

Chapter Two

1. The U.S. Department of Homeland Security was established on November 25, 2002, by the Homeland Security Act of 2002. In his memoir, Tom Ridge

wrote extensively about the politics of terrorism and counterterrorism inside and outside the Bush administration, especially, in chapter 6 ("The Politics of Terrorism, Part I") and chapter 14 ("The Politics of Terrorism, Part II").

2. From a CNN report aired on March 12, 2002.

3. Leno made the remark on *The Tonight Show*, March 14, 2002.

4. From "Martha Stewart Jokes" at http://www.101funjokes.com/martha_stewart_jokes_8.htm.

5. Because the Vanderbilt TV news summaries provided the airtimes for each segment but the Lexis/Nexis transcripts did not, we compared the length of news segments concerning changes in the official terror alert levels in minutes and seconds and in word counts.

6. According to a survey conducted for *Time* magazine by Schulman, Ronca, and Bucuvalas, August 22–24, 2006.

7. For our demographical comparisons we relied on three surveys that the Marist College Institute for Public Opinion conducted for the Children's Health Fund over three years: August 5–20, 2003; July 19–26, 2004; and July 15–22, 2005.

8. Responses to most of these four questions also correlate noticeably with each other. The correlations are for great concern about major terrorist attacks, average $r = .60$; very worried about an attack occurring soon, average $r = .46$; thinking that an attack will occur in the next few months, average $r = .59$; and personal worry, average $r = .40$ for very worried or worried in figure 2.11.

9. The responses over time to the two Bush approval questions were highly correlated ($r = .94$).

10. For the survey data, see the appendix to this chapter and the general appendix, available at http://www.press.uchicago.edu/books/nacos/.

11. We did not find evidence for serial correlation in the results that we report. As described in chapter 1, we rely substantially on close analyses of time periods during which there are corresponding changes in news media content and in public perceptions and attitudes.

12. Reuters, "Report: Bush Says bin Laden Aided in Elections," February 28, 2006. http://www.msnbc.com/id/11604530/, accessed June 19, 2006.

13. Ibid.

14. "Exclusive: Kerry Says UBL Tape Cost him Election," Fox News.com, November 21, 2004. http://www.foxnews.com/printer_friendly_story/0,3566,139060,00.html, accessed June 20, 2006.

15. Ridge's session with journalists was reported by Hall 2005.

Chapter Three

1. From a speech that Anthony Lewis delivered at the Benjamin N. Cardozo School of Law at Yeshiva University in a conference called "Weapons of Mass

Destruction, National Security, and a Free Press" on March 2, 2004. The full text is available at http://www.nieman.harvard.edu/reportsitem.aspx?id=100829.

2. Even after the Abu Ghraib revelations, the media themselves rarely used the term "torture" in this context and instead preferred "abuse," "alleged abuse," or "mistreatment."

3. "Remarks by President George W. Bush at Signing of Anti-Terrorism Legislation," October 26, 2001.

4. Ibid.

5. Florida International University, College of Law and Jack D. Gordon Institute for Public Policy and Citizenship Studies, Overview for Conference "At War with Civil Rights and Civil Liberties: A Constitutional Symposium," October 17, 2003. Available at http://www.fiu.edu/~ippcs/oct17_f03_confoverview .html, accessed June 4, 2008.

6. Public Law 107-40 (2001).

7. From a speech by Anthony Lewis delivered at the Benjamin N. Cardozo School of Law at Yeshiva University during the conference "Weapons of Mass Destruction, National Security, and a Free Press," March 2, 2004.

8. From the attorney general's testimony before the Senate Judicial Committee on December 6, 2001, according to the transcript available at Lexis/Nexis.

9. When asked shortly after the Oklahoma City bombing whether they thought it necessary for the average person to give up some civil liberties in order to curb terrorism in this country, 49% of respondents to a *Los Angeles Times* poll conducted April 26–27, 1995, said it was necessary, 43% did not deem it necessary. Two years later, 62% of the public said it was not necessary and only 29% believed it was necessary to give up some civil liberties to fight terrorism, according to a poll conducted for the Pew Research Center for the People and the Press, April 3–6, 2007.

10. We used the search term combination of "civil liberty or civil liberties or USA PATRIOT Act and terrorism or terrorist."

11. President Bush addressed a Joint Session of the Congress of the United States on September 20, 2001.

12. According to surveys conducted for the Pew Center for the People and the Press September 14–17, 2001, and August 14–25, 2002.

13. According to Harris polls conducted September 19–24, 2001; March 13–19, 2002; February 12–16, 2003; February 9–16, 2004; and September 9–13, 2004.

14. This particular question was asked in *Newsweek* surveys conducted June 27–28, 2002, and August, 28–29, 2002.

15. According to Gallup polls for CNN/*USA Today*. The most notable change in public opinion occurred from February 2004, when 26% of respondents said that the PATRIOT Act "goes too far," to December 2005, when this number increased to 34%. During the same period, the percentage of "don't know" responses declined from 10% to 4%.

16. The only two surveys on profiling were conducted for *Newsweek* June 27–28, 2002, and August 28–29, 2002. In the first survey, 14% of respondents were strongly in favor of profiling, 34% were willing to accept such a measure, 48% said it "goes too far," and 4% had no opinion. In the second, 12% expressed strong support, 26% were willing to accept it, 59% said such a measure "goes too far," and 3% did not know.

17. According to surveys conducted by the Media and Society Research Group at Cornell University, October/November 2002 and 2004. The report is available at http://www.comm.cornell.edu/msrg/report1a.pdf, accessed June 20, 2008.

18. According to polls by Princeton Survey Research Associates for *Newsweek*: In late June 2002, 44% of respondents were either strongly in favor or willing to accept such power, and 52% rejected it as going too far. By late August, only 34% were strongly in favor or willing to accept and 63% opposed such government power as going too far.

19. For Linda Greenhouse's report on the 2008 Supreme Court ruling in the *New York Times*, see http://www.nytimes.com/2008/06/13/washington/13scotus.html?_r=1&oref=slogin, accessed June 20, 2008.

20. According to surveys conducted for the *Los Angeles Times* on September 13–14, 2001; the Pew Research Center for the Press and the People on September 14–17, 2001, January 9–13, 2002, June 27–28, 2002, July 14–August 5, 2003, July 8–18, 2004, and July 13–17, 2005; *Newsweek* on September 20–21, 2001, June 27–28, 2002, and August 28–29, 2002; and National Public Radio/Kaiser/Harvard on October 31–November 12, 2001.

21. This question was asked by Gallup for CNN/*USA Today* on January 25–27, 2002; June 21–23, 2002; June 21–23, 2002; September 2–4, 2002; April 22–23, 2003; August 25–26, 2003; and November 11–12, 2003.

22. *New York Times Co. v. United States*, 403 U.S. 713 (1971).

Chapter Four

1. From Ajami's appearance on the *CBS Evening News* on September 11, 2001.

2. Haig made the remarks during a Fox News special on September 15, 2001.

3. From an NBC News transcript of the *Today* show on September 12, 2001, that was retrieved from the Lexis/Nexis archives on July 20, 2008.

4. The report was aired on *NBC Nightly News* on September 13, 2001, and retrieved from the Lexis/Nexis archives on July 20, 2008.

5. From the official transcript of Powell's speech on February 5, 2002, available at http://www.state.gov/secretary/former/powell/remarks/2003/17300.htm.

6. From the transcript of a White House press briefing on September 26, 2001, that is available at http://www.whitehouse.gov/news/releases/2001/09/20010926-5 .html.

7. We were unable to access the study at FAIR's online site and therefore relied on a summary available at http://athensfreepress.blogspot.com/2008/01/ coverage-of-colin-powells-address-to-un.html.

8. For the *New York Times*' editors apology, see http://www.nytimes.com/ 2004/05/26/international/middleeast/26FTE_NOTE.html?ex=1217304000&en= f7f8b43912a5d721"&ei=5070.

9. Wilkerson was interviewed on CNN; see http://www.cnn.com/2005/ WORLD/meast/08/19/powell.un/.

10. Mentioned by Bill Schneider, "Marketing Iraq: Why Now," CNN online, September 12, 2002. The article was accessed July 28, 2008, at http://archives .cnn.com/2002/ALLPOLITICS/09/12/schneider.iraq/

11. We retrieved the transcript of the *CBS Morning News*, September 12, 2002, from the Lexis/Nexis news archive.

12. UN Secretary-General Kofi Annan said, "There is no substitute for the unique legitimacy provided by the United Nations." And former ambassador Richard Holbrooke said, "The administration is laying the basis for military action by creating a Security Council resolution which they suspect, if not hope, Saddam can't comply with." The transcript of the *CBS Evening News*, September 12, 2002, was retrieved from the Lexis-Nexis archives.

13. The term "government's little helper" was used by Zaller and Chiu 2000.

14. Geoffrey Nunberg wrote in mid-2004 about the White House shift from using mostly "terrorism" to preferring "terror," and about an equally dramatic shift in the media the previous year. Since our research period was significantly longer, covering the 18-months after 9/11, it is entirely possible that the media followed the White House's lead strongly throughout 2003 in this respect. We, too, found strong correlations in the latter part of the period we studied.

15. According to Harris and FOX News/Opinion Dynamics surveys conducted on September 13, 2001; October 31–November 1, 2001; November 28–29, 2002; October 23–24, 2002; and February 6, 2003.

16. According to Time/CNN/Harris surveys of October 13–24, 2002, and February 6, 2003; Newsweek/PSRA polls conducted on September 26–27, 2002, and February 6–7, 2002.

17. Gallup/CNN/USA TODAY polls in August, November, and December 2002 found that 55%, 66%, and 63% of the public, respectively, thought that Iraq had WMD at the time, and 39%, 27%, and 28% believed that Iraq was trying to develop such weapons.

18. From Fox/Opinion Dynamics survey conducted on October 31, 2001– November 1, 2001.

19. ABC News/Washington Post asked the following question between November 1, 2001, and March 3, 2003, 18 times: "Would you favor or opposed having U.S. troops take military action against Iraq to force Saddam Hussein from power?" See online appendix (available at http://www.press.uchicago.edu/books/nacos/).

20. For the transcript of President Bush's address to the General Assembly of the United Nations on September 12, 2002, see http://www.whitehouse.gov/news/releases/2002/09/20020912-1.html.

21. Based on ABC News/Washington Post polls conducted on August 29, 2002, and September 12–14, 2002.

22. Ibid.

23. The poll was conducted by ABC News/Washington Post on February 5, 2003.

24. According to ABC/Washington Post surveys conducted on January 30–February 1, 2003, and February 6–9, 2003.

25. According to a Harris poll conducted on July 5–11, 2006.

26. Based on a Gallup/USA TODAY survey conducted on February 21–24, 2008.

27. According to a survey conducted for NBC and the *Wall Street Journal* by Teeter Research Companies on June 25–28, 2004.

28. From a CBS News poll of October 3–5, 2005.

29. Since most of the public opinion change seemed to occur during the later period, as the trend lines suggest, to make sure any correlations we estimated were not driven only by that, we divided the entire period in to two parts (October 2001 to August 2002 and September 2002 to May 2003) and estimated the separate correlations. The results were essentially the same.

Chapter Five

1. Clarke was the National Coordinator for Counterterrorism before and after 9/11. The quote is from Clarke 2004, 236–37.

2. From the transcript of a hearing of the National Commission on Terrorist Attacks upon the United States on April 8, 2004, available at http://govinfo.library.unt.edu/911/archive/hearing9/9–11Commission_Hearing_2004–04–08.pdf.

3. From President Bush's speech at the FBI Academy Commencement on July 11, 2005.

4. Council on Foreign Relations Task Force, "America—Still in Danger, Still Unprepared," http://www.cfr.org/publication.html?id=5099, accessed February 25, 2007.

5. Thomas H. Kean made these statements during the final press conference

of the 9/11 Commission held on December 5, 2005, in the Ronald Reagan Building in Washington, DC.

6. The White House press conference with President George W. Bush was held on December 19, 2005.

7. From Senator Susan Collins's remarks as contained in the Federal News Service transcript of the Senate Committee on Homeland Security and Governmental Affairs hearing on December 11, 2008, available at the Lexis/Nexis electronic archives.

8. Tom Ridge made these remarks in interviews with the BBC on January 14, 2005, and with Reuters on January 28, 2005.

9. National Commission on Terrorism, "Countering the Changing Threat of Terrorism," report, pursuant to Public Law 277, 105th Congress, 49.

10. Surveys conducted by the Marist College Institute for Public Opinion for the National Center for Disaster Preparedness at the Mailman School of Public Health in August 2002 and 2003, July 2004 and 2005, October 2005, and July/August 2006, asked respondents, "Overall, are you very confident, confident, not too confident, or not confident at all in government to protect the area where you live from a terrorist attack?"

11. In surveys conducted on September 7, 2003, January 18, 2004, August 29, 2004, September 8, 2004, August 10, 2004, and August 21, 2005, ABC News asked respondents, "Compared to before September 11, 2001, do you think the country today is safer from terrorism? If safer, would you say the country is much or somewhat safer?"

12. According to surveys conducted by the Marist College Institute for Public Opinion for the National Center for Disaster Preparedness at the Mailman School of Public Health in August 2002 and 2003, July 2004 and 2005, and October 2005.

13. Surveys conducted by the Marist College Institute for Public Opinion for the National Center for Disaster Preparedness at the Mailman School of Public Health in July 2005 and October 2005 asked respondents, "Overall, are you very confident, confident, not too confident, or not confident at all in the government to protect public transportation such as trains and busses from terrorist attacks?"

14. In a poll conducted by ABC News on August 21, 2005, respondents were asked, "For each situation I name, please tell me if you think the United States is or is not doing enough to try to prevent it . . . b. Car bombs or suicide bombers"; 45% answered "doing enough," 51% said "not doing enough," and 4% did not express an opinion.

15. The Marist College Institute for Public Opinion surveys asked about respondents' party identification only in July and October 2005 and in August 2006.

Chapter Six

1. National Commission on Terrorist Attacks upon the United States 2004, 323.

2. From the dust jacket of Flynn 2007.

3. http://www.nola.com/katrina/pdf/hs_katrinarpt_lieberman.pdf, accessed January 12, 2007.

4. For the Brian Williams report, see http://www.msnbc.msn.com/id/9216831/#050905, accessed July 5, 2009.

5. *NBC Nightly News*, December 8, 1997, according to the program's transcript retrieved from the Lexis/Nexis archive.

6. The data on the attitudes of different groups was taken from the previously cited surveys conducted by the Marist College Institute for Public Opinion for the National Center for Disaster Preparedness at the Mailman School of Public Health in August 2002 and 2003, July 2004 and 2005, October 2005, and August 2006.

7. For the Final Report on the 9/11 Commission Recommendations, see http://www.9–11pdp.org/press/2005–12–05_report.pdf.

8. From ABC *World News Tonight* on December 5, 2005.

9. For the press release about the Lieberman/Collins letter, see http://hsgac.senate.gov/public/index.cfm?FuseAction=PressReleases.Detail&Affiliation=C&PressRelease_id=3993a0e0-0622-4918-b06d-bd127729 fa86&Month=4&Year=2007.

10. Jamie Gorelick made these remarks during her appearance on ABC's *Good Morning America*, December 4, 2005.

Chapter Seven

1. From Edward R. Murrow's "A Report on Senator Joseph R. McCarthy" on CBS's *See It Now* program of March 9, 1954. For Murrow's full closing statement, see http://honors.umd.edu/HONR269J/archive/Murrow540309.html, accessed July 28, 2009.

2. Giuliani made this claim on ABC's *Good Morning America* on January 8, 2010.

3. Perino made the remark on the Hannity show of November 24, 2009.

4. Mary Matelin, former assistant to President George W. Bush and counselor to Vice President Cheney, also got into the act. She said during an appearance on CNN on December 27, 2009, "We inherited a recession from President Clinton and we inherited the most tragic attack on our own soil in our nation's history."

5. The volume of coverage of the pros and cons of the administration's charge

that Iraq had WMDs, had ties to Al Qaeda, and some involvement in the 9/11 attacks was actually higher than the above numbers indicate, in that we shortened the 39-month post-9/11 period for the other four issues we studied to only the 30 months that constituted the buildup before the Iraq invasion in March 2003.

6. According to Bok (1998, 4), "Crowds in many societies have watched hangings and other public executions with awe and relish. People have thrilled since the beginning of time to hearing horror stories and war epics, and to viewing combat between every kind of living being that could be induced or compelled to fight in front of spectators, from cocks to cobra, from mongooses to human beings."

7. From Anthony Lewis's speech at the conference "Weapons of Mass Destruction, National Security, and a Free Press" at the Benjamin N. Cardozo School of Law at Yeshiva University. The transcript of his remarks was published in the *Nieman Reports* 58, no. 2 (Summer 2004).

8. The full text of the "ASNE Statement of Principles" is available at http://www.asne.org/kiosk/archive/principl.htm, accessed March 26, 2009.

9. Alex Jones cited in Hunt 2009.

Postscript

1. Jim F. Harris et al., "Cheney Warns of New Attacks," *Politico*, February 4, 2009. See http://www.politico.com/news/stories/0209/18390.html, accessed March 16, 2009.

2. Ibid.

3. Former Vice President Cheney made the remarks during an interview with CNN's John King on March 15, 2009. http://www.cnn.com/2009/POLITICS/03/15/cheney.interview/index.html, accessed March 17, 2009.

4. For CNN's report on bin Laden's message of January 14, 2009, see http://www.cnn.com/2009/WORLD/meast/01/14/binladen.message/index.html?section=cnn_latest, accessed March 18, 2009.

5. See the post "Napolitano Avoids Terror Terminology" at http://www.cbsnews.com/stories/2009/02/24/national/main4826437.shtml, accessed May 2, 2010.

6. Examples of such cases were the killing of abortion provider Dr. George Tiller in Wichita, Kansas, by a violent antiabortion activist on May 31, 2009; the shooting of guard Stephen Johns at the Washington, DC, Holocaust Museum by a neo-Nazi, on June 10, 2009; and the killing of Internal Revenue Service manager Vernon Hunter by an antigovernment extremist who crashed his small plane into the Austin, Texas, IRS office on February 18, 2010, in an act of suicide terrorism.

7. For the "dithering" charge, see http://www.cbsnews.com/stories/2009/10/21/ap/preswho/main5407819.shtml, accessed May 4, 2010.

8. Jordan Fabian, "Pataki Not Satisfied with Arrest in Times Square Bomb Plot," *The Hill's Blog Briefing Room*, May 4, 2010, available at http://thehill.com/blogs/blog-briefing-room/news/95883-pataki-not-satisfied-with-arrest-in-times-square-bomb-plot, accessed May 5, 2010.

9. Glenn Thrush and Josh Gerstein, "Despite Arrest, White House on Defensive," *Politico*, available at http://www.politico.com/news/stories/0510/36842_Page3.html, May 5, 2010; accessed May 6, 2010.

10. For a more recent case, see Charlie Savage, "Court Dismisses a Case Asserting Torture by C.I.A." *New York Times*, September 8, 2010.

11. Poll data were taken from "Few See Personal Upside to Health Care Reform; Obama Image Unscathed by Terrorism Controversy," Pew Research Center for the People and the Press, January 14, 2010, available at http://www.people-press.org.

12. Ibid.

13. According to data on terrorism incidents and foiled incidents compiled by Brigitte L. Nacos.

14. Based on the data available at this writing, public approval of Obama's handling of terrorism ranged from 49% to 55% in seven Associated Press–GFK polls from January to September 2010, and approval of his handling of the "war on terror" stood at 44% in June and 48% in August 2010 in Newsweek Polls conducted by Princeton Survey Research Associates International. See http://pollingreport.com/terror.htm and http://www.ap-gfkpoll.com/pdf/AP-GfK%20Poll%20September%20Topline%20091510_1.pdf. Accessed September 24, 2010.

References

Abramowitz, Alan I. 2010. *The Disappearing Center: Engaged Citizens, Polarization, and American Democracy.* New Haven, CT: Yale University Press.

Abramowitz, Alan I., and Kyle L. Saunders. 1998. "Ideological Realignment in the U.S. Electorate." *Journal of Politics* 60:634–52.

———. 2005. "Why Can't We All Just Get Along? The Reality of Polarized American." *The Forum* 3 (June): http://www.bepress.com/forum/v013/iss2/art 1. Accessed July 23, 2005.

Alali, A. Odasuo and Kenoye Kelvin Eke, 1991. *Media Coverage of Terrorism: Methods of Diffusion.* Newbury Park, CA: Sage Publications.

Alden, Edward. 2001. "Report Warned of Attack on American Soil." *Financial Times*, September 12, 5.

Alter, Jonathan. 2001. "Time to Think about Torture." *Newsweek*, November 5.

———. 2010. *The Promise: President Obama, Year One.* New York: Simon and Schuster.

Althaus, Scott, and Devon Largio. 2004. "When Osama Became Saddam: Origins and Consequences of the Change in America's Public Enemy #1." *PS: Political Science and Politics* 37 (October): 795–99.

Anker, Elisabeth. 2005. "Villains, Victims and Heroes: Melodrama, Media, and September 11." *Journal of Communication* 55, no. 1 (March): 22–37.

Associated Press. 2009. "Huffington Post Starts Project to Investigate the Economy." *New York Times*, March 30. http://www.nytimes.com/2009/03/30/business/media/30huff.html?ref=business. Accessed March 30, 2009.

Auletta, Ken. 2010. "Non-Stop News." *New Yorker*, January 25.

Bachrach, Peter, and Morton S. Baratz. 1962. "Two Faces of Power." *American Political Science Review* 56 (December): 947–52.

———. 1963. "Decisions and Nondecisions: An Analytical Framework." *American Political Science Review* 57 (September): 632–42.

Bafumi, Joseph, and Robert Y. Shapiro. 2009. "A New Partisan Voter." *Journal of Politics* 71 (January): 1–24.

Baker, Al, and William K. Rashbaum. 2006. "U.S. Feared Cyanide Attack on New York Subway." *New York Times*, June 18, 25.

Baker, Peter. 2010. "A Renewed Debate over Suspect Rights." *New York Times*, May 4, New York Region.

Bandura, Albert. 2004. "The Role of Selective Moral Disengagement in Terrorism and Counterterrorism." In *Understanding Terrorism: Psychological Roots, Consequences and Interventions*, ed. Fathali M. Mogahaddam and Anthony J. Marsella. Washington, DC: American Psychological Association Press.

Barstow, David. 2008. "One Man's Military-Industrial-Media Complex." *New York Times*, November 29.

Baumgartner, Frank R., Suzanna L. De Boef, and Amber E. Boydstun. 2008. *The Decline of the Death Penalty and the Discovery of Innocence*. New York: Cambridge University Press.

Bennett, W. Lance. 1990. "Toward a Theory of Press-State Relations in the United States." *Journal of Communication* 40 (Spring): 103–25.

———2001. *News: The Politics of Illusion*. 4th ed. New York: Pearson Longman.

Bennett, W. Lance, Regina G. Lawrence, and Steven Livingston. 2007. *When the Press Fails: Political Power and the News Media from Iraq to Katrina*. Chicago: University of Chicago Press.

Bennett, W. Lance, and William Serrin. 2007. "The Watchdog Role of the Press." In *Media Power in Politics*, ed. Doris Graber, 326–36. Washington, DC: Congressional Quarterly Press.

Berinsky, Adam J. 2009. *In Time of War: Understanding American Public Opinion from World War II to Iraq*. Chicago: University of Chicago Press.

Bloch-Elkon, Yaeli. 2007. "The Polls—Tends: Preventing Terrorism after the 9/11 Attacks." *Public Opinion Quarterly* 71 (Spring): 142–63.

Bobbitt, Philip. 2008. *Terror and Consent: The Wars for the Twenty-First Century*. New York: Knopf.

Bobo, Lawrence, and Frederick C. Licari. 1989. "Education and Political Tolerance: Testing the Effects of Cognitive Sophistication and Target Group Affect." *Public Opinion Quarterly* 53:285–308.

Bok, Sissela. 1998. *Mayhem: Violence as Public Entertainment*. Reading, MA: Perseus Books.

Bowden, Mark. 2003. "The Dark Art of Interrogation." *Atlantic Monthly*, October.

Brody, Richard. A. 1991. *Assessing the President: The Media, Elite Opinion, and Public Support*. Stanford, CA: Stanford University Press.

———. 1994. "Crisis, War, and Public Opinion: The Media and Public Support for the President." In *Taken by Storm: The Media, Public Opinion, and U.S. Foreign Policy in the Gulf War*, ed. W. Lance Bennett and David L. Paletz, 210–30. Chicago: University of Chicago Press.

Brody, Richard A., and Catherine R. Shapiro. 1989. "A Reconsideration of the Rally Phenomenon in Public Opinion." In *Political Behavior Annual*, vol. 2, ed. Samuel Long. Boulder, CO: Westview.

Buffalo News. 2002. "A Question of Torture." December 30, B8.

Cappella, Joseph N., and Kathleen H. Jamieson. 1997. *Spiral of Cynicism: The Press and the Public Good*. New York: Oxford University Press.

Carey, James W. 1992. *Communication as Culture: Essays on Media and Society*. New York: Routledge.

———. 1998, "Political Ritual on Television: Episodes in the History of Shame, Degradation and Excommunication." In *Media, Ritual and Identity*, ed. James Curran and Tamar Liebes, 42–70. London: Routledge.

Carter, Bill, and Felicity Barringer. 2001. "At U.S. Request, Networks Agree to Edit Future bin Laden Tapes." *New York Times*, October 11.

Carsey, Thomas M., and Geoffrey C. Layman. 2006. "Changing Sides or Changing Minds? Party Identification and Policy Preferences in the American Electorate." *American Journal of Political Science* 50 (April): 464–77.

Choi, Sang Ok. 2008. "Emergency Management: Implications from a Strategic Management Perspective." *Journal of Homeland Security and Emergency Management* 5(1): 1–21.

Clarke, Richard A. 2004. *Against All Enemies: Inside America's War on Terror*. New York: Free Press.

Cohen, Jeffrey E. 2008. *The Presidency in the Era of 24-Hour News*. Princeton, NJ: Princeton University Press.

Cohen, Richard. 2001. "The Terrorism Story—and How We Blew It." *Washington Post*, October 4, A31.

Cole, David. 2008. "The Brits Do It Better." *New York Review of Books*, June 12, 68–71.

Cole, David, and James X. Dempsey. 2006. *Terrorism and the Constitution: Sacrificing Civil Liberties in the Name of National Security*. New York: New Press.

Crenshaw, Martha. 1986. "The Psychology of Political Terrorism." In *Political Psychology: Contemporary Problems and Issues*, ed. Margaret G. Hermann. London: Josey-Bass.

———. 2006. "The American Debate over 'New' vs. 'Old' Terrorism." Unpublished paper, Stanford University.

Davis, Darren W. 2007. *Negative Liberty: Public Opinion and the Terrorist Attacks on America*. New York: Russell Sage Foundation.

Davis, Darren W., and Brian D. Silver. 2004. "Civil Liberties vs. Security in the Context of Terrorist Attacks on America." *American Journal of Political Science* 48(1):28–46.

Davis, James A. 1975. "Communism, Conformity, Cohorts, and Categories: American Tolerance in 1954 and 1972–73." *American Journal of Sociology* 81:491–513.

Dayan, Daniel, and Elihu Katz. 1992. *Media Events: The Live Broadcasting of History*. Cambridge, MA: Harvard University Press.

Deese, David. A. 1994. "Making American Foreign Policy in the 1990s." In *The New Politics of American Foreign Policy*, ed. David A. Deese. New York: St. Martin's Press.

de la Garza, Rodolfo O., Angelo Falcon, and F. Chris Garcia. 1996. "Will the Real Americans Please Stand Up: Anglo and Mexican-American Support of Core American Political Values." *American Journal of Political Science* 40(2):335–51.

Downie, Leonard, Jr., and Michael Schudson. 2009. "The Reconstruction of American Journalism." *Columbia Journalism Review*, October 19. http://www.cjr.org/reconstruction/the_reconstruction_of_american.php. Accessed May 22, 2010.

Dworkin, Ronald. 2003. "Terror and the Attack on Civil Liberties." *New York Review of Books*, November 6.

Edwards, George C. 1990. *Presidential Approval: A Sourcebook*. Baltimore: Johns Hopkins University Press.

Entman, Robert M. 2000. "Declaration of Independence: The Growth of Media Power after the Cold War." In *Decisionmaking in a Glass House: Mass Media, Public Opinion, and American and European Foreign Policy in the 21st Century*, ed. Brigitte L. Nacos, Robert Y. Shapiro, and Pierangelo Isernia, 11–26. Lanham, MD: Rowman and Littlefield.

———. 2003, "Cascading Activation: Contesting the White House's Frame After 9/11." *Political Communication* 20 (October–December): 415–32.

———. 2004. *Projections of Power: Framing News, Public Opinion, and U.S. Foreign Policy*. Chicago: University of Chicago Press.

Erikson, Robert S., Michael B. MacKuen, and James A. Stimson. 2002. *The Macro Polity*. New York: Cambridge University Press.

Erikson, Robert S., and Kent L. Tedin. 2001. *American Public Opinion: Its Origins, Content, and Impact*. 6th ed. Boston: Allyn and Bacon.

———. 2005. *American Public Opinion: Its Origins, Content, and Impact*. 7th ed. New York: Pearson Longman.

Farnsworth, Stephen J., and S. Robert Lichter. 2007. *The Nightly News Nightmare: Television Coverage of U.S. Presidential Elections, 1988–2004*. Lanham, MD: Rowman and Littlefield.

Fiorina, Morris P., with Samuel J. Abrams and Jeremy C. Pope. 2006. *Culture Wars? The Myth of Polarized America*. 2nd ed. New York: Pearson Longman.

Flynn, Stephen. 2007. *The Edge of Disaster*. New York: Random House.

Foyle, Douglas C. 2004. "Leading the Public to War? The Influence of American Public Opinion on the Bush Administration's Decision to Go to War in Iraq." *International Journal of Public Opinion Research* 16(3):269–94.

Friedman, Benjamin H., Jim Harper, and Christopher A. Preble, eds. 2010. *Terrorizing Ourselves: Why U.S. Counterterrorism Policy Is Failing and How to Fix It*. Washington, DC: Cato Institute.

Gadarian, Shana Kushner. 2010. "The Politics of Threat: How Terrorism News Shapes Foreign Policy Attitudes." *Journal of Politics* 72 (April):469–83.

Gans, Herbert J. 1979. *Deciding What's News*. New York: Random House.

Gershkoff, Amy, and Shana Kushner. 2005. "Shaping Public Opinion: The 9/11-Iraq Connection in the Bush Administration's Rhetoric." *Perspectives on Politics* 3 (September): 525–37.

Graber, Doris A. 1997. *Mass Media and American Politics*. Washington, DC: Congressional Quarterly Press.

Green, Joshua. 2001. "Weapons of Mass Confusion: How Pork Trumps Preparedness in the Fight against Terrorism." *Washington Monthly*, May, 15–21.

Grimm, Juergen. 2009. "Culture of Fear: Media Logic and Its Impact on a Loss of Aggression Control." Unpublished paper, University of Vienna.

Hall, Mimi. 2006. "Ridge Reveals Clashes on Alerts." *USA Today*, May 10, 2005. http://www.usatoday.com/news/washington/2005–05–10-ridge-alerts_x.htm?POE=NEWISVA. Accessed March 10.

Hallin, Daniel C. 1992. "Sound-Bite News: Television Coverage of Elections, 1968–1988." *Journal of Communications* 42(2):5–24.

Hamilton, James T. 2004. *All the News That's Fit to Sell: How the Market Transforms Information into News*. Princeton, NJ: Princeton University Press.

Hayes, Danny, and Matt Guardino. 2010. "Whose Views Made the News? Media Coverage and the March to War in Iraq." *Political Communication* 27 (January–March): 59–87.

Healy, Andrew, and Neil Malhotra. 2009. "Myopic Voters and Natural Disaster Policy." *American Political Science Review* 103 (August): 387–406.

Herman, Edward S. 1993. "The Media's Role in U.S. Foreign Policy." *Journal of International Affairs* 47(1):23–45.

Herman, Edward S., and Noam Chomsky. 2002. *Manufacturing Consent: The Political Economy of the Mass Media*. New York: Pantheon.

Herman, Edward, and Gerry O'Sullivan. 1989. *The "Terrorism" Industry: The Experts and Institutions That Shape Our View of Terror*. New York: Pantheon.

Heatherington, Marc J. 2001. "Resurgent Mass Partisanship: The Role of Elite Polarization." *American Political Science Review* 95 (September): 619–31.

Heatherington, Marc J., and Michael Nelson. 2003. "Anatomy of a Rally Effect: George W. Bush and the War on Terrorism." *PS: Political Science and Politics* 36 (January): 37–42.

Heatherington, Marc J., and Jonathan D. Weiler. 2009. *Authoritarianism & Polarization in American Politics*. New York: Cambridge University Press.

Hillygus, D. Sunshine, and Todd G. Shields. 2005. "Moral Issues and Voter Decision Making in the 2004 Presidential Election." *PS: Political Science and Politics* 38 (April): 201–9.

Hinckley, Ronald H. 1992. *People, Polls, and Policy Makers: American Public Opinion and National Security*. New York: Lexington.

Holsti, Ole R. 2004. *Public Opinion and American Foreign Policy*. Rev. ed. Ann Arbor: University of Michigan Press.

Holzer, Henry Mark. 2003. "Terrorism Interrogations and Torture." *Milwaukee Journal Sentinel*, March 16.

Hoskin, Andrew, and Ben O'Loughlin. 2007. *Television and Terror: Conflicting Times and the Crisis of News Discourse*. Houndsmills, Hampshire: Palgrave MacMillan.

Huddy, Leonie, Stanley Feldman, Gallya Lahav, and Charles Taber. 2003. "Fear and Terrorism: Psychological Reactions to 9/11." In *Framing Terrorism: The News Media, the Government, and the Public*, ed. Pippa Norris, Montague Kern, and Marion Just, 255–78. New York: Routledge.

Huddy, Leonie, Stanley Feldman, Charles Taber, and Gallya Lahav. 2005. "Threat, Anxiety, and Support of Antiterrorism Politics." *American Journal of Political Science* 49, no. 3 (July): 593–608.

Hugick, Larry, and Alec M. Gallup. 1991. "Rally Events and Presidential Approval." *Gallup Poll Monthly*, June.

Hunt, Albert R. 2009. "Nothing Creative about Newspapers' Destruction." *Bloomberg Wire*, March 23.

Huntington, Samuel P. 1997. "The Erosion of American National Interest." *Foreign Affairs* 76 (5).

Ignatieff, Michael. 2004. "Lesser Evils." *New York Times Magazine*, May 2.

Iyengar, Shanto, and Donald R. Kinder. 1987. *News That Matters*. Chicago: University of Chicago Press.

Jacobs, Lawrence R., and Robert Y. Shapiro. 2000. *Politicians Don't Pander: Political Manipulation and the Loss of Democratic Responsiveness*. Chicago: University of Chicago Press.

Jacobson, Gary C. 2008. *A Divider, Not a Uniter: George W. Bush and the American People*. New York: Pearson/Longman.

———. 2010. "Perception, Memory, and Partisan Polarization on the Iraq War." *Political Science Quarterly* 125 (Spring): 31–56.

———. 2011. *A Divider, Not a Uniter: George W. Bush and the American People*. 2nd ed. New York: Pearson/Longman.

Jamieson, Kathleen H. 1992. *Dirty Politics*. New York: Oxford University Press.

Jamieson, Kathleen Hall, Bruce W. Hardy, and Daniel Romer. 2007. "The Effectiveness of the Press in Serving the Needs of American Democracy." In *A Republic Divided*, ed. Annenberg Democracy Project. New York: Oxford Press.

Jervis, Robert. 2010. *Why Intelligence Fails: Lessons from the Iranian Revolu-tion and the Iraq War.* Ithaca, NY: Cornell University Press.

Katz, Elihu, and Tamar Liebes. 2007. "'No More Peace!': How Disaster, Terror and War Have Upstaged Media Events." *International Journal of Communi-cation* 1:157–66.

Kean, Thomas H., and Lee H. Hamilton. 2005. "Sept. 11th Unfinished Busi-ness." *Mercury News*, September 11.

Kellner, Douglas. 2005. *Media Spectacle and the Crisis of Democracy.* Boulder, CO: Paradigm Publishers.

———. 2006. "September 11, Social Theory, and Democratic Politics." In *Media, Terrorism, and Theory*, ed. Anandam P. Kavoori and Tood Fraley. Lanham, MD: Rowman and Littlefield.

Kern, Montague. 1981. "The Invasion of Afghanistan: Domestic vs. Foreign Stories. In *Television Coverage of the Middle East*, ed. William C. Adams, 106–27. Norwood, NJ: Ablex Publishing.

Kern, Montague, Marion Just, and Pippa Norris. 2003. "The Lessons of Framing Terrorism." In *Framing Terrorism: The News Media, the Government, and the Public*, ed. Pippa Norris, Montague Kern, and Marion Just, 281–302. New York: Routledge.

Kernell, Samuel. 2007. *Going Public: New Strategies of Presidential Leadership, Fourth Edition.* Washington, DC: Congressional Quarterly Press.

Kinder, Donald R., and D. Roderick Kiewiet. 1979. "Economic Discontent and Political Behavior: The Role of Personal Grievances and Collective Eco-nomic Judgments in Congressional Voting." *American Journal of Political Science* 23:495–527.

Koppel, John S. 2001. "To the Editor." *New York Times*, September 12, 26.

Krebs, Ronald R., and Jennifer Lobasz. 2007. "Fixing the Meaning of 9/11: He-gemony, Coercion, and the Road to War in Iraq." *Security Studies* 16 (July–September): 409–51.

Kull, Steven, Clay Ramsay, and Evan Lewis. 2003–4. "Misperceptions, the Me-dia, and the Iraq War." *Political Science Quarterly* 118 (Winter): 569–98.

Kurtz, Howard. 2004. "The Post on WMDs: An Inside Story." *Washington Post*, August 12, A1.

Kushner, Shana A. 2005. "Threat, Media, and Foreign Policy Opinion." Paper prepared for the Annual Meeting of the Midwest Political Science Associa-tion, Chicago, April 7–10.

Langer, Gary, and Jon Cohen. 2005. "Voters and Values in the 2004 Election." *Public Opinion Quarterly* 69:744–59.

Laqueur, Walter. 2003. *No End to War: Terrorism in the Twenty-First Century.* New York: Continuum.

Lawrence, Bruce, ed. 2005. *Messages to the World: The Statements of Osama bin Laden.* London and New York: Verso.

Layman Geoffrey C., Thomas M. Carsey, and Juliana Menasce Horowitz. 2006. "Party Polarization in American Politics: Characteristics, Causes, and Consequences." *Annual Review of Political Science* 9:83–110.

Lerner, Jennifer S., Roxana M. Gonzales, Deborrah A. Small, and Baruch Fischoff. 2003. "Effects of Fear and Anger on Perceived Risks of Terrorism: A National Field Experiment." *Psychological Science* 14 (March): 144–50.

Levendusky, Matthew. 2009. *The Partisan Sort: How Liberals Became Democrats and Conservatives Republicans.* Chicago: University of Chicago Press.

Lewis, Anthony. 2001. "Abroad at Home; a Different World. *New York Times*, September 12, 27.

Lippmann, Walter. 1997 [1922]. *Public Opinion.* New York: Free Press.

Lustick, Ian S. 2006. *Trapped in the War on Terror.* Philadelphia: University of Pennsylvania Press.

Martin, David V., and John Walcott. 1988. *Best Laid Plans: The Inside Story of America's War against Terrorism.* New York: Harper and Row.

Martin, James. 2002. "The Year in TV." *America*, June 17.

Massing, Michael. 2004. *Now They Tell Us.* New York: New York Review of Books.

Mayer, Jane. 2008. *The Dark Side: The Inside Story Of How the War on Terror Turned into a War on American Ideals.* New York: Doubleday.

McClellan, Scott. 2008. *What Happened: Inside the Bush White House and Washington's Culture of Deception.* New York: Public Affairs.

Mermin, Jonathan. 1999. *Debating War and Piece: Media Coverage of U.S. Intervention in the Post-Vietnam Era.* Princeton, NJ: Princeton University Press.

Merolla, Jennifer L., and Elizabeth J. Zechmeister. 2009. *Democracy at Risk: How Terrorist Threats Affect the Public.* Chicago: University of Chicago Press.

Merskin, Debra. 2005. "Making Enemies in George W. Bush's Post-9/11 Speeches." *Peace Review* 17(4):373–81.

Milbank, Dana. 2001. "On Fortress Capitol Hill, United Roars of Approval." *Washington Post*, September 21, sect. A, 22.

Miller, Abraham H. 1980. *Terrorism and Hostage Negotiations.* Boulder, CO: Westview.

———. 1982. *Terrorism, the Media and the Law.* Dobbs Ferry, NY: Transnational.

Mills, C. Wright. 2000 [1956]. *The Power Elite.* New York: Oxford University Press.

Moore, David W. 2008. *The Opinion Makers: An Insider Exposes the Truth behind the Polls.* Boston: Beacon Press.

Mueller, John E. 1985 [1973]. *War, Presidents and Public Opinion.* Lanham: University Press of America. .

———. 1988. "Trends in Political Tolerance." *Public Opinion Quarterly* 52:1–25.

———. 2006. *Overblown: How Politicians and the Terrorism Industry Inflate National Security Threats and Why We Believe Them*. New York: Free Press.

Nacos, Brigitte L. 1990. *The Press, Presidents and Crises*. New York: Columbia University Press.

———. 1996. *Terrorism and the Media: From the Iran Hostage Crisis to the Oklahoma City Bombing*. New York: Columbia University Press.

———. 2002. *Mass-Mediated Terrorism: The Central Role of the Media in Terrorism and Counterterrorism*. Lanham, MD: Rowman and Littlefield.

———. 2006. *Terrorism and Counterterrorism: Understanding Threats and Responses in the Post-9/11 World*. New York: Longman.

———. 2007a. *Mass Mediated Terrorism*. 2nd ed. Lanham, MD.

———.2007b. "The 'New' Terrorism: Result of Changes in the Global Environment." Paper presented at the Annual Meeting of the American Political Science Association, Chicago, August 31–September 3.

National Commission on Terrorist Attacks upon the United States. 2004. *The 9/11 Commission Report*. New York: Norton.

National Geographic Society. 2001, "Inside 9/11." Available at http://channel.nationalgeographic.com/series/inside-911#tab-Interactive.

Neuman, Russell W., Marion Just, and Ann N. Crigler. 1992. *Common Knowledge: News and the Construction of Political Meaning*. Chicago: University of Chicago Press.

Nisbet, Eric C., and James Shanahan. 2004. "Restrictions on Civil Liberties, Views of Islam and Muslim Americans." Media and Society Group, Cornell University, December.

Nolan, Martin F. 2005. "Orwell Meets Nixon: When and Why 'the Press' Became 'the Media.'" *Press/Politics* 10(2):69–84.

Norris, Pippa, Montague Kern, and Marion Just. 2003. *Framing Terrorism: The News Media, the Government, and the Public*. New York: Routledge.

Nunberg, Geoffrey. 2004. "How Much Can a Simple Word Pack?" *New York Times*, July 11.

Omaha World-Herald. 2000. "Secure, Yes, but Also Free," June 12, 6.

Page, Benjamin I., and Robert Y. Shapiro. 1984. "Presidents as Opinion Leaders: Some New Evidence." *Policy Studies Journal* 12 (June): 649–61.

———. 1992. *The Rational Public: Fifty Years of Trends in Americans' Policy Preferences*. Chicago: University of Chicago Press.

Page, Benjamin I., Robert Y. Shapiro, and Glenn R. Dempsey. 1987. "What Moves Public Opinion?" *American Political Science Review* 81:23–43.

Paletz, David L., and Alex P. Schmid. 1992. *Terrorism and the Media*. Newbury Park, CA: Sage Publications.

Parenti, Michael. 1986. *Inventing Reality: The Politics of the Mass Media*. New York: St. Martin's.

Patterson, Thomas E. 1994. *Out of Order.* New York: Knopf.

Paumgarten, Nick. 2010. "Fallout." *New Yorker,* May 10. Available at http://www.newyorker.com/talk/2010/05/10/100510ta_talk_paumgarten?printable=true#ixzz0nlCaf5eN. Accessed September 11, 2010.

Pew Project for Excellence in Journalism. 2009. *The State of the News Media: An Annual Report on American Journalism.* Washington, DC: Pew Project for Excellence in Journalism.

Pious, Richard M. 2006. *The War on Terrorism.* Los Angeles: Roxbury Publishing.

Pratkanis, Anthony, and Elliott Aronson. 1991. *Age of Propaganda: Everyday Use and Abuse of Persuasion.* New York: W. H. Freeman.

Priest, Dana, and Barton Gelman. 2001. "US Decries Abuse but Defends Interrogations." *Washington Post,* December 26.

Redlener, Irwin, and David A. Berman. 2006. "National Preparedness Planning: The Historical Context and Current State of the US Public's Readiness, 1940–2005." *Journal of International Affairs* 59(2):87–103.

Ridge, Tom. 2009. *The Test of Our Times.* New York: St. Martin's Press.

Roberts-Miller, Patricia. 2005. "Democracy, Demagoguery, and Critical Rhetoric." *Rhetoric and Public Affairs* 8(3):459–76.

Rose, Richard. 2000. *The Post Modern President.* Chatham, NJ: Chatham House.

Schattschneider, E. E. 1960. *The Semi-Sovereign People.* Hinsdale, IL: Dryden Press.

Schell, Orville. 2004. "Preface." In *Now They Tell Us,* ed. Michael Massing. New York: New York Review of Books.

Schlagheck, Donna M. 1988. *International Terrorism.* New York: Lexington Books.

Schneider, William. 1994. "Introduction: From Foreign Policy to Politics as Usual." In *The New Politics of American Foreign Policy,* ed. David A. Deese. New York: St. Martin's Press.

Schmid, Alex, and Janny de Graaf. 1982. *Violence and Communication: Insurgent Terrorism and the Western News Media.* London: Sage.

Schudson, Michael. 2007. "Why Democracies Need an Unlovable Press." In *Media Power in Politics,* ed. Doris Graber, 36–47. Washington, DC: Congressional Quarterly Press.

Shapiro, Robert Y., and Yaeli Bloch-Elkon. 2005. "Partisan Conflict, Public Opinion, and U.S. Foreign Policy." Paper presented at the Inequality and Social Policy Seminar, John F. Kennedy School of Government, Harvard University, Cambridge, MA, December 12.

———. 2006. "Political Polarization and the Rational Public." Paper presented at the Annual Conference of the American Association for Public Opinion Research, Montreal, May 18–21.

———. 2007. "Ideological Partisanship and American Public Opinion towards Foreign Policy." In *Power and Superpower: Global Leadership and Exceptionalism in the 21st Century*, ed. Morton H. Halperin et al., 49–68. New York: Century Foundation Press.

———. 2008a. "Foreign Policy, Meet the People." *National Interest* 97 (September/October): 37–42.

———. 2008b. "Do the Facts Speak for Themselves? Partisan Disagreement as a Challenge to Democratic Competence." *Critical Review* 20 (1–2): 115–39.

Shapiro, Robert Y., and Lawrence R. Jacobs. 2000. "Who Leads and Who Follows? U.S. Presidents, Public Opinion, and Foreign Policy. In *Decisionmaking in a Glass House: Mass Media, Public Opinion and American and European Foreign Policy in the 21st Century*, ed. Brigitte L. Nacos, Robert Y. Shapiro, and Pierangelo Isernia, 223–45. Lanham, MD: Rowman and Littlefield.

Shapiro, Robert Y., and Harpreet Mahajan. 1986. "Gender Differences in Policy Preferences: A Summary of Trends from the 1960s to the 1980s." *Public Opinion Quarterly* 50 (Spring): 42–61.

Shenk, David. 1997. *Data Smog: Surviving the Information Glut*. New York: HarperCollins.

Sheppard, Ben. 2009. *The Psychology of Strategic Terrorism: Public and Government Responses to Attack*. London: Routledge.

Simon, Steven, and Daniel Benjamin. 2001. "The Terror." *Survival* 43, no. 4 (Winter): 5–18.

Snyder, Jack, Robert Y. Shapiro, and Yaeli Bloch-Elkon. 2009. "Free Hand Abroad, Divide and Rule at Home." *World Politics* 61 (January): 155–87.

Spencer, Alexander. "Questioning the Concept of 'New Terrorism.'" *Peace, Conflict and Development 8* (January 2006). Available at: http://www.peacestudiesjournal.org.uk/docs/Feb%2006%20SPENCER.pdf. Accessed December 12, 2006.

Starr, Paul. 2004. *The Creation of the Media: Political Origins of Modern Communications*. New York: Basic Books.

Steele, Catherine, and Kevin Barnhurst. 1996. "The Journalism of Opinion: Network News Coverage of U.S. Presidential Campaigns, 1868–88." *Critical Studies in Mass Communication* 13 (September): 187–209.

Stouffer, Samuel A. 1955. *Communism, Conformity, and Civil Liberties*. New York: Doubleday.

Stroembaeck, Jesper. 2008. "Four Phases of Mediatization: An Analysis of the Mediatization of Politics." *Press/Politics* 13(3):228–46.

Sullivan, John L., James E. Pierson, and George E. Marcus. 1982. *Political Tolerance and American Democracy*. Chicago: University of Chicago Press.

Taylor, Jr., Stuart. 2003. "Is It Ever Right to Torture Suspected Terrorists?" *National Journal*, March 8.

Weimann, Gabriel. 1987. "Media Events: The Case of International Terrorism."
    Journal of Broadcasting and Electronic Media 31, no. 1 (Winter): 21–39.
Washington Post. 2002. "Torture Is Not an Option." December 27, A24.
Weimann, Gabriel, and Conrad Winn. 1994. *The Theater of Terror: Mass Media
    and International Terrorism*. New York: Longman.
Western, Jon, 2005. *Selling Intervention and War: The Presidency, the Media,
    and the American Public*. Baltimore, MD: Johns Hopkins University Press.
White, Theodore H. 1973. *The Making of the President 1972*. New York: Ban-
    tam Books.
Wilkinson, Paul. 2001. *Terrorism versus Democracy*. London: Frank Cass.
Willer, Robb. 2004. "The Effects of Government-Issued Terror Warnings on
    Presidential Approval Ratings. *Current Research in Social Psychology*
    10(1):1–12.
Woodward, Bob. 2002. *Bush at War*. New York: Simon and Schuster.
———. 2004. *Plan of Attack*. New York: Simon and Schuster.
Wright, Robin. 2007. "From the Desk of Donald Rumsfeld . . ." *Washington
    Post*, November 1.
Zaller, John R. 1992. *The Nature and Origins of Mass Opinion*. New York: Cam-
    bridge University Press.
———. 1998. "Monica Lewinsky's Contribution to Political Science." *PS: Politi-
    cal Science and Politics* 31(2):182–89.
Zaller, John, and Dennis Chiu. 2000. "Government's Little Helper: U.S. Press
    Coverage of Foreign Policy Crises." In *Decisionmaking in a Glass House*,
    ed. Brigitte L. Nacos, Robert Y. Shapiro, and Pierangelo Isernia, 61–84. Lan-
    ham, MD: Rowman and Littlefield.

Index

ABC News, 20; and Bush's speech to Congress after 9/11, 29; and the Christmas Day bomber, 182; and civil liberties, 4–5, 67, 70–71, 72; and emergency preparedness, 157, 162, 163, 180; and Hurricane Katrina, 143, 148, 160, 166, 168; and the Iraq War, 94, 98, 101, 107, 109, 113; and 9/11, 1, 3, 96, 185; and prevention of terrorism, 132, 133; self-censorship of, 33; and threat of terrorism, 36, 38–39, 163; and war on terror, 111–12
Abdulmutallab, Umar Farouk, 203
Abu Ghraib, 62, 66, 75, 198
Afghanistan: detainees from, 75, 196–97; media attention on, 123; military action against, 3–4, 5, 16, 93–94, 108, 203; and 9/11, 3–4, 93–94, 113, 185; support for bin Laden in, 2, 3–4, 97
age, public opinion by, 23–24; on civil liberties vs. national security, 82; on the Iraq War, 118–19; on the threat of terrorism, 46
Ajami, Fouad, 96
Alden, Edward, 130
alerts, threat. *See* threat alerts
Alien and Sedition Acts 1798, 63, 68
Al Jazeera, 14, 34
Allard, Ken, 125
Alluni, Taysir, 63
Al Qaeda: alleged links with Iraq, 2, 94, 98, 105, 106, 107, 108, 112–16, 145, 192; tapes of, 14, 33–34, 37, 40; and threat of terrorism, 25, 53–54, 56, 58, 186, 191; U.S. retribution against, 3–4; use of media coverage, 14. *See also* bin Laden, Osama

Alter, Jonathan, 61, 205
American Civil Liberties Union, 73, 74
American Society of Newspaper Editors: Statement of Principles, 10, 197
Anker, Elisabeth, 16, 185
Annan, Kofi, 104, 105, 106, 215n12
anthrax, 113, 160–61, 169
approval ratings, presidential. *See* presidential approval ratings
Aronson, Elliot, 35, 196
Ashcroft, John, 30, 31, 51, 66–67, 70, 71, 72, 73
Atlantic Monthly, 61
Auletta, Ken, 20
Aum Shinrikyo, 13

Bachmann, Michele, 205
Baker, Al, 155
Baker, James, 8
Bandura, Albert, 31
Barringer, Felicity, 33
Barstow, David, 104
Bennett, W. Lance, 12, 67, 97, 99, 124, 150, 154, 156, 187
Berinsky, Adam J., 80
Berman, David A., 152
Berra, Yogi, 202
Biden, Joe, 4–5
bin Laden, Osama: alleged links with Iraq, 4, 94, 105, 106, 107, 108, 145; Bush on, 109–12; Cheney on, 109–12; on civil liberties, 25, 63; and the news media, 15–16, 33, 42, 109–11, 184–85, 188; and 9/11, 3–4, 15–16; tapes of, 14, 33–34, 37, 40, 56, 202; and threat of terrorism, 34,

bin Laden, Osama (*continued*)
   35, 36–37, 53–54, 184, 191, 195; and war
   on terror, 108–11. *See also* Al Qaeda
bipartisanship, 6, 8
Blitzer, Wolf, 31–32
blogosphere, 20, 27, 198, 199–200
Bobbitt, Phillip, 65
Bok, Sisela, 191, 219n6
Boren, David, 4, 95
Bowden, Mark, 61
BP oil spill, 208
Brody, Richard, 7, 18
Brokaw, Tom, 2–3, 8, 29, 39, 71–72, 157,
   161–62
Brown, Michael, 154
Buchanan, Patrick, 11
Buffalo News, 62
Bush, George H. W., 93
Bush, George W.: and Afghanistan, 93; approval ratings, 7–8, 18, 49, 50, 54–55,
   56, 57, 58, 121–22, 140–41, 147, 171–
   72, 177–78, 198; on bin Laden, 109–12;
   and CIA intelligence assessment before 9/11, 125–26; and civil liberties,
   25, 63–64, 71, 73, 76, 89, 185; election
   victory aided by bin Laden, 56; and
   emergency preparedness, 163, 164–65,
   171–72, 177–78, 180, 185–86; and Hurricane Katrina, 166, 167, 171–72, 187;
   on Iraq's weapons of mass destruction, 107, 113–14; and the Iraq War, 25,
   103, 104–5; on links between Iraq and
   9/11, 108; on links between Iraq and Al
   Qaeda, 108; and 9/11, 2, 6, 7, 15–16, 28,
   29, 108, 182, 203; and prevention of terrorism, 126, 127, 136–37, 140–41, 144,
   147, 149, 185–86; on Saddam Hussein,
   109–12; and shoe bombing attempt,
   203–4; speech to Congress after 9/11,
   29; speech to United Nations General
   Assembly, 105–6, 113–14; and threat of
   terrorism, 29, 31, 41, 50–51, 188, 191,
   201–2; on Tom Ridge, 30; and USA PA-
   TRIOT Act, 63–64, 71, 73; on war on
   terror, 110–12

Cannistraro, Vince, 5
Cantor, Eric, 205
Card, Andrew, 102
Carey, James W., 15
Carter, Bill, 33

CBS News, 20; and anthrax scare, 160–61;
   and Bush's speech to Congress after
   9/11, 29; and civil liberties, 67, 71, 72;
   and emergency preparedness, 157, 160–
   61, 163; and Hurricane Katrina, 143,
   168; and the Iraq War, 98, 101, 104–6,
   107; and 9/11, 3, 94–95, 185; and prevention of terrorism, 132, 133, 134; self-
   censorship of, 33; and threat of terrorism, 36, 37–38, 39, 163
censorship: self-censorship of television
   networks, 33–34
Central Intelligence Agency (CIA),
   125–26, 196–97
Cheney, Richard: criticism of Obama,
   201–2, 203, 206; on Iraq's weapons of
   mass destruction, 103, 107; on links between Iraq and Al Qaeda, 108; and prevention of terrorism, 126; on Saddam
   Hussein, 96, 109–12; and threat of terrorism, 28, 201–2, 206; on war on terror, 110–12
Chertoff, Michael, 180
Chicago Tribune, 66
Choi, Sang Ok, 152
Chomsky, Noam, 12
Christmas Day bombing attempt, 182,
   203–4, 207
CIA (Central Intelligence Agency),
   125–26, 196–97
civil liberties vs. national security, 2, 19, 20,
   60–92; and counterterrorism measures,
   25, 63–66; domestic eavesdropping, 74,
   86, 87, 89, 185, 194, 202, 203; extraordinary rendition, 196–97, 202, 203, 206;
   and fear, 67–68, 194–95; methodology
   for collection of data, 20–21, 69–70;
   Miranda rights, 204–5, 206, 207; news
   coverage of, 4–5, 5, 25, 60–62, 66–67,
   70–76, 85–90, 91–92, 185, 186–87, 188,
   189, 194–95; and Obama, 201–3, 206,
   207; personal records, 74, 88–89; public opinion on, 67–69, 76–90, 189,
   190, 193–95, 213n9; torture, 61–62,
   75, 197, 201, 202, 206; in the United
   Kingdom, 65
Claiborne, Ron, 133
Clarke, Richard A., 93, 125
Clayson, Jane, 38
Clinton, Bill, 18, 93, 94, 182, 203
CNN, 4, 6, 31–32, 33, 61, 67, 157

Cohen, Richard, 130
Colbert Report, The, 198
Cold War, 26, 56–57, 68, 97, 110
Cole, David, 64, 65, 77, 193
Collins, Susan, 127, 180
communication, transmission vs. ritual,
   15–16
counterterrorism: and media politics, 182–
   89, 191–93, 196–98; military force, 3,
   65; Obama's policies, 20, 27, 201–8;
   public opinion of, 19, 189–90; use of
   fear to justify, 34–36, 183, 196–97, 201–
   2; use of threat of terrorism to justify,
   14, 30–31, 34, 56, 58–59, 150, 183, 186,
   196–97, 201–2. *See also* Afghanistan;
   Iraq War; prevention of terrorism; war
   on terror
Crenshaw, Martha, 35
Crigler, Ann N., 17

Daily Show, The, 198
Daschle, Tom, 6
Davis, Darren W., 45, 46, 68, 142
Dayan, Daniel, 15
de Graaf, Janny, 14
demagoguery, 16, 185
Democracy at Risk (Merolla and Zech-
   meister), 42
Dempsey, James X., 64, 65
Department of Homeland Security (DHS),
   30, 126, 163, 179, 180, 187, 211n1 (ch. 2)
detainees, 61–62, 75, 76, 78, 194, 196–97
disaster preparedness. *See* emergency
   preparedness
domestic eavesdropping, 74, 86, 87, 89, 185,
   194, 202, 203
Donaldson, Sam, 29
Douglass, Linda, 4–5
Downie, Leonard, Jr., 100, 200
Dworkin, Ronald, 76–77

eavesdropping, domestic. *See* domestic
   eavesdropping
education, public opinion by, 23–24; on
   civil liberties vs. national security,
   83–85, 190; on the Iraq War, 119; on the
   threat of terrorism, 46
emergency preparedness, 20–21, 152–81,
   208–9; effect of Iraq War on, 159,
   167–69; methodology for collection
   of data, 20–21, 158–60; and the news

media, 5, 26, 154–56, 157–69, 176–81,
   185–89, 195; before 9/11, 156–58; public
   opinion of, 159, 160, 169–78, 189, 190;
   relief vs. preparedness, 153–54
enemy combatants. *See* unlawful
   combatants
Entman, Robert, 10, 18–19, 26
Erikson, Robert S., 23–24, 189
Espionage Act 1917, 63
evil, use of the word in the news, 16, 185
extraordinary rendition, 196–97, 202, 203,
   206

Fairness and Accuracy in Reporting
   (FAIR), 98–99, 100
Farnsworth, Stephen, 22
FBI (Federal Bureau of Investigation),
   125–26
fear: after 9/11, 10–11, 28–29, 34–35, 43–44,
   63, 192–93, 201–2; and civil liberties re-
   striction, 67–68, 194–95; personal vs.
   national risk, 192; use of by terrorists,
   34–36, 63, 90, 188, 195, 196; use of to
   justify counterterrorism, 34–36, 150,
   183, 196–97, 201–2. *See also* threat of
   terrorism
Federal Bureau of Investigation (FBI),
   125–26
Federal Emergency Management Agency
   (FEMA), 163, 179, 187
Fleischer, Ari, 98
Flynn, Stephen, 127, 150, 152, 155
Ford, Gerald, 7
Fort Hood shooting, 182
Fournier, Ron, 28
Fox, Jim, 94
Fox News, 16, 33, 62, 96, 112, 182
Friedman, Benjamin H., 208

Gadahn, Adam, 30
Gans, Herbert J., 91
Gelman, Barton, 197
gender, public opinion by, 23–24; on civil
   liberties vs. national security, 82–83,
   190; on emergency preparedness,
   172–73, 174–76, 190; on the Iraq War,
   117–18, 190; on prevention of terrorism, 141, 190; on the threat of terrorism, 45, 190
Giuliani, Rudy, 157, 182
Goodwin, Doris Kern, 6

Gorelick, Jamie, 180–81
Graber, Doris, 156
Green, Joshua, 157
Gregory, David, 161–62
Grimm, Juergen, 192
Guantanamo detention facilities, 202, 207
Gulf War (first), 93

Hagel, Chuck, 5
Haig, Alexander, 96
Hamburg, Margaret, 162
Hamilton, James T., 9–10
Hamilton, Lee H., 153, 180
Hannity, Sean, 182
Harper, Jim, 208
Harris polls, 112
Healy, Andrew, 153, 166, 181
Herman, Edward, 12–13
Hinckley, Ronald, 42
Holbrooke, Richard, 106, 215n12
Holder, Eric, 206
Holtermann, Keith, 161
Holzer, Henry Mark, 62
homeland security. See Department of
   Homeland Security (DHS); emergency
   preparedness; prevention of terrorism
Hoskin, Andrew, 11
Huddy, Leonie, 45, 192
Huffington, Arianna, 200
Huffington Post, 199, 200
Hughes, Pat, 30
Hunt, Albert, 198–200
Hunter, Vernon, 219n6
Hurricane Katrina, 26, 132, 140, 141,
   142–43, 147–49, 150–51, 153, 154,
   159–60, 166–69, 170–79, 181, 186,
   187–89, 208
Hussein, Saddam: alleged involvement in
   9/11, 4, 94–97, 111, 112–16, 145; alleged
   links with Al Qaeda, 112–16, 145; Bush
   on, 109–12; capture of, 145; Cheney
   on, 109–12; first Gulf War, 93; and the
   news media, 109–11; and war on terror,
   108–11. See also Iraq
Hutchinson, Asa, 38, 39

Ignatieff, Michael, 63, 64
indexing of the news. See news indexing
infotainment, 9, 10
intelligence services, 5, 125–26, 204.
   See also CIA (Central Intelligence

Agency); FBI (Federal Bureau of
   Investigation)
Internet news, 8, 20, 27, 198–200
internment of Japanese Americans, 63, 68
iPOLL. See Roper Center's iPOLL archive
IRA. See Irish Republican Army (IRA)
Iran: alleged involvement in 9/11, 4, 95
Iraq: alleged involvement in 9/11, 2, 4,
   93–97, 105, 106, 107, 108, 112–16, 154,
   185, 192; alleged links with Al Qaeda,
   2, 94, 98, 105, 106, 107, 108, 112–16, 145,
   192; alleged weapons of mass destruction (WMD) in, 98, 99, 104–7, 112–16,
   186, 192. See also Hussein, Saddam
Iraq War, 5, 16, 19–20, 93–124; as Al
   Qaeda recruiting tool, 56; effect of on
   emergency preparedness, 159, 167–69;
   marketing of, 25, 102–8; media coverage of opposition voices to, 98–100;
   methodology for collection of data, 21,
   100–102; news coverage of, 25, 98–100,
   103–12, 119–24, 183, 195; public opinion
   on, 44, 113–22, 189, 190, 192–93; and
   the United Nations, 104–7
Irish Republican Army (IRA), 65
Iyengar, Shanto, 17

Jamieson, Kathleen Hall, 130
Japanese Americans, internment of, 63,
   68
Jennings, Peter, 1, 3, 5, 29, 38–39, 70–71,
   94, 96
Jervis, Robert, 99
Johns, Stephen, 219n6
Jones, Alex, 199
Just, Marion R., 17

Kaledin, Elizabeth, 161
Kallstrom, James, 6
Katrina, Hurricane. See Hurricane
   Katrina
Katz, Elihu, 15
Kay, David, 107
Kean, Thomas H., 51, 127, 153, 180
Kellner, Douglas, 15, 16
Kelly, Raymond, 39
Kennedy, Edward, 99
Kennedy, John F., 60
Kinder, Donald, 17
King, Peter, 202, 203, 204–5
Kurtz, Howard, 100

Larson, Randall, 38
Lawrence, Bruce, 14
Lawrence, Regina G., 12, 67, 99, 124, 150, 154, 187
Leno, Jay, 32
Lewinsky, Monica, 18, 182
Lewis, Anthony, 60–61, 66, 194, 211n6
Lexis/Nexis archives, 21, 36, 101, 129, 131, 132, 160
liberal democracies: vulnerability to terrorism, 62–66
Lichter, Robert, 22
Lieberman, Joseph, 153, 180, 205
Liebes, Tamar, 15
Lincoln, Abraham, 68
Lippmann, Walter, 9, 16, 182
Livingston, Steven, 12, 67, 99, 124, 150, 154, 187
London transport bombings, 58, 126, 137, 140

Madrid train bombings, 135
Maher, Bill, 98
Malhotra, Neil, 153, 166, 181
Marist College Institute for Public Opinion, 23, 69
Marshall, Josh, 200
Martin, David, 38
Martin, James, 2
Massing, Michael, 99
Matelin, Mary, 218n4
Mayer, Jane, 93, 97
McCain, John, 204
McCarthy era investigations, 90, 218n1 (ch. 7)
McClellan, Scott, 100
McCullough, David, 4
McGinnis, Susan, 71
McWethy, John, 3
media. See news media
media politics, 11–13, 18, 182–89, 191–93, 196–98
Mermin, Jonathan, 184
Merolla, Jennifer, 42
Merskin, Debra, 76
Meserve, Jeanne, 32
methodology: for analysis of public opinion, 22–24, 37, 102, 131–32, 159, 160; for collection of civil liberties data, 20–21, 69–70; for collection of emergency preparedness data, 20–21, 158–60; for collection of Iraq War data, 21, 100–102; for collection of prevention of terror-

ism data, 20–21, 130–32; for collection of threat of terrorism data, 20–21, 36–37; for content analysis of news coverage, 20–22, 36–37, 69–70, 100–102, 130–32, 158–60
Miklazewski, Jim, 97
Milbank, Dana, 29
military force, 3, 65. See also Afghanistan; Iraq War
Mills, C. Wright, 12
Miranda rights, 204–5, 206, 207
Mitchell, Andrea, 3–4, 39, 96
Mohammed, Khalid Sheikh, 62, 207
Moore, David, 120
Mueller, John, 7, 127–28
Mueller, Robert, 30
Murrow, Edward R., 182

Nacos, Brigitte, L., 67
Napolitano, Janet, 202
National Commission on Terrorism, 129
National Commission on Terrorist Attacks, 125–27, 152, 153, 179
National Public Radio (NPR), 67, 157
national security vs. civil liberties. See civil liberties vs. national security
NBC News, 20; and Bush's speech to Congress after 9/11, 29; and civil liberties, 61, 67, 71–72; and emergency preparedness, 157, 161–62, 163; and Hurricane Katrina, 143, 154, 160, 166, 168; and the Iraq War, 98, 101, 107; and 9/11, 2–4, 6, 8, 96, 185; and prevention of terrorism, 125, 126, 132–33; self-censorship of, 33; and threat of terrorism, 36, 39, 163
Neuman, W. Russell, 17
news indexing, 12–13, 27, 57, 59, 97, 154, 178–79, 183–89
news media: and Al Qaeda communications, 33–34, 40–41, 42, 50, 53, 56; and anthrax scare, 160–61; and bin Laden, 15–16, 33, 42, 109–11, 184–85, 188; and Bush's speech to Congress after 9/11, 29; and civil liberties vs. national security, 4–5, 25, 60–62, 66–67, 70–76, 91–92, 185, 186–87, 188, 189, 194–95; and the Cold War, 56–57, 110; as conveyer of emergency information, 156–57; decline of the newspaper industry, 8–9, 198–200; effect on public opinion, 17–18, 48–55, 85–90, 119–22, 176–78,

news media (*continued*)
191–95; and emergency preparedness,
5, 26, 154–56, 157–69, 176–81, 185–89,
195; and Hurricane Katrina, 143, 147–
49, 150–51, 154, 159–60, 166–69, 176–
79, 181, 186, 187–89; as infotainment, 9,
10; international/domestic divide, 6–7;
Internet news, 8, 20, 27, 198–200; and
Iraq's alleged involvement in 9/11, 94–
95; and the Iraq War, 25, 103–12, 119–
24, 183, 186, 195; media politics, 11–13,
18, 182–89, 191–93, 196–98; methodology for content analysis of, 20–22, 36–
37, 69–70, 100–102, 130–32, 158–60;
news as commodity, 8–11; news as public good, 9–11; and 9/11, 1–6, 8, 10–11,
13–14, 16, 185; and opposition voices
to Iraq War, 98–100; and presidential
approval ratings, 56–59; and prevention of terrorism, 5, 26, 128–37, 144–51,
185–87, 188, 189, 195; and propaganda,
196–97; public dependence on, 17–18;
and Saddam Hussein, 109–11; self-
censorship of, 33–34; and terrorism,
13–14, 15–16, 19; terrorism vs. terror
in, 110–12; and the threat of terrorism,
31–34, 37–42, 48–55, 51–52, 56, 90, 158,
163, 183, 184–85, 186, 188, 191–93, 195;
and the United Nations, 104–7; and violence, 10, 191; watchdog role of, 6, 27,
154–56, 194, 196, 197–98, 208. *See also
names of individual television networks
and newspapers*
Newsweek, 61
New York City: effect of 9/11 on public
concern, 43–44, 139, 140
New York Daily News, 129
New York Times: and civil liberties, 60–61,
66; and Hurricane Katrina, 132, 143,
147–48, 160, 166, 168; and the Iraq War,
25, 99–100, 101, 102, 104, 110–11; and
Saddam Hussein, 109
9/11: and Afghanistan, 3–4, 93–94, 113,
185; as an act of war, 1, 2–3, 5, 10–11,
28–29, 96; anniversary used to market
the Iraq War, 102–3; and bipartisanship, 6, 8; and Bush, 2, 6, 7, 15–16, 28,
29, 182, 203; compared to Pearl Harbor,
1, 2–3, 5, 29, 96, 125; intelligence services, 5, 125–26, 204; Iran's alleged involvement in, 4, 95; Iraq's alleged in-

volvement in, 2, 4, 93–97, 105, 106, 107,
108, 111, 112–16, 154, 185, 192; news
coverage of, 1–6, 8, 10–11, 13–14, 16,
185; news media as conveyer of emergency information, 157; 9/11 Commission Report, 125–27, 179; and patriotism, 6, 7–8; public fear after, 10–11,
28–29, 34–35, 43–44, 63, 192–93,
201–2
Nisbet, Eric C., 68, 80
Nixon, Richard, 11
Nolan, Martin F., 11
NPR. *See* National Public Radio (NPR)
nuclear weapons, 106–7
Nunberg, Geoffrey, 110–11
Nunn, Sam, 13

Obama, Barack, 201–9; and civil liberties,
201–3, 206, 207; counterterrorism poli-
cies of, 20, 27, 201–8; public opinion of,
20, 206–8, 220n14; use of new technol-
ogy, 199
O'Brien, Conan, 32
O'Brien, Soledad, 61
Office of Homeland Security, 29–30, 126.
See also Department of Homeland Se-
curity (DHS)
O'Hare, Brian, 133
Oklahoma City bombing, 42, 67, 137, 152,
156, 157, 213n9
O'Loughlin, Ben, 11
Omaha World-Herald, 129
Orr, Bob, 37–38, 134
O'Sullivan, Gerry, 13

Padilla, Jose, 51, 85
Page, Benjamin, 17, 44
Palin, Sarah, 205
Palmer Raids, 68
Parenti, Michael, 155
partisanship, public opinion by, 23–24; on
civil liberties vs. national security, 80–
81, 189; on counterterrorism, 189–90;
on emergency preparedness, 173–74,
175–76, 189; on the Iraq War, 116, 118,
189; on Obama's handling of terrorism, 206–7; on prevention of terrorism,
141, 143, 189; on the threat of terrorism, 46–47
Pataki, George, 204
PATRIOT Act. *See* USA PATRIOT Act

patriotism, 6, 7–8, 98
PBS *NewsHour with Jim Lehrer*, 4, 6, 20, 94, 95, 98
Pearl Harbor, 9/11 compared to, 1, 2–3, 5, 29, 96, 125
Perino, Dana, 182
personal records, government access to, 74, 88–89
Pious, Richard M., 65
Plant, Bill, 105
political party. *See* partisanship
Polling the Nations archive, 23, 69
Popper, Laura, 161
Powell, Colin: on Iraq's weapons of mass destruction, 98, 100, 107, 114, 117, 118, 121, 190; and the Iraq War, 93, 94, 103, 190; on links between Iraq and Al Qaeda, 97, 98, 108
Pratkanis, Anthony, 35, 196
Preble, Christopher A., 208
preparedness, emergency. *See* emergency preparedness
presidential approval ratings, 7–8, 17–18, 49, 50, 54–55, 56–59, 121–22, 140–41, 147, 171–72, 177–78, 198
Presidential election 2004, 55, 56
prevention of terrorism, 20, 125–51; before 9/11, 129–30; methodology for collection of data, 20–21, 130–32; and the news media, 5, 26, 128–37, 144–51, 185–87, 188, 189, 195; public opinion of, 19, 131–32, 137–49, 189, 190; research on, 19. *See also* counterterrorism
Priest, Dana, 196–97
print media. *See* news media
profiling, 78, 214n16
propaganda, 12–13, 16, 196–97
public dependence on the news media, 17–18
public opinion
    on civil liberties vs. national security, 67–69, 76–85, 89–90, 193–95, 213n9; by age, 82; by education, 83–85, 190; by gender, 82–83, 190; by political party, 80, 189; by race, 81–82, 190
    of counterterrorism, 19, 189–90; by political party, 189–90
    dynamics of, 48–55, 85–90, 119–22, 176–78, 193–95
    effect of news media on, 17–18, 48–55, 85–90, 119–22, 176–78, 191–95

    on emergency preparedness, 159, 160, 169–78; by gender, 172–73, 174–76, 190; by political party, 173–74, 175–76, 189; by race, 160, 172–73, 174–76, 190
    on Hurricane Katrina, 170–78, 179, 181
    on the Iraq War, 112–22; by age, 118–19; by education, 119; by gender, 117–18, 190; by political party, 116, 118, 189; by race, 116–17, 190
    methodology for analysis of, 22–24, 37, 102, 131–32, 159, 160
    of Obama's handling of terrorism, 20, 206–8, 220n14
    on prevention of terrorism, 19, 131–32, 137–49; by gender, 141, 190; by political party, 141, 143, 189; by race, 141–43, 190
    on the threat of terrorism, 42–47, 57–58, 191–93; by age, 46; by education, 46; by gender, 45, 190; by political party, 46–47; by race, 45–46, 190
    on USA PATRIOT Act, 78, 213n15

race, public opinion by, 23–24; on civil liberties vs. national security, 81–82, 190; on emergency preparedness, 160, 172–73, 174–76, 190; on the Iraq War, 116–18, 190; on prevention of terrorism, 141–43, 190; on the threat of terrorism, 45–46, 190
Raddatz, Martha, 180
Rashbaum, William K., 155
Rather, Dan, 3, 5, 6, 29, 34, 37–38, 94–95, 105–6, 160–61
Redlener, Irwin, 152, 209
Reid, Richard, 87, 133, 146, 203–4, 205
Rice, Condoleezza, 33, 93, 108, 126
Ridge, Tom, 30–32, 51, 58, 128, 162, 163, 164–65, 211n1 (ch. 2)
Ritter, Scott, 107–8
Roberts, John, 106
Roberts-Miller, Patricia, 16, 185
Roosevelt, Franklin D., 28, 29
Roper Center's iPOLL archive, 23, 69, 102
Rumsfeld, Donald, 30, 34, 93–94, 96, 103, 107, 108
Russert, Tim, 126

Schell, Orville, 98, 123, 124
Schlagheck, Donna M., 35

Schmid, Alex, 14
Schudson, Michael, 154, 200
security alerts. *See* threat alerts
Sedition Act 1918, 63
September 11th. *See* 9/11
Serrin, William, 150, 156
sex, public opinion by. *See* gender, public opinion by
Shahzad, Faisal, 204
Shanahan, James, 68, 80
Shapiro, Catherine, 7
Shapiro, Robert, 17, 44
Shelby, Richard, 4
Shenk, David, 48
shoe bomber. *See* Reid, Richard
Sick, Gary, 94–95
Silver, Brian D., 68
Smith, Tracey, 104
social networks, 20, 27, 198
Spain: Madrid train bombings, 135
SS *Mayaguez*, 7
Stark, Lisa, 133
Starr, Paul, 9, 11
Stein, Sam, 199
Stephanopoulos, George, 182
Stewart, Potter, 92
Stouffer, Samuel, 83

Taliban, 2, 3–4, 94, 97, 108–9, 113. *See also* Afghanistan
Taylor, Stuart, Jr., 61
Tea Party movement, 205
Tedin, Kent L., 23–24, 189
television news. *See* news media
Tenet, George, 93, 130
terrorism: as a criminal activity, 64–65; news coverage of, 13–14, 15–16, 19; as theater, 35; transnational, 7, 13, 184; use of fear, 34–36, 63, 90, 188, 195, 196; and vulnerability of liberal democracies, 62–66; war against, 110–11
terrorism, prevention of. *See* prevention of terrorism
terrorism, threat of. *See* threat of terrorism
terrorism preparedness. *See* emergency preparedness
Thomas, Pierre, 38, 70–71, 162
threat alerts, 24–25, 30–33, 34, 36–40, 50–51, 54–55, 56, 58, 183
threat of terrorism, 19, 24–25; in Bush's speeches, 29; and civil liberties, 63, 67–

68; Iraq War and, 44; methodology for collection of data, 20–21, 36–37; news coverage of, 31–34, 37–42, 48–55, 51–52, 56, 128, 158, 163, 183, 184–85, 186, 188, 191–93, 195; and presidential approval ratings, 49, 50, 54–55, 56, 57, 58; public opinion of, 42–47, 48–55, 57–58, 128, 190, 191–93; threat alerts, 24–25, 30–33, 34, 36–40, 50–51, 54–55, 56, 58, 183; use of by bin Laden, 34, 35; use of to justify counterterrorism, 14, 30–31, 34, 56, 58–59, 150, 183, 186, 196–97, 201–2; volume of threat messages, 50. *See also* fear
Tiller, George, 219n6
Times Square bombing attempt, 204–5
Tokyo subway sarin gas attack, 13
torture, 61–62, 75, 197, 201, 202, 206
TPM (Talking Points Memo), 200
transnational terrorism, 7, 13, 184
trust in government. *See* public opinion

United Kingdom: and civil liberties, 65; London transport bombings, 58, 126, 137, 140
United Nations, 104–7
unlawful combatants, 61, 64–65, 75, 78, 204–5
U.S. Commission on National Security in the 21st Century, 130
USA PATRIOT Act, 5, 60, 64, 67, 70–76, 78, 185, 213n15
USS *Pueblo*, 7

Vaillant, Auguste, 48
Vanderbilt University Television News Archive, 21, 36, 101, 131
violence and the news media, 10, 191
Viverette, Mary Ann, 180

war, 9/11 as an act of, 1, 2–3, 5, 10–11, 28–29, 96
war on terror, 25. 108–12, 202. *See also* counterterrorism; prevention of terrorism
Washington Monthly, 157
Washington Post, 25, 61–62, 66, 100, 113, 130, 196
watchdog role of the news media, 6, 27, 154–56, 194, 196, 197–98, 208

weapons of mass destruction (WMD), 98,
    99, 104–7, 112–16, 186, 192
Weimann, Gabriel, 15
White, Theodore, 11, 211n4
White House online archive, 101
Wilkerson, Lawrence, 100
Wilkinson, Paul, 65–66
Willer, Rob, 55
Williams, Brian, 154
Williams, Pete, 39, 133
WMD. *See* weapons of mass destruction
    (WMD)
Wolfowitz, Paul, 93, 96, 97

Woodward, Bob, 93, 94
Woolsey, James, 4, 93, 94
World Trade Center 1993 bombing, 42, 43,
    94, 137, 152, 156, 157
World War II, 96. *See also* internment of
    Japanese Americans; Pearl Harbor

Yousef, Ramzi, 94

Zaller, John, 8, 18, 182, 197–98
Zawahiri, Ayman al-, 34, 155
Zechmeister, Elizabeth, 42